B   8 1978

'HOMO RELIGIOSUS' IN MIRCEA ELIADE

An Anthropological Evaluation

SUPPLEMENTA AD NVMEN, ALTERA SERIES

DISSERTATIONES

AD HISTORIAM RELIGIONUM PERTINENTES

EDENDAS CURAVIT

C. J. BLEEKER

VOLUMEN QUINTUM

LEIDEN

E. J. BRILL

1976

'HOMO RELIGIOSUS' IN MIRCEA ELIADE

An Anthropological Evaluation

BY

JOHN A. SALIBA

LEIDEN
E. J. BRILL
1976

ISBN 90 04 04550 3

TABLE OF CONTENTS

INTRODUCTION

An interdisciplinary book is faced with the problem of relating subjects which, in spite of their many similarities, have frequently existed in opposition to one another. There are, therefore, a number of assumptions which are crucial to the discussion which is the preoccupation of this study.

It is assumed from the start that anthropology has something positive to offer to the study of religion. This book thus rejects from the outset the attitude which spurns anthropological research or the whole anthropological effort, labelling it "reductionistic." Though many anthropological studies on religion, past and present, are open to such a charge, not all contemporary contributions fall under this category. It is assumed that even those studies which tend to be reductionistic can be of some value to the student of religions because they contain the source material of many non-literate religions which would otherwise have not been recorded.

Another major assumption stems from the great changes in anthropology that have taken place in the last few decades. Like many other disciplines anthropology has witnessed, in its first hundred years, a radical change in method and theory as well as in the training of an anthropologist. Even though there are different schools of anthropological thought, these changes have left a lasting and universal impact on anthropology as a discipline. It is therefore assumed that contemporary anthropology has made genuine advances since its birth in the second half of the last century, and that its rejection of so many early theories and conclusions about non-literate cultures has been a step in the right direction. This presupposition is in fact necessary for an anthropological evaluation of Mircea Eliade's views. It follows that any defense of Eliade's main tenets which is based on the hypothesis that the revolution in anthropology has been a kind of degeneration is considered off the mark.

Basic to this study is the assumption that the history of religions and related disciplines have a right to exist academically on their own. More specifically, the history of religions is not merely a discipline which unites the works on religion done in other fields; the study of religion is not a monopoly of any one discipline. The history of religions has contributed to the general understanding of religions and religious man. Hence the work of Eliade is worthy not only of critical evaluation but also of positive analysis of the contribution he has made to the field in question. Thus it follows that this work does not accept as academically tenable the general neglect by anthropologists of what Eliade has said on the religions of non-literate societies.

Another set of hypotheses is inevitable when one deals with the subject matter of man and his religions. Rather than feign complete detachment and impartiality, which are difficult, if not impossible to achieve, it is wiser to recognize and state one's own religious assumptions. This book is written by a religious believer with the simple aim of examining whether Eliade's interpretation of the religions of non-literate societies conforms to contemporary anthropological research. While the data examined are not viewed from one particular religious tradition, they are nevertheless seen through the eyes of a person who takes religion seriously. Anthropologists have stated their belief or unbelief quite openly, and they deserve praise, if not for the opinions they hold, at least for their candor. It follows, then, that this work evaluates not only Eliade's views but also anthropological writings on religion. The extent and limit of anthropological research on religious matters will be fairly obvious, as will the fact that the writer has been strongly influenced by a particular group of British anthropologists who share his own religious convictions. It is precisely because of these religious assumptions that the task of evaluating Eliade's works can be taken up with some assurance that his opinions will be criticized without any attempt to go into the question of religious truth or falsehood. For Eliade, like many historians of religions, writes primarily as a believer who looks on religion as a manifestation of the divine or the holy.

The task of evaluating Eliade from an anthropological viewpoint faces inevitable limitations. Anthropology is a vast field to which many schools in different countries have made lasting contributions. No single work could possibly take into consideration all the available anthropological resources. Eliade's concept of "Homo Religiosus" is seen, therefore, in the light of anthropological studies done in the English language, in particular those studies contributed by anthropologists from Great Britain and the United States of America. This necessary self-imposed limitation is justified, in part at least, because some of Eliade's main works on religion have appeared originally in the English language, while the rest have all been translated into English. Further, because of his long teaching career in the United

States, his scholarly achievement can be seen in the perspective of his academic background.

The final problem which this study entails is the fact that it challenges the position of a leading historian of religions who has left a lasting impact in his field. One must insist that Eliade's position in, and contribution to, the history of religions remains intact even if many of his views are here seriously questioned and many of his principal opinions abandoned. That the history of religions as a discipline is at a turning point is admitted by Eliade himself. One of the steps in scholarly development is the re-examination of currently held views; academic progress and critical examination go hand in hand. This work, therefore, claims to be nothing else but a first attempt to re-examine some of the fundamental positions of a leading historian of religions who deals at length with the religions of non-literate societies.

CHAPTER ONE

ANTHROPOLOGY AND THE HISTORY OF RELIGIONS

THE STUDY OF MAN AND HIS RELIGIONS

The study of man is as old as man himself. Man has always been interested in himself. The earliest literature we know of reveals this quest for self-knowledge. Speculations on man's origins, on his place in the universe and on what the future holds for him belong to the cultural heritage of all peoples. To speak of the beginnings of the study of man and of his religions is thus almost futile. The roots of anthropology and the history of religions, therefore, lie deep. [1] Ethnographic discoveries and philosophical reflections gradually paved the way for the rise of both anthropology and the history of religions as academic disciplines. Scholars have undertaken to write the history of man in different ways. Some have selected early writers for comment with the intention of emphasizing a particular anthropological theory. [2] Others have concentrated on a specific historical period, thus producing a penetrating study of one historical phase in the study of man. [3] Still others have tried to give an over-all sweep of the whole vast area, supplying the reader with selected passages and thereby showing how rich and abundant the material really is. [4] Particular aspects of religion and individual branches of anthropology have often served as a unifying device in historical reflections. [5] Most historical reconstructions, though by no means all, have not gone further back than the nineteenth century. [6] As a rule, with some notable exceptions, [7] those who have attempted to write a history of the study of man have limited themselves to the Western world. A complete history of man's search for knowledge has still to make its appearance.

In spite of this universal and ageless pursuit for learning it has

---

[1] Tax, 1964a, p. 15; Kessing, 1958, p. 9; Ashby, 1965, p. 5.

[2] A typical example is Harris, 1968.

[3] Kluckhohn, 1961; Hodgen, 1964.

[4] Slotkin, 1965; Darnell, 1974.

[5] For instance, De Vries, 1967, deals mainly with the history of the study of mythology; Penniman, 1952, concentrates his work on the history of archaeology and physical anthropology; and Hays, 1958, is concerned with social anthropology.

[6] Lowie, 1937; Lienhardt, G., 1966, pp. 1-32; Eggan, 1968, pp. 119 ff. For an exception, see Evans-Pritchard, 1951, pp. 21-42.

[7] Dundes, 1968, pp. 14-22.

been established that the scientific knowledge of man is a relatively recent phenomenon. [8] It was during the nineteenth century that both anthropology and the history of religions began to emerge as distinct disciplines. Frazer and Tylor in England are considered among the pioneers in the rise of anthropology, while Max Muller introduced the West to the Indian scriptures. [9] That anthropology and the history of religions should have a common origin need not come as a surprise. As one historian of anthropology has written: "The historical process that truly fathered social anthropology was Europe's gradual domination of the world through successive waves of exploration and colonization." [10] Many of the early contributors to the study of man and his religions were travellers, traders, explorers and missionaries. The nineteenth century saw a prolific growth of colonization with the consequent increase in the knowledge of man. [11] Such expansions have been supplying anthropology with new material even in the twentieth century. With the founding of the new capital of Brazil, hitherto unknown tribes were discovered and studied as among the few human specimens untouched by Western civilization. [12]

The two disciplines in question did not only share a common origin, but, at first, they also shared the same theories. Max Muller occupies a prominent place in the history of anthropology because of his linguistic and mythological studies. [13] Frazer and Tylor supplied the theoretical framework and the data to many historians of religions. The theories of Marrett, Durkheim, Lévi-Bruhl and Schmidt were read not only by anthropologists but also by influential scholars of religion. Historians of religions, reflecting on the history of their own discipline, have included these theories as part of their background. [14] The early anthropological views on religion often formed the speculative basis of historians of religions. It is an accepted fact that anthropology contributed to the advance of the history of religions more than any other discipline. One can even say that anthropology and the history of religions, both still looking for self-identity, were closely allied well into the twentieth century.

---

[8] Kessing, 1958, p. 9.
[9] Kardiner and Preble, 1961, pp. 50-94; Lowie, 1937, pp. 68-85 and 101-104; Ashby, 1965, p. 9; Earhart, 1967, p. 198.
[10] Hays, 1958, ix.
[11] Lienhardt, G., 1966, pp. 3 ff.
[12] Lévi-Strauss, 1966, p. 125.
[13] Evans-Pritchard, 1965b, pp. 20-23; Malefijt, 1968, pp. 45-48.
[14] Ashby, 1965, p. 12; Eliade, 1969a, pp. 12-30.

The breakdown of the early anthropological theories on religion was to have repercussions not only on anthropology but also on the history of religions. By the 1930's these theories were already losing their hold on the then younger generation of anthropologists who directed their attention to the functional theories of Malinowski and Radcliffe-Brown. [15] The interest in religion, though it never died down, gradually subsided. It is only in the last two decades that one can notice an increase in anthropological studies on religion. Even so, contemporary anthropologists have complained that in this recent phase "our conceptual tools have developed only slightly beyond those which were forged by Tylor, Durkheim or Van Gennep." [16] And the omission of recent writings on religion by Professor Evans-Pritchard in his book *Theories of Primitive Religion* (1965), an omission for which he has been mildly rebuked, [17] may be an indication that he held a similar view. While, however, anthropologists neglected or treated superficially the study of religion, they still made progress in other areas. The development in theory and method, the advances in linguistics, the study of kinship, and the refinements in personality and culture have balanced the lack of progress in the field of religion. [18] The advances made in these areas are already having some impact on newer studies on religion.

The history of religions seems to have inherited this apathy from anthropology. Philip Ashby has remarked that "scholarship in the area was limited to teachers of the history of religions or comparative religion, in theological schools and centers preparing students for the ministry or, occasionally, for the teaching of religion." [19] Religion did not play a key role in the curricula of colleges and universities. The problem which the history of religions had to face was that, when the interest in the study of religions subsided, it had nothing to turn to. Anthropologists could and did become absorbed in many other cultural traits, all of which fell within their comprehensive discipline. Consequently, anthropology had a better chance than the history of religions of developing as a discipline. It has to be admitted that the history of religions had more success on the European continent than

---

[15] Malinowski, 1925 and 1926; Radcliffe-Brown, 1952. Cf. Lowie, 1937, pp. 230-239.
[16] Spiro, 1964a, p. 1.
[17] Turner, V., 1966.
[18] See Siegel, 1965-1971, 1972 and 1973.
[19] Ashby, 1965, p. 13. Cf. Kitagawa, 1959, pp. 4-5.

it did in the United States. [20] The latter country's deficiency in this respect is clearly borne out by a comparison between the university departments of the two disciplines. [21] Besides, the numerous institutes of anthropology have had, till recently, no parallel in the history of religions. [22] Major scholars, like Van der Leeuw, Wach, Pettazzoni and Eliade have not only kept the history of religions alive but are also responsible for the state of the discipline as we know it today. During the last two decades, however, the history of religions, especially in the United States, has taken great strides toward becoming a fully independent discipline with its own theories and method. It is necessary, therefore, to outline the two disciplines as they now stand and to compare them, marking their similarities and differences.

ANTHROPOLOGY — AIMS AND METHODS

Anthropology is the study of man. As a discipline it is the most comprehensive of the academic disciplines dealing with mankind. It treats both the physical and the cultural aspects of man; and it covers an extensive geographic area and a broad range of topics. As knowledge of man and his many cultures expanded, it became clear that further specialization was needed. The title "anthropology" now covers a number of areas which have almost become disciplines in their own right.

The study of anthropology in colleges and universities in the United States is usually divided into two areas, namely, physical anthropology and cultural anthropology. [23] The former has links with human biology, but concentrates on human origins, on the evolution of man and on his adaptation to his environment. It comprises such interests as genetics, nutrition, sex differences and the comparative anatomy and physiology of races. It also includes the comparative study of the human species with sub-human species like monkeys and apes. [24] This latter concern is already branching out into a new sub-discipline, called

---

[20] Cf., for example, Waardenburg, 1972.

[21] See Mclean, 1967; Welch, 1971 and 1972; American Anthropological Association, 1972. The growth of departments of religion or of religious studies in the United States is a relatively recent phenomenon.

[22] International Directory of Anthropological Institutions, 1967.

[23] The academic separation of the various branches of human knowledge differs in other countries. Evans-Pritchard, 1950, supplies some information on the European scene. In general the term "Anthropology" is often used in Europe to refer mainly to physical anthropology. Cf. Kottack, 1974, p. 3.

[24] Pelto, 1966, p. 2; Barnouw, 1971, vol. I, pp. 1-3; Pearson, 1974, pp., 2-3.

ethology. [25] Cultural anthropology, on the other hand, embraces a number of sub-divisions, the most important being ethnography, ethnology, social anthropology and psychological anthropology. Archaeology is often incorporated in cultural anthropology, though departments of archaeology are common and some scholars list archaeology as a separate anthropological field of study. [26] Ethnography is defined as the description of a specific culture and is looked upon as the raw material of cultural anthropology. It refers to the process of collecting data by direct inquiry and to the task of describing a particular culture; it makes no explicit attempts to draw up theoretical positions. Its task is to record as accurately as possible the modes of life of other peoples. [27] Ethnology adds two elements to ethnography, the concepts of comparison and historical reconstruction. [28] It has been labelled "the comparative study of peoples from the ethnographics that have been produced about them," [29] or "the study of culture by the method of historical reconstruction." [30] Some anthropologists are thus inclined to see ethnology as closely allied with archaeology, which is concerned with the study of civilizations and cultures of the past. [31] This is more so in English-speaking countries since World War II. On the European continent, ethnology still has a broader connotation and often implies cultural and/or social anthropology. Purely descriptive studies, or simple ethnography, seem to have become less common. Anthropologists are realizing that they cannot but approach the field of study with some theoretical formulations. [32] Some explicit or implicit generalization and comparison are found even in descriptive studies. Here ethnographic reporting has in some quarters a derogatory

---

[25] Morris, 1967.
[26] American Anthropological Association, 1972. Cf. Hammond, 1971, p. 4.
[27] Clifton, 1968, pp. 8-9; Mair, 1965, p. 7; Lévi-Strauss, 1963, p. 2; Kroeber, 1963, pp. 131-133; Greenberg, 1968, p. 307.
[28] Kessing, 1958, p. 5; Lévi-Strauss, 1963, p. 2.
[29] Bohannan, 1963, p. 8. Cf. Kottack, 1974, p. 6.
[30] Radcliffe-Brown, 1958, p. 8; cf. Schmidt, 1939, pp. 12-18; Pearson, 1974, p. 3. One must note, however, that the distinction between ethnology and ethnography is not always clear. Different definitions of both terms are available in anthropological literature. Thus, for example, Haviland, 1974, p. 10, describes ethnology as the study of contemporary cultures, while Ember and Ember, 1973, p. 11, state that the ethnographer "may also suggest explanations for some of the customs he has observed."
[31] Mair, 1965, p. 7; Evans-Pritchard, 1951, p. 5. Ember and Ember, 1973, p. 11, sees the aims of the ethnologist as being largely the same as those of the archeologist.
[32] Evans-Pritchard, 1951, pp. 87-88; Firth, 1958, p. 2; Berreman, 1968a, p. 339.

connotation. [33] Even if the production of a purely descriptive work is no longer considered feasible, there can be no doubt that the first step an anthropologist attempts is to a certain degree an ethnographic one.

One of the most specialized branches of anthropology is social anthropology. Such a title is common in the British Commonwealth, though the implied method and interests are found in many other countries. Though many scholars identify cultural with social anthropology, or include social anthropology as a sub-division of cultural anthropology, as we did above, there are important differences in emphasis and perspectives among those scholars who classify themselves either as social or as cultural anthropologists. Social anthropology is the study of institutionalized, that is standardized, social relationships. It aims at understanding, or making more intelligible, the diversity of human behavior by a comparative study of social relationships, especially those which are customary or the norm in society. [34] For social anthropologists an institution denotes relationships "in which people are regularly concerned as members of a particular social group or categories." [35] Social relations refer to the prescribed ways in which people relate to each other, and these relations are never at random; they follow a customary pattern accepted as normal by the members of that society which adheres to such behavior. A typical example of such social relationships are kinship relations. Not only are relatives called by a standard terminology, but also the way they address one another and the social behavior they expect from one another are often highly formalized and predictable. [36] It is precisely these uniformities and regularities in social life that put some order in society and thus makes its study feasible. These patterns of behavior imply that there is a system; and the social anthropologist's task is to reveal it. [37]

Like social anthropology, cultural anthropology owes its origin to English anthropologists. The word "culture," with its modern technical or anthropological meaning, can be traced to Edward Tylor who identifies culture with civilization and then goes on to define culture as "that complex whole which includes knowledge, belief, art, morals, law,

[33] Beattie, 1964, p. 19; Lewis, I. M., 1968, xii.
[34] Beattie, 1959b, pp. 46-47; Nadel, 1951, p. 29; Firth, 1968a, p. 320. Cf. Bock, 1974, pp. 17-18.
[35] Firth, 1968a, p. 320.
[36] Cf., for example, Schusky, 1965.
[37] Evans-Pritchard, 1951, pp. 19-20.

custom, and any other capabilities and habits acquired by man as a member of society." [38] Since Tylor's time anthropologists have not ceased in their attempts to analyze and define this concept. So much has been written on the subject that some twenty years ago two American anthropologists published a book reviewing the concepts and definitions of the word "culture." [39] Many anthropologists have just taken over Tylor's definition, expressing his basic idea in different words and with varying emphasis. Culture has been described as "all that a man learns to do as a member of his society. It includes knowledge, common understanding and expectations that the people of a group share and that their children learn." [40] The emphasis here is on the fact that culture is learned behavior and can thus be defined as "a learned pattern of thinking, believing and acting." [41] Culture has also been defined as man's most important instrument of adaptation, that is, "as an extension of his (man's) physiology, and an artificial instrument for maintaining a viable relationship with human habitats." [42] Yehudi Cohen writes:

> A Culture is made up of energy systems, the objective and concrete artifacts, the organizations of social relations, the modes of thought, the ideologies and the total range of customary behavior that are transmitted from one generation to another by a social group and that enable it to maintain life in a particular habitat. [43]

While many anthropologists who describe culture stress its material content, some focus on its symbolic aspect. [44] Others prefer to look on cultures as systems of communication, thus taking language as their model. [45] Though anthropological studies have shown that culture is subject to many definitions, they seem to point to a consensus among anthropologists that culture is the most unique characteristic of being human. Culture distinguishes men from animals and is, thus contrasted with nature. [46]

---

[38] Tylor, 1871, vol. 1, p. 1.
[39] Kroeber and Kluckhohn, 1952.
[40] Mandelbaum, 1968, p. 313.
[41] Clifton, 1968, p. 4. Cf. Bock, 1974, pp. 14-16; Ember and Ember, 1973, pp. 16 ff.; Kottack, 1974, p. 20.
[42] Cohen, 1968, vol. 2, p. 40. Cf. Haviland, 1974, p. 272.
[43] Cohen, 1968, vol. 2, p. 1. Cf. Montagu, 1968c.
[44] Geertz, 1965, pp. 17-29. Cf. Haviland, 1974, pp. 269-270 who holds that this symbolic aspect is one of the characteristics of culture.
[45] Lévi-Strauss, 1963, pp. 67-69; cf. Leach, 1968b, p. 341.
[46] Brace, 1967, p. 51; Geertz, 1964, pp. 37-48; Holloway, 1969, pp. 395-412; Mandelbaum, 1968, p. 313; Hoebel, 1972, pp. 6-7.

The difference between social and cultural anthropology is that the former is devoted to the study of social institutions, the latter to the study of techniques which implement social life. Cultural anthropology deals with cultural systems rather than with social ones; it handles objects, values and ideals, rather than people. Its main concern is the relationship between the items of culture, the culture traits, rather than, as in social anthropology, the relations and interactions between people. [47] In general it can be said that British and French anthropologists prefer to use the concept "society," while American and German scholars would opt for the term "culture." Though there are historical reasons why this should be the case, [48] it must be borne in mind that the differences can be overplayed. For society and culture can only be analytically distinguished. Both are aspects of the same subject matter, that is, human beings living in groups. Some anthropologists have, consequently, insisted that the distinction between social and cultural anthropology is more apparent than real; others have pointed out that the difference is one of emphasis. Some also see signs that the two are being reconciled by the stressing of the commonly shared aspects and perspectives. [49]

Not all anthropologists, however, portray clearly this important distinction between social and cultural anthropology and its implications. Some definitions of social anthropology [50] would fit more properly psychological anthropology which has gained in respectability since it took its first steps to establish itself as a branch of anthropology in the 1920's. Also known as "personality and culture," psychological anthropology studies the effects of society and culture on human personality; it also deals with the role of personality characteristic in the development, formation and change of culture. [51] While psychological anthropology is indebted to psychiatry and psychoanalysis, few anthropologists are psychoanalytically minded. [52] There has been continuous collaboration, especially in the United States of America, between psychologists and anthropologists; at times, however, many anthropologists have seriously questioned some basic psychoanalytic tenets. [53] Psychological anthropology, which is practically ignored by

---

[47] Lévi-Strauss, 1963, p. 3; Beattie, 1964, p. 12; Mair, 1965, p. 8.
[48] Wolf, 1964, pp. 16 ff.
[49] Bidney, 1967, p. 101; Beattie, 1956, p. 254; Hammond, 1971, pp. 4-5.
[50] See, for example, Hays, 1958, vii.
[51] Hsu, 1972, pp. 6 ff.
[52] Hunt, 1967, xviii.
[53] The works of Mead and Erikson are among the best examples of the col-

British anthropologists, is more closely linked with social psychology than with any other branch of psychology. [54]

There is a basic interest underlying these various sub-disciplines of anthropology. All are concerned with the study of customs found in diverse societies. All look upon these customs as related with one another. The difference lies in the perspective under which such interrelations are analyzed. A cultural anthropologist will see them as forming a cultural pattern, a mosaic of culture traits. A social antropologist views them as operating within a system of social relations; for him it is through personal social relations that culture traits are maintained and passed on from one generation to the next. [55] The psychological anthropologist directs his attention to customs with the aim of seeing them as structuring the various types of personality in different groups. The study of customs as forming an interdependent pattern is one of the main characteristics which distinguishes anthropology from the other disciplines. [56]

Another characteristic of anthropology is the "holistic" approach. [57] Anthropologists deal with culture or society as a whole; they study all aspects of a given culture or society and see them as constituting one unit composed of interrelated parts. This approach is to some extent imposed by the anthropologists' main field of study, namely, small-scale societies without a written literature. Anthropologists have generally taken it for granted that the study of these societies is their major concern. [58] They have, however, insisted, sometimes rather strongly, that even though the significantly creative work of anthropologists has been largely in the field of non-literate societies, anthropologists have never as a group restricted their interest to these societies. [59] More recently some anthropologists have stated that they "no longer study primarily primitive society." [60] In fact, anthropologists have produced village and community studies of most of the main

---

laboration between the two disciplines. For an example questioning a major psychoanalytic tenet see Parsons, 1964.

[54] Hsu, 1972, p. 11.

[55] Lienhardt, G., 1966, p. 154.

[56] Gluckman and Eggan, 1965, x.

[57] Clifton, 1968, p. 5; Dubois, 1963, pp. 30-31; Brown, I., 1963, p. 15; Ember and Ember, 1973, pp. 4-5; Kottack, 1974, p. 3.

[58] Mair, 1965, p. 2; Beattie, 1964, p. 12; Mead, 1964, p. 5; Hammond, 1971, pp. 23-24.

[59] Firth, 1958, p. 12; Pelto, 1966, pp. 5-6; Beattie, 1959b, p. 46; Mair, 1965, p. 6; Evans-Pritchard, 1951, p. 10.

[60] Kottack, 1974, pp. 439.

cultures and civilizations. There are studies which take into account European countries, such as the British Isles, France, Greece, Italy and Spain. Most of the East, in particular India and Indo-China has been the object of intensive anthropological research. There is a growing literature on Mediterranean cultures, and anthropological works on Latin America have not been restricted to obscure and remote tribes. [61] As one anthropologist has aptly expressed it: "the primitive world continues to belong to anthropology, but not anthropology to the primitive world." [62] There are theoretical reasons why the anthropologist cannot restrict himself to the world of non-literate societies. When an anthropologist is engaged in studying a small-scale society in some remote region he is still doing so with the same social and philosophical categories of his own cultural background. Moreover, no matter how much he tries to concentrate his study on one particular society, he is always, at least implicitly, comparing it with his own. Some have argued that it is necessary for anthropologists to direct their attention also to literate societies because lack of concern with these societies can lead to defective anthropological theory. [63] The stress on the study of literate societies has grown in the last few decades. This is due in part to the fact that most of the traditional societies studied by anthropologists have come in contact with one of the great civilizations and have adapted themselves to some degree to the new situation. The societies which have been the stamping ground of anthropologists are undergoing vast changes under the influence of Western technology. It is impossible to understand these changing societies and cultures without taking into account the impact of both Eastern and Western civilizations. [64]

Another bond uniting anthropological disciplines is their methodology. Reacting against an earlier approach which relied mainly on very unreliable accounts of non-literate societies and which tended to select that data which fitted preconceived theories, the twentieth century anthropologists realized that the best way to study non-literate cultures is to go and live with the people. Today there is no other way of making an anthropologist except to send him to live among the people he intends to study. [65] It is an accepted principle in anthropology

---

[61] See bibliography in Hsu, 1969, pp. 104-120 and in Goldschmidt, 1968, pp. 337-339; cf. Kottack, 1974, pp. 459-463.

[62] Clifton, 1968, p. 11; Evans-Pritchard, 1951, pp. 10-11; Hsu, 1969, pp. 52-55.

[63] Hsu, 1969, p. 34.

[64] Wolf, 1964, p. 22.

[65] Mead, 1964, p. 5.

that the first step an anthropologist should take is to study the language of the people with whom he will be living during his field-work period. [66] The goal of an anthropologist is to be able to dispense with interpreters as soon as possible. It is because of this insistence on the study of native languages that anthropologists have made a noteworthy contribution to linguistics. [67]

One of the main tasks an anthropologist has in the field is that of observation. [68] Most of his attempts to gather information, however, will be futile if he does not participate in some of the tribal activities. He should try and behave in such a way that he is accepted as a regular member of the community. In other words, the anthropologist must find a social position within the group he is studying. [69] This method is called participant-observation. [70] It involves assuming at least a few of the traditional roles of the community under study. The anthropologist has to immerse himself in the society, to think, feel, see and sometimes act as one of its members. Though it is agreed that complete involvement in a particular society may be an obstacle to its understanding, some involvement is deemed to be necessary. [71] The anthropologist is thus faced with the problem of adaptation and this could be a source of personal difficulties. [72] Field-work has, therefore, been appropriately called the "rite of passage" of the anthropologist, who experiences a form of culture shock. [73] Through this method the researcher will have a better chance of understanding a people's way of life than by merely observing outward behavior. Participant-observation enables a field-worker to see the actions of the people he is studying from their own point of view. Only then will he be able to give an idea of how people conceive of their own social life. The ideals, values and behavior of a community can be evaluated correctly

[66] Malinowski, 1925, pp. 146-147. One to three years of field work are required for a doctoral degree. Fieldwork is preceded by academic anthropological training which includes the study of the language of the society where the anthropologist intends to do fieldwork. Books and articles have been written to help anthropologists learn an unwritten language. Cf. Gudschinsky, 1967.

[67] Cf. Durbin, 1967, pp. 209-51.

[68] In this he is helped by manuals which guide the anthropologist through the maze of information he has to accumulate; see Murdock, 1961 and Royal Anthropological Institute, 1951.

[69] Pelto, 1966, p. 41; Bock, 1974, p. 385.

[70] Taylor, R. B., 1973, pp. 107 ff.; Bock, 1974, p. 386.

[71] Powdermaker, 1966, pp. 11 ff. See Taylor, R. B., 1973, pp. 108-110, who warns that participant observation is not immune from problems.

[72] Holmberg, 1968, pp. 136-41; Beattie, 1965, pp. 8 ff; Hammond, 1971, p. 23.

[73] Bock, 1970, ix-xii; Pearson, 1974, p. 172; Taylor, R. B., 1973, p. 108.

only in the light of meaning they have for the members of the society itself. [74] While it is difficult, perhaps even impossible, for a scholar to get a complete inside view of another culture, yet the anthropologist must not desist in his endeavors to do so. Participant-observation, investigating from within, taking an inside view of another culture is probably the most important methodological approach in anthropology. [75]

To what degree will an anthropologist get this inside view may depend not only on the personality of the field-worker but also on the members of the society he is studying. Anthropologists have had to explain on arrival in the field that they were neither government agents nor missionaries. [76] The participant-observation technique is often supplemented by surveys, questionnaires and interviews. Anthropologists have often recruited native informants to help them in their research. [77] Another means used is the writing of biographies of leading natives, a method which could lead one to understand how people visualize their own culture and social life. [78] Since the late 1940's the use of photography has been common, and photography has now acquired the status of a significant research tool, adding a new dimension to anthropological studies. [79] Not all these methods can be applied with the same beneficial results to the study of all cultures. Research methods are never completely fool-proof. Anthropologists are aware that error, misinformation and bias can always destroy what they are aiming at, namely, the understanding of another way of life.

While participant-observation is the most stressed method in anthropology, it has to be noted that anthropologists are becoming increasingly aware that they cannot approach the field without a theoretical background. As some anthropologists have stated:

> Observation is always selective and requires some interest, some point of view, or some theoretical framework if it is to be meaningful. Not only do we not want to observe and describe everything, but it is not clear what describing everything could possibly mean. Thus what we choose to call "observed" or "ethnographic" fact is very much dependent upon the conceptual or theoretical framework within which the observation is carried out. [80]

[74] Beattie, 1965, p. 14; Brown, I., 1963, p. 15.
[75] Manners and Kaplan, 1968, p. 3; Lévi-Strauss, 1967, p. 137.
[76] Beattie, 1965, p. 14.
[77] Beattie, 1965, pp. 24 ff.; Williams, 1966, pp. 28-31; Taylor, R. B. 1973, pp. 110-112.
[78] Langness, 1965; Mandelbaum, 1973.
[79] Collier, 1967.
[80] Manners and Kaplan, 1968, p. 5.

Theory supplies a set of hypotheses toward which the collection of data must be oriented. [81] Anthropology here follows the scientific procedure. First there is the formation of a hypothesis which is rigorously tested and validated by cross-cultural studies. If the test of the hypothesis proves negative, the hypothesis itself will be refined, drastically amended or possibly dropped. [82] The use of hypotheses, like that of theories, concepts and models, is not and end in itself. Hypotheses and the like are theoretical assumptions directed towards the understanding of peoples and cultures.

One of the main disadvantages inherent in the subject-matter of anthropology is that one cannot experiment with human societies. Anthropologists have, therefore, looked on the comparative method as an equivalent or substitute of laboratory experimentation. [83] Others point out that the comparative method does, to some degree, make up for the absence of written sources. [84] There is unanimous agreement that comparison is essential to anthropological research; after all, comparison is a generic aspect of human thought. Even thought anthropology has been the most comparative of the social sciences, the method is certainly not a particular property of anthropological investigation. Comparison is needed for some degree of accuracy and for reaching some general conclusions. A science of man cannot be developed out of individual cases. [85] Some are in favor of using the comparative method for formulating universal statements; others are more cautious. [86] From a practical point of view it must be admitted that comparison always takes place when an anthropologist studies another culture, even though the comparisons may not be explicit. [87]

The first attempts to apply the comparative method in anthropology were mostly unsuccessful. Earlier writers tended to cite indiscriminately reports of undetermined reliability about customs col-

---

[81] Firth, 1958, p. 11; Haviland, 1974, pp. 11-12.

[82] Hsu, 1972, p.10.

[83] Nadel, 1951, p. 222; cf. Hoebel, 1972, pp. 7-8.

[84] Lévi-Strauss, 1963, p. 16.

[85] On the comparative method confer the following essays: Ackerknecht, 1954; Radcliffe-Brown, 1951; Schapera, 1953; Lewis, O., 1956; Evans-Pritchard, 1963; Eggan, 1953 and 1962; Chaney, 1973.

[86] Cf., for example, Radcliffe-Brown, 1951, p. 127; Bock, 1974, p. 411-412; Barth, 1974, p. 207. Some anthropologists, like Eggan, 1962, p. 368, Evans-Pritchard, 1963, pp. 28-31, Schapera, 1953, p. 61 and Hoebel, 1972, p. 7, are more cautious.

[87] Hsu, 1969, pp. 53-54; Lewis O., 1956, p. 56; Evans-Pritchard, 1963, p. 13; Bohannan, 1963, p. 10; Beattie, 1964, p. 14.

lected by untrained observers from all parts of the world. [88] The comparative method, consequently, lost much of its appeal and many anthropologists either criticized it openly or just ignored it. [89] Besides, many others rejected the use of the comparative method to reconstruct the stages of evolution as unscientific. [90] The change in anthropological attitude came about with Murdock's *Social Structure* and with Nadel's assertion that anthropology "is wedded to the comparative method." [91]

It is generally agreed that in comparing different societies or cultures the differences must be explored as well as the similarities; the former may at times be more significant than the latter. [92] A general principle is that cultural items can only be intelligently compared when they are first understood in their own cultural context. [93] Customs, beliefs and objects do not exist in isolation but in relation to other cultural traits. The understanding of these relations may be necessary for a meaningful comparison which goes beyond the superficial listing of traits. [94] Another principle, put forward by Boas as early as 1896, states that legitimate comparison must be restricted to those customs and objects which have been proved to be the effects of the name causes. [95] Some anthropologists have taken ideological postulates in societies as a basis for comparison, while others have suggested that one could compare processes, that is, the way comparable things are done in different societies. [96] There seems to be no single method of comparison applicable in all cases. Like fieldwork, the approach one takes depends largely on the problem. [97]

---

[88] Typical examples are Spencer, H., 1876 and Frazer, 1890. Cf. Golderweiser, 1925, pp. 214-25 and Jacobs, 1964, p. 39. Tylor, 1889, is an exception in that it is a much more rigorous attempt to apply the comparative method to anthropological data.

[89] Boas, 1896. Cf. Jacobs, 1964, p. 39; Evans-Pritchard, 1963, pp. 18-19; Haddon, 1910, p. 142.

[90] Taylor, R. B., 1973, p. 9.

[91] Nadel, 1951, p. 193. Cf. Ackerknecht, 1954, pp. 117-118; Lewis, O., 1956, p. 56; Hoebel, 1972, p. 7. The contemporary approach is best seen in the Human Relations Area Files which are intended to provide a selected sample of cultures, organized in terms of standard classifications to provide for comparison and for the testing of generalizations. Cf. Textor, 1967. For an evaluation of these files, see Jacobs, 1964, pp. 39-40.

[92] Hsu, 1969, p. 41; Evans-Pritchard, 1963, p. 25.

[93] Beattie, 1964, p. 10.

[94] Cf. Evans-Pritchard, 1963, p. 33; Nadel, 1951, p. 222. For two very specific examples of comparison, see Evans-Pritchard, 1929 and Nadel, 1952.

[95] Boas, 1896, p. 275.

[96] Gluckman, 1952, pp. 1 ff.; Hsu, 1969, pp. 61 ff.

[97] Lewis, O., 1956, pp. 73-75.

Anthropology shares with other disciplines many other theoretical formulations and methods besides the attempt to generalize and the use of the comparative method. One of the most written about problems is the place of anthropology in the academic world. The classical debate has been whether anthropology is a science or an art, whether it belongs to the natural or social sciences or to the humanities. The question was framed as long ago as the fourteenth century and an unanimous solution has not yet been found. [98] The heart of the problem lies in the fact that anthropology is probably unique, in that it is an attempt by the scholar to understand another style of life by the most direct form of investigation. [99] Today, anthropology is classified with the social sciences and it has been called the youngest among them. [100] But its roots lie equally in the humanities and in the natural sciences. Its mood is certainly scientific. [101] But there can hardly be any doubt that anthropology is also a humanistic inquiry, and this explains why the interest of anthropologists in humanistic studies has increased in the last two decades. [102] In like manner anthropological method is both scientific and humanistic. [103] Hence one must examine briefly the relation of anthropology to sociology and psychology and to history, the humanistic discipline to which anthropology has been often compared. There are differences both in the field of study, in the area covered, in the methods used and in the main interests. Anthropology's chief concern has been non-literate societies, while sociology and psychology have dealt with Western civilization. The area covered by anthropology is much wider and more inclusive. The anthropological method of fieldwork, the studying of a society face-to-face, has no parellel in the other social sciences which have concentrated on the use of sampling, statistics and the like. Moreover, anthropology is not an experimental science, for, as has been pointed out above, cultures and societies cannot be subjected to laboratory tests. Again, the anthropological approach has been a holistic one; the sociological and psychological approaches have concerned themselves as a rule with particular problems in culture. Anthropology is much

---

[98] Herskovits, 1965, p. 407.

[99] Lévi-Strauss, 1966, p. 126; Ember and Ember, 1973, p. 3; Taylor, R. B., 1973, pp. 18 ff.

[100] Lienhardt, G., 1966, p. 1; Lévi-Strauss, 1963, p. 361; Hoebel, 1972, p. 15.

[101] Jennings, 1963, p. 5; Wolf, 1964, p. 13; Kessing, 1958, p. 3; Lévi-Strauss, 1963, p. 361; Clifton, 1968, p. 3.

[102] Dubois, 1963, p. 33; Hoebel, 1972, p. 5.

[103] Berreman, 1966, pp. 346-347.

broader in its theory formation than either sociology and psychology and has utilized concepts from both these disciplines. [104] Social anthropology, in particular, borrows concepts from sociology and not from psychology, and it is thus inclined to be more sharply distinguished from psychology. Psychological anthropology, on the other hand, is more akin to psychology. Many of these traditional differences now seem to be breaking down. [105]

Anthropologists have been recently re-examining the relation of their discipline to history. The interest in history subsided when the evolutionary theories of the nineteenth and early twentieth centuries were discredited. Since the history of non-literate societies was not recorded in writing, anthropologists abandoned the historical approach. Studies of society or culture became functional or synchronic, that is, of the present in terms of the present, rather than historical or diachronic, that is, of the present in terms of the past. When Professor Evans-Pritchard, after having himself produced two historical studies, suggested that the relation between anthropology and history should be carefully considered, the reaction of his colleagues was almost an uproar. [106] This hostile anthropological attitude Evans-Pritchard later ascribed to antihistorical prejudice. [107] Even though Evans-Pritchard's view on the nature of anthropology as a humanistic discipline is not universally accepted, the relationship between anthropology and history is now hardly disputable. The 1966 meeting of the Association of Social Anthropologists of the British Commonwealth was dedicated to anthropology and history. [108] Social anthropology in particular would have greater links with history, especially social history. Evans-Pritchard suggests that social anthropology and history do not differ in aim and method "for fundamentally both are trying to do the same thing, to translate one set of ideas into terms of another, their own, so that they may become more intelligible, and they employ similar methods to that end." [109] There are, of course, some differences. The historian studies societies through historical documents and has directed his research to civilizations. [110] The historian does his work in the

---

[104] Pelto, 1966, pp. 8-9.

[105] Beattie, 1964, pp. 26 ff.

[106] Cf. Evans-Pritchard, 1940a and 1949. This suggestion was made in Evans-Pritchard, 1950, pp. 139 ff.

[107] Evans-Pritchard, 1961, p. 172.

[108] Lewis, I. M., 1968.

[109] Evans-Pritchard, 1961, p. 184; cf. Beattie, 1964, pp. 24-25; Bohannan, 1963, p. 12.

[110] Mead, 1964, p. 156; cf. Anderson, 1971, p. 3.

library and not in the field. [111] In the Western world at least, the interest of many historians has been been directed to a large extent to political events, while anthropologists have been just as concerned with domestic and community affairs. The anthropologist approaches his data from a different angle and perspective and thus he writes about society or culture in a different way. But the anthropologist who tries to understand the present condition of a society as fully as possible can hardly fail to ask questions about how it came to be as it is. The past may be directly relevant to explain and understand the present. Another reason why the anthropologist cannot neglect history is that the account of past events, even if historically undocumented, constitutes a body of contemporary ideas which people have about those events. History is therefore an aid to understanding, even though it is not the only means. [112] Margaret Mead, approaching the question from a different angle, draws attention to the fact that both anthropology and history place special value on the unique event. Psychological anthropology has close links to history, for the study of personality and culture leads a scholar to place man in society which has a long social history. [113] And Lévi-Strauss, though his views on anthropology may not square with Evans-Pritchard's or Mead's, holds that anthropology and history must cooperate. Especially when both the historian and the anthropologist are studying literate societies, the difference between them is one of orientation and of organizing the data. In the study of non-literate societies a little history is better than no history at all. [114] In fact, discussing the future of anthropology, Lévi-Strauss maintains that, in those non-literate societies which are being westernized, anthropology will eventually be taken over by local scholars who will adopt the aims and methods similar to those which have been found useful for the study of our own culture. [115] One of these methods is no doubt the historical one. There are probably two reasons why anthropologists are looking more favorably towards history. The first is the study of social change. Many non-literate societies are undergoing great social changes through the impact of the great civilizations. Anthropologists who have revisited their original field of study have realized that the study of change involves the study of

[111] Hoebel, 1972, pp. 15-16.
[112] Beattie, 1964, pp. 23-24; Schapera, 1962, p. 154.
[113] Mead, 1964, pp. 155 ff.
[114] Lévi-Strauss, 1963, pp. 12 ff.
[115] Lévi-Strauss, 1966, p. 126.

the recent historical past. [116] Secondly, the increasing interest in literate societies by anthropologists brings with it the realization that the historical documents of the particular culture under investigation cannot be ignored; and the anthropologist has no other alternative but to turn to the historical method.

Finally, the few anthropologists who have tried to examine the relation between anthropology and philosophy have tended to align anthropology with history. "It's (i.e., anthropology's) type of validity," write Northrop and Livingston, "should be compared to that of history in which a large place is left to the interpretative ability of the historian in his reconstruction of the past." [117] The knowledge produced by anthropological research belongs "epistemologically to the sphere of the humanistic disciplines rather than to the sphere of the physiomathematical sciences." [118] The relation between anthropology and philosophy has not yet been worked out in any detail. One reason why the two disciplines cannot pursue their own paths independently of each other is due to the fact that anthropologists have made important statements on the nature of man. [119] Further, anthropology has also its practical applications; hence the title "applied anthropology." [120] Moral and philosophical issues are often brought to the surface by anthropological studies. David Bidney has, therefore, attempted to work out what he has called a meta-anthropology, which refers to the theory concerned with the problems of cultural reality and man's nature. [121] Such attempts, however, are still in their infancy.

RELIGION IN ANTHROPOLOGICAL STUDIES

Religion forms only one of the areas covered by anthropological research. Since religion is a universal phenomenon, any study of a society or culture which aims at taking a holistic approach cannot ignore it. The task of social anthropology is to study the different kinds of social relations. But there are beliefs and religious values which are intrinsic to these relationships. [122] In other words, an an-

---

[116] Schapera, 1962, p. 153. Kottack, 1974, p. 13, points out that both the historian and the anthropologist are interested in change, the former in change in personnel, the latter in change in form.

[117] Northrop and Livingston, 1964, p. 24.

[118] Northrop and Livingston, 1964, p. 25. Cf. Bidney, 1967, p. 177.

[119] Montagu, 1962b.

[120] Mair, 1969b; Evans-Pritchard, 1951, pp. 109-29; Mead, 1964, pp. 12-13; Ember and Ember, 1973, pp. 512-529.

[121] Bidney, 1967, pp. 156-82.

[122] Fortes, 1961, pp. 166-91.

thropologist often discovers that to understand, for instance, certain kinship relations, he must know some of the religious beliefs of the society itself. One of the tasks of social anthropology is, therefore, to show the relation of religion to social life in general. [123] Also, one of the most common religious beliefs is that man does have continuing relations with God and the spirits. These relations are institutionalized. Man's behavior and attitude to the deity or deities are thus important standardized human actions having repercussions on other aspects of human life. The study of religion need not always take into account social relations. Religious beliefs form a system of interrelated ideas and can at times be understood without direct reference to society. [124] The anthropologist is interested in people's attitudes towards the world, and religious beliefs often form part of the world view. Thus some anthropologists have preferred to discuss religious beliefs under the heading "world view." [125] Moreover, since religious beliefs and practices are learned, they form an integral part of culture which some have defined as an instrument for handing down learned behavior from one generation to the next. Religion is thus a system in itself which forms part of the cultural heritage of a people. Anthropologists agree that religions could also be studied as systems of thought independent of other cultural traits. One American anthropologist has complained that his colleagues have tended to neglect such studies; a complaint which seems more applicable to American anthropologists themselves than to their British colleagues. [126] In fact American anthropologists have themselves admitted that the best studies on the religions of non-literate peoples have been made by British social anthropologists. [127]

Anthropologists have applied their general methodology to the study of religion. They realize that one has to go beyond external features. [128] While religious rites are easily observable, their meaning often eludes the investigation of the observer. [129] The outsider's interest in religious matters is often looked upon with suspicion, much more so if the observer's attitude tends to deride or minimize their value. Mere

---

[123] Evans-Pritchard, 1959b, p. 6.
[124] Beattie, 1959b, p. 58. This topic is further discussed in Chapter V.
[125] Hostetler and Huntington, 1967; Hallowell, 1960. The use of the concept "worldview" in anthropological literature is summarized in Chapter V.
[126] Spiro, 1964a, p. 1.
[127] Wolf, 1964, pp. 71-72; Eggan, 1953, p. 118. Cf. Jacobs, 1964, p. 32.
[128] Lévi-Strauss, 1966, p. 127.
[129] Hultkrantz, 1965, p. 77; Evans-Pritchard, 1953b, p. 110.

observation of religious rites is not sufficient to understand them. [130] Some insist that, following the method of participant-observation, one should take active part in some of the rites he is studying. [131] For the anthropologist the study of religions is not merely the accumulation of facts. He must also evaluate and interpret them. He sees the rites and beliefs in perspective; in other words, he sees them as part of the total life-style and cultural background. He is thus able to judge their significance, that is, to elicit a more comprehensive meaning these religious beliefs and rites have for their adherents and for social life in general. [132]

The application of the comparative method to the study of religions has lagged behind in anthropological studies. In nineteen fifty-nine, Evans-Pritchard noted that "it cannot be said that anthropologists have yet built a science of comparative religion." [133] More than a decade after its pronouncement, this statement is still valid. Lessa and Vogt's mis-named book, *Reader in Comparative Religion*, shows how little comparative work has been done. [134] When one turns to the so-called great religions, one has to admit that anthropological studies in this area are relatively few. Recent bibliographies on anthropological studies of literate societies are conspicuous for the few, if any, works on religion they refer to. [135] There have been some studies on Indian religions and on Islam, but these have concentrated on local beliefs. [136] This, naturally, does not suffice. One must also study the scriptures, for they express ideals which influence religious beliefs and practices. And the relation between the ideal and the real should also be taken into consideration. [137]

The History of Religions — Aims and Method

Religious phenomena are so numerous that a scholar can dedicate his whole life to their study. To such a scholar the questions arise: how does one order the vast material; how does one approach the data; how does one account for the origin of religion; and how does one

---

[130] Berndt and Berndt, 1967, pp. 73-74; Furer-Haimendorf, 1962, p. 1.
[131] Hultkrantz, 1965, pp. 79-80.
[132] Cf. Evans-Pritchard, 1959b, p. 10.
[133] Evans-Pritchard, 1959b, p. 7.
[134] Lessa and Vogt, 1972.
[135] Cf. Hsu, 1969, pp. 104-20; Goldschmidt, 1968, pp. 337-39; Geertz, 1968, p. 407.
[136] Bellah, 1965, pp. 230-35; Harper, 1964.
[137] Hsu, 1969, p. 49.

deal with the problem of religious change? While the sociologist, psychologist and anthropologist can take the general approach to human phenomena elaborated in their respective discipline and apply it to religious data, the historian of religions has to devise a specific theoretical and methodological framework. Students of religion have concentrated their efforts on various religious problems, often portraying different interests and perspectives in their study of religious beliefs and practices. [138]

The history of religion is the study of the origin and development of religion. It tries to embrace all the world's religions, past and present, in one single field, as one whole phenomenon evolving in time. [139] It aims at unfolding the one great pattern of religion and also at interpreting the status of any one religion in its particular historical milieu. The result of this approach should be a general classification of religions. Such attempts have a long history and they abounded in the eighteenth and nineteenth centuries. [140] This approach has become, however, much less common today. Similarly, the evolutionary perspective has lost most of its appeal. Some scholars still look for the origin of religion, but as a rule this search has been abandoned. The common opinion maintains that it is not easy to determine the history of many religions, and that the question of origins is an insoluble puzzle. [141] Historians of religion hold that, after having classified all religions, then one can move into comparative religion or the history of religions. [142]

The term "comparative religion," like the "history of religions" means different things to different people. The former phrase is more in use in Great Britain than in the United States of America. Comparative religion denotes in general the task of discovering and comparing data. [143] There are certain characteristic features in all religions which can be compared because they have the same basic meaning; and it is the aim of the student of comparative religion to draw up these features. The material used by scholars varies. Some, like E. O. James and G. Parrinder, have incorporated in their works data from non-literate societies. These two scholars have also made use of archaeo-

---

[138] Parrinder, 1962, pp. 10-11; Kitagawa, 1959, p. 15: Ashby, 1965, p. 29.

[139] Parrish, 1965, Preface.

[140] Parrish, 1941, p. 47.

[141] Brandon, 1959. Cf. Bleeker, 1963, p. 19; Parrinder, 1962, p. 122; 1966, pp. 257 ff.; Eliade, 1969a, p. 52.

[142] Parrish, 1941, p. 63.

[143] Kitagawa, 1959, p. 14; Streng, 1969, p. 37.

logical material to outline religions of the past. R. C. Zaehner and S. F. G. Brandon prefer to ignore the religions of non-literate peoples and to concentrate on the great religions. Both Zaehner and C. J. Bleeker have complained that too much emphasis has been given to non-literate cultures. [144] The latter has asked whether the study of the great religions is not really the better starting point. [145] Zaehner has thus described the comparative study of religion:

> [It is] concerned with the great religions and ethical systems of the East, the setting forth of their development and spiritual meaning, and the interpretation of them by comparison and contrast with each other and with the religions and ethics of the West. [146]

The tendency among students of comparative religion is to emphasize the similarities between the various religions. [147] External features often occupy the leading place in their studies and similar features are frequently given an identical meaning. [148] The preference of American scholars for the title "history of religions" is in part due to the fact that they recognize that such stress on similarities may be misleading as well as superficial. [149] In fairness, it must be noted that at least some students of comparative religion are aware of the need of historical studies on each religion. James has remarked that religion can only be rightly understood if it is placed in its proper cultural setting; and Gualtieri has noted that contemporary students seem more ready to admit that activities which are outwardly similar may have quite different meanings. [150]

The historian of religions studies the religions of the world in their historical setting. [151] His first aim is to draw a general outline of the history of each religion, which is studied in its own environment, in its development within that environment, and in relation to other cultural values belonging to the same social conditions. Religious data are seen in their historical connections. [152] Whether the emphasis is placed on the historical development of a particular religion, or on seeing the religion in its cultural setting, depends on the choice of the

---

[144] Zaehner, 1962, p. 11; Bleeker, 1963, p. 13; cf. Parrinder, 1962, pp. 9-10.
[145] Bleeker, 1963, p. 13.
[146] Zaehner, 1962, p. 12.
[147] Kitagawa, 1967, p. 42.
[148] Gualtieri, 1967, p. 32.
[149] Kitagawa, 1967, pp. 41-43.
[150] James, 1938, p. 33; Gualtieri, 1967, p. 35.
[151] Bleeker, 1963, p. 36.
[152] Pettazzoni, 1954, p. 217; King, W. L., 1968, p. 6.

historian of religions. The historical approach brings to the fore the uniqueness and the significance of the religious data. It also assumes that changes in history result from interactions with other conditions surrounding the religious event. [153]

Yet such historical studies are only preliminary steps. [154] The general aims of the history of religions are conceived in different fashions. Some see its main objective as "a scholarly inquiry into the nature and structure of the religious experience of the human race and its diverse manifestations in history." [155] Others prefer to describe its primary role and function as that of "describing and interpreting the religious data, past and present." [156] Still others see the special task of the history of religions as that of explaining the historical conditions in which a religious person or community lives. [157] Mircea Eliade states that the historian of religions also tries to discern the function of religious symbolism in general. [158] The historian of religions aims at coherence, at understanding and interpreting the religious data on their own plane of reference. The prime object of investigation is the nature of religious experience and expression. [159] Some historians of religions have insisted that their main concern is with persons who believe. [160]

Religion is held by historians of religions to be more than a system of beliefs, doctrines and ethics. It is a total orientation and a way of life which aims at enlightenment, deliverance and salvation. What is of primary importance is the way the believer experiences this total orientation. The historian of religions does not abandon the comparative method. It is of the very nature of his discipline that he is not just a specialist in a single field. Nor does it suffice for him to use exclusively historical method and theory. He must study at least a few religions so as to be able to compare them, and thereby to understand the modalities of religious behavior, institutions and ideas. [161] Eliade complains that too many historians of religions have specialized in one small area and have produced highly technical work. "In short," he writes, "we have neglected this essential fact: that in the title

---

[153] Streng, 1969, pp. 38-39.
[154] Ashby, 1965, p. 25.
[155] Kitagawa, 1968, p. 199.
[156] Ashby, 1965, p. 5.
[157] Streng, 1969, pp. 39-40.
[158] Eliade, 1959b, p. 97.
[159] Eliade, 1969a, pp. 6-7; Long, 1967, p. 77.
[160] Smith, W. C., 1959, pp. 37-38; 1962, p. 17.
[161] Eliade, 1969a, p. 28.

'history of religions' the accent ought not to be on the word *history*, but on the word *religions*." [162] This emphasis is shared by others in the same field of study. [163]

A few students have pointed out that neither the term "comparative religion" nor "history of religions" adequately designate the scope of the modern study of religions. [164] Hideo Kishimoto has thus coined a new term, "religiology," which has its closest parallel in the German "religionswissenschaft." [165] This new term, however, has not become common usage in the English-speaking world. For Kishimoto religiology is a branch of science and its aim is the scientific study of religion. It is also a humanistic study in that human values are included in the study of cultural religious phenomena. The object of such a study would be religion as a cultural or social fact and as observable human behavior. Religiology is thus a scientific pursuit because it studies religions empirically and it deals with objects which are empirically observable by any student, while metaphysical perspectives are not directly treated. [166] Religious experience is also dealt with in religiology for, even though experience is intimately personal and unobservable, yet it still is human behavior which affects man not only inwardly but also outwardly. Religiology is, therefore, an objective study and belongs to the descriptive disciplines. It would differ from the history of religions in that the latter treats the data as expressing unique phenomena, while religiology looks on the same data as manifestations of typical phenomena. For the historian of religions religious events occur in one particular historical situation; for the student of religiology religious events are typical phenomena which recur in many cultures. [167] Religiology also collects all the verifiable knowledge and material on religion and classifies and organizes them. Such material includes religious experience, thought, behavior, doctrine and organizations.

These studies on religion lead straight into the phenomenology of

---

[162] Eliade, 1969c, p. 29.

[163] Cf., for example, Smart, 1969, p. 17.

[164] Ashby, 1965, p. 39. Pummer, 1972, pp. 102 ff., lists the terminology used to describe the study of religions.

[165] Kishimoto, 1967, pp. 81-86. Cf. Sharpe, 1971, p. 2 and Pummer, 1972, pp. 104-106. The latter raises serious questions regarding the identification of "religionswissenschaft" with the history of religions. Penner and Yoman, 1972, p. 107, use the term "religionswissenschaft" to mean the science of religion, a discipline which restricts itself to the study of religions as such. Smart, 1973a, pp. 4 ff. opts for the term "the study of religion."

[166] Kishimoto, 1967, p. 84.

[167] Kishimoto, 1967, pp. 84-85.

religion, which can refer to the philosophical school of Husserl. [168] The phenomenology of religion could, therefore, be part of the philosophical study of religion. Some scholars, however, while explicitly disavowing the claim to philosophical speculation, [169] have used broad phenomenological methods to study and explore religions. For them, the phenomenology of religion is a study which seeks to discover the phenomena, that is, that which "appears." [170] The word phenomena refers both to the objective and subjective elements which a person experiences. Applied to the study of religion, this implies that phenomenologists are not concerned with the truth or falsehood of religious beliefs. What is important to them is the objective fact that people profess religious beliefs and express these in ritual form. Whether the beliefs are true or false, or whether the gods and spirits believed in exist apart from the believer or not, the religious attitude of the believer remains the same.

Schleiermacher and Otto are to a large degree responsible for the early development of the phenomenology of religion. The former insisted on the element of feeling and emotion in religious life. In order to describe the basic attitude of the behavior, which is to some extent concealed, Schleiermacher coined the phrase "religious experience."[171] Otto, specifying further Schleiermacher's ideas looked on religious experience as a feeling of awe in the presence of the sacred or holy. Religious experience is a unique feeling brought into being by man's confrontation with the holy which is grasped by the whole man as a mystery—a "mysterium tremendum et fascinans." [172] Following Otto, phenomenologists consider religious phenomena as primarily a manifestation or a revelation of the sacred; religious experience is seen as an experience or profound awareness of the divine or holy. [173]

This is also the starting point of most historians of religions who, whenever they go beyond giving an historical account of a particular religion, try to assume a phenomenological approach. The historian of religions, Eliade tells us, begins as a historian and "completes his historical task as a phenomenologist or philosopher of religion." [174] Bleeker states that "the history of religions leads with logical necessity

---

[168] Husserl, 1931. Cf. Bettis, 1969, pp. 1-4; Smart 1973b, pp. 19-20; 49 ff.
[169] Bleeker, 1972, p. 41.
[170] Leeuw, 1933, vol. 2, pp. 671 ff. Cf. James, 1956, p. 229; Smart, 1969 p. 3.
[171] Schleiermacher, 1893.
[172] Otto, 1950.
[173] Pettazzoni, 1959, p. 10.
[174] Eliade, 1959b, p. 88.

to phenomenological investigations." [175] The phenomenology and history of religions are thus closely linked; the first is clearly dependent on the matter which the second has to offer. Phenomenology is a necessary approach to the study of religions because there is no other way of penetrating into the significance of any religious fact. [176] Phenomenology has thus been the helpful tool of the historian of religion. [177]

There are, however, important differences in perspective between the phenomenology and the history of religions. The historian examines the cults and beliefs within a particular religious tradition, the phenomenologist makes a systematic analysis of the phenomena itself. The former is more interested in the origin and development of the historical religions and in the influences which may have contributed to their growth and expansion; the latter sees his task as describing the thing in itself, that is the religious fact, and not as it stands in the world of interdependent and contingent objects. Religious facts are, therefore, to some degree abstracted from their historical and cultural context, or prescinded from history. This is the only process, it is claimed, by which the meaning and over-all picture of religious phenomena can be attained. [178]

To what degree do phenomenologists attempt to grasp the essence of religion is not very clear. Some unhesitatingly affirm that phenomenology is not the pursuit of the essence or nature of religion and that, consequently, its main concerns are descriptive and typological. [179] Others, including Eliade, find no difficulty in stating that the aim of phenomenology is the essence of religion. This quest for the essence can create tension between the historian and the phenomenologist. [180] Bleeker suggests that phenomenology seeks the "eidetic" vision, that is, its aim is the search for the "eidos," the essentials. [181] The main quest here appears to be the essential characteristics of religious phenomena. Bleeker thinks that the definition of religion should be the final goal of the phenomenologist — a position not shared unanimously by his colleagues. [182] The disagreement between phenomeno-

---

[175] Bleeker, 1963, pp. 2-3.
[176] Bleeker, 1963, p. 10; Pettazzoni, 1954, p. 217.
[177] Ashby, 1965, p. 26; Bleeker, 1972, pp. 43-45.
[178] Ashby, 1965, pp. 28-29; Kristensen, 1957, p. 2; Pettazzoni, 1959, p. 8.
[179] Kristensen, 1957, p. 9. Cf. Bleeker, 1972, p. 39.
[180] De Vries, 1967, xi; Eliade, 1969a, pp. 35-36.
[181] Bleeker, 1954, p. 148; 1963, pp. 3-4. Cf. Husserl, 1931, pp. 51 ff., where the "eidos" is defined as "pure essence."
[182] Bleeker, 1963, p. 15.

logists stems from the fact that the phenomenology of religion has a number of tasks each of which could be pursued on its own. Bleeker himself has clearly summarized these tasks into three separate, though obviously related, inquiries into i) the *theoria* of the phenomena, which discloses the essence and the significance of the facts; ii) the *logos* of the phenomena, which penetrates into the structure of the different forms of religious life; and iii) the *entelecheia* of the phenomena, which is seen in the dynamics of religious life. [183] There seems to be more agreement on the principle that phenomenology seeks to uncover the structure and significance of general religious conceptions, such as sacrifice, god and spirit. The hidden structures of the different religions is laid open by getting at the inner laws which lie behind them. [184] There is also agreement that the history of religions uses the same methodology as phenomenology. [185]

The methodological approach of the historian of religions is first of all an empirical one; that is, it deals with observable data, the recording of which is the first step taken. [186] As in the empirical sciences any a priori judgment on what should be counted as religious is disallowed, and religions are looked upon from a neutral value viewpoint. [187] Religious phenomena, it is asserted, must be investigated on their own merits, historically and comparatively, independent of any preconceived theory or accepted loyalty. [188] The historian of religions is encouraged to have definite attitudes when studying religions: attitudes such as a sympathetic understanding of religions other than his own and a critical approach to his own religious background. [189] The whole atmosphere has to be one of impartiality.

It is also insisted that a religion must be studied from within, that is, on its own terms. [190] Not that the objective observer does not offer a helpful viewpoint, but his observations tend to scrape the surface and to miss any depth of meaning. [191] To study a society from within implies that one has to ask what value has religion for the believer and what is the point of view of the believer himself. No statement

[183] Bleeker, 1972, p. 42.
[184] James, 1956, p. 229; Bleeker, 1963, pp. 11 and 36.
[185] Smart, 1968, p. 197; Ashby, 1965, p. 29.
[186] Kishimoto, 1967, p. 82; Eliade, 1961a, p. 15.
[187] McDermott, 1968, p. 12; Kishimoto, 1967, p. 82.
[188] James, 1956, p. 18.
[189] Kitagawa, 1959, p. 15.
[190] Eliade, 1961a, p. 165; Wach, 1967, p. 16; Smart, 1968, p. 104.
[191] Streng, 1969, pp. 7-8.

about religion is valid unless it can be acknowledged by the adherent of that religion. [192]

Winston King has recently elaborated the several methods of studying religion. He explains that the methods differ in nature and are dependent on the student's own attitude to religious beliefs. He writes:

> These methods of study may be classified in terms of their basic perspectives or positions vis-à-vis religion itself. By so classifying them, we shall gain some sense of why the various methods operate as they do, of why each produces its own special kind of result and of what relations each has to the others. [193]

He then goes on to distinguish five ways of studying religion current today. First, one can study religion from within. This would be the kind of investigation a believer would make of his own faith; it is a faith-perspective. Secondly, one can approach religious data from the semi-within. The attitude of a questioning believer is a typical example of a scholar who follows this path. A missionary, for example, in looking at his own faith as his prospective converts would, has to assume a semi-within method of understanding his own beliefs. While the student who studies religion from within needs to be aware of other faiths, the scholar who assumes a semi-within stance is keenly conscious of the problems which the existence of other religions present to his own faith. Thirdly, religions can be investigated from the semi-without position. This has been ordinarily the Western philosopher's approach. The scholar here tries to evaluate all truth without taking his own religious standard as the absolute criterion. The study of religion from without is the fourth method which King ascribes to the social sciences. Their approach is not normative; they do not assume an absolute standard under which they can judge their investigations; neither do they approach religious data from a religious standpoint. Finally, there is the study of religion from the detached-within; which is the method of the history of religions. King admits that this method is somewhat ill-defined. It implies that the student is not an adherent of the religion he is studying, or that he feels detached from any one particular religion. The student, however, is still within religion in the general sense, that is within religion as a whole. Probably, many statements by historians of religions and

---

[192] Smith, W. C., 1959, p. 42.
[193] King, W. L., 1968, pp. 1-8.

phenomenologists that religion must be studied from within refer to King's fifth type, namely, the detached-within. [194]

One of the most important methodological positions of historians of religions is the insistence that religious phenomena must be studied as religious. Religion must be taken as something "sui generis." [195] Religious phenomena have to be given a religious meaning and explanation. Among the most vociferous exponents of this position is Mircea Eliade. He writes:

> A religious phenomena will only be recognized as such if it is grasped on its own level, that is to say, if it is studied as something religious. To try and grasp the essence of such a phenomenon by means of physiology, psychology, sociology, linguistics, art, or any other study is false; it misses the one unique and irreducible element in it, the element of the sacred. [196]

This is in harmony with the phenomenological approach which concentrates on the essentials of religious beliefs and practices.

The comparative approach is part of the methodological procedure of all the disciplines which deal with religion; some scholars think that this method is essential to all studies of religion. [197] Comparison leads to the understanding of all religious experience, ideas and institutions in terms of other elements in the same religion and comparable elements in other traditions. [198] Analogous religious phenomena are placed side by side. The comparative method is thus an interpretative tool. [199] Its aim is to look for generalizations. Historians of religions are aware of the problems involved in comparison and of the blunders of earlier writers. But is has been the tendency of historians of religions to maintain, with students of comparative religion, that similarity in religious behavior "is infinitely more important" than the divergences. [200] This is particularly true of Eliade whose works are inclined to show the similarity in structure and meaning of religious beliefs and experience, rather than to draw up differences. It seems, however, that contemporary historians of religions are dedicating their efforts more to specialization in one field than to generalizations about man's religious nature and experience. Hence the differences in religious

---

[194] Wach, 1967, p. 16; Parrinder, 1962, p. 104. Cf. Smart, 1973b, pp. 19 ff. who seems to hold the same view.

[195] Bleeker, 1954, p. 143; King, W. L., 1968, p. 7; Fenton, 1970, pp. 67-71.

[196] Eliade, 1958b, xiii.

[197] Pettazzoni, 1959, p. 8.

[198] McDermott, 1968, p. 12.

[199] Zaehner, 1962, pp. 11-12.

[200] Eliade, 1961a, pp. 15-17.

manifestation are certainly not being neglected by all contemporary historians of religions.

The history of religions depends greatly on other disciplines. Since the historian of religions studies all religions, he must rely on the data of archaeology for the religions of the past and on the data of anthropology for the religions of non-literate societies. [201] Yet the history of religions goes beyond the interpretations of archaeology and of the social sciences. As historians of religions view it, their discipline is neither a normative one, nor solely a descriptive one; it lies somewhere in between. [202]

The normative disciplines are theology and philosophy. The latter is normative in the sense that it can give a value judgment on a religion or on a particular religious belief or practice. The former is equally normative because it approaches other religions with a specific orientation and assumption of what is true and false. Philosophers and historians of religions have often shared common problems and areas of study. Philosophy, however, has tried to bear witness to the statement that religion is not an illusion or an emotional allurement, and that, on the contrary, it answers to the most rigorous test of reason. Philosophy also attempts to purify religion from its distortions. [203] Some writers would also insist that the search for the essence of religion is a philosophical task. The historian of religions provides material for further reflection by the philosopher. Like philosophy, theology is normative because it starts from clearly defined convictions, that is, statements about religious truth which come from revelation and which are accepted as worthy of belief by the faithful. Theology takes a dogmatic stance and, though theological speculations on the history of religions have changed over the centuries, it still asks the same fundamental questions. [204] How, for instance, can the Christian understand the co-existence of the different religions and the competition that exists among them? How grasp the plurality as it is related to the Christian concepts of God, man and salvation? What is the nature of religion and of religious truth? Theology makes a definite metaphysical stance on which is the one true religion. [205] Thus theology has a dual function: first, to defend its own position against

---

[201] Brauer, 1967, ix-x.

[202] Kitagawa, 1959, pp. 18-19.

[203] Danielou, 1959, p. 68.

[204] Bleeker, 1954, p. 142; Meland, 1961, p. 267; Benz, 1959, pp. 120 ff.

[205] James, 1954, p. 104. For the relation between theology and the History of religions, see Bleeker, 1971, Dhavamony, 1969 and Kim, 1972.

other claims, and secondly to widen the understanding of the insights, experience and norms upon which it is itself based. [206] The precise tasks of theology is a long debated problem, but the very attitude of the theologian as he approaches other faiths is a commonly accepted norm. Belief in God is taken for granted, even if recognized as problematic. The relationship between man and God are worked out not from an empirical study of man, but from accepted principles derived from normative scriptural texts. Truly enough, theology has not remained uneffected by other disciplines, including the social sciences, and many theologians hold that new historical and scientific outlooks cannot be ignored. [207] The theologian is essentially performing a task for the believing community of which he is a member. The historian of religions, on the other hand, does not have the obligation of serving a religious community. [208] He does not start from a dogmatic position and as a rule he does not approach the study of religions from the standpoint of an adherent of a particular faith. Like the phenomenologist he suspends his judgment. Nor, incidentally, does he aim at creating a new universal synthetic religion. [209] The historian of religions can make great contributions to theology, but he does not approach the data in the same light as the theologian, and for method he might look with more profit to the social sciences.

Historians of religions admit that they are indebted to the social sciences. They look on the sciences as descriptive disciplines supplying materials for their own reflection and interpretation. From sociology, the history of religions has accepted insights into the action and reaction of all kinds of human groupings. Wach's *Sociology of Religion* (1944) is a case in point. Man's behavior tells us more about the actual religious level of a person than his confession of faith, and the structure of a religious community and its celebrations can supply us with better information about the characteristics of a given religion than do doctrines and myths. [210] From psychology, the historian of religions has taken the emphasis on the individual. This is more obvious in the works of some historians of religions whose stress lies on the faith of individuals. Hence the insistence by some that one

[206] Wach, 1947, p. 163.
[207] Benz, 1961, pp. 1-16.
[208] Wach, 1947, p. 162.
[209] Kitagawa, 1959, p. 15; Wach, 1947, pp. 176-77.
[210] Bleeker, 1954, p. 144.

should not study Hinduism but Hindus. [211] The study of the effects of religion on man is one of the major preoccupations of both the psychologists and the historians of religions. Bleeker maintains that the history of religions has also been of service to sociology and psychology by supplying them materials for study. [212]

While sociology and psychology have left an impact on the history of religions, it must be noted that the historian does not always approve of the work of the social sciences. These are suspected of a reductionistic tendency. [213] In other words, as the historians of religions view it, there seems to be an inclination in psychology to reduce religious phenomena to a pathological state or to a purely psychic condition in man. Similarly, sociology is suspected of looking on religion as nothing more than a group activity explainable by the fact that man is a social animal. Bleeker goes as far as to say that the historian of religions "has to keep an eye on the manner in which these materials are used, and must even give a serious warning or make frank criticism, if the historical material is made use of in an unscientific way to the detriment of the history of religions." [214]

In English speaking countries, Anthropology is probably the most neglected social discipline by the historians of religions. With some exceptions, like Eliade and Kitagawa in the United States of America, and James and Parrinder in Great Britain, few historians of religions are familiar with contemporary anthropological literature. It is therefore not surprising that the relations between anthropology and the history of religions are nowhere spelled out. Scholarly articles dealing with the relation of the history of religions with other disciplines and outlining approaches to the study of religion have omitted references to anthropological aims and methods and even to anthropological sources. [215] Historians of religions would classify anthropology with the social sciences as a descriptive discipline. They are just as hesitant in accepting interpretations by anthropologists as they are cautious in incorporating sociological analyses. "It is solely through timidity," writes Eliade, "that historians of religions have at times accepted interpretations proposed by sociologists and anthropologists." [216] The

---

[211] Smith, W. C., 1959, p. 34.
[212] Bleeker, 1954, p. 150.
[213] Danielou, 1959, p. 81; Penner, 1969, p. 52. This accusation is discussed in Chapter IV.
[214] Bleeker, 1954, p. 150.
[215] McDermott, 1968, pp. 11-13; Bleeker, 1954, p. 150.
[216] Eliade, 1959b, p. 89.

need, however, to define the relation between the history of religions and anthropology is crucial if the material collected and analysed by anthropologists is to be used meaningfully by historians of religions.

The scientific study of religion cannot abstain from relating itself to the humanities. Religion is a specifically human action and is concerned with human interests and ideals. Since the history of religions includes the study of past religions as well as the historical developments of contemporary ones, the student has to turn to history both for his material and for his method. In Brandon's words: "He [that is, the historian of religions] is concerned to understand ideas, actions and institutions of a specific kind of past generations of men and women. He used the same methods and techniques of history." [217] The history of religions starts with facts. Thus careful procedure, as practiced both in the natural and humanistic disciplines, is necessary. As in history, the facts and events have to be evaluated. Genuine history is not a mere catalogue of events. This historical method, Wach assures us, is the same in the history of religions as in all other historical studies. [218] It is possible that the history of religions is more akin to history than to any other discipline, both in its aims and method.

RELATION OF THE HISTORY OF RELIGIONS TO ANTHROPOLOGY

It has been remarked that "breaking down the barriers between the disciplines has usually been presented as a very arduous and consequently moral and exacting form of intellectual activity." [219] Relating anthropology to the history of religions is no exception, for the two disciplines have not been engaged in dialogue for some decades. Historians of religions have often explicitly neglected or ignored the theories elaborated by anthropologists. Eliade, for instance, has in fact suggested that the explanations according to the principles of the empirical sciences prejudge the issue, and he thus proposes another approach to the study of religions which apparently bypasses the viewpoint of anthropologists. [220] Anthropologists, on the other hand, have not paid much attention to the works of historians of religions, often neglecting the writings of even the leading scholars like Eliade. [221]

---

[217] Brandon, 1967, ix.
[218] Wach, 1947, pp. 260-261.
[219] Mead, 1964, p. 149.
[220] Eliade, 1960a, pp. 209-210; 1964a, pp. 57-58.
[221] While Eliade has been included in the International Directory of Anthro-

There are, however, important links between the two disciplines in question. They both have a scientific and humanistic dimension. The history of religions is an interpretative art, rather than a pure science, and anthropology is classified with the "soft" sciences rather than with the "hard" natural sciences. Anthropology has been more scientific in that it has borrowed its theories, models and methods from the scientific disciplines rather than from philosophy and theology as the history of religions has done.

The object and area of study of both disciplines overlap. Religious man is the concern of both the anthropologist and the historian of religions. [222] The latter scholar, however, takes religious man as his exclusive field of study, the former is interested in all dimensions of mankind. Both disciplines are interested in the variety of religious manifestations, in religions rather than in religion. Anthropologists have tended to stress the differences, historians of religions the similarities. Another difference lies in the fact that the majority of historians of religions have concentrated their studies on the great religions which have voluminous scriptures and theological writings, while anthropologists have been concerned mainly with the religions of non-literate societies. The history of religions has been broader than anthropology, in the sense that it has covered all religions of mankind, past and present. Anthropologists are more interested in folk religions, an aspect which has been largely ignored by historians of religions. Finally, historians of religions are mainly concerned with religious experience and they study all aspects of religion under this dimension. Religious experience has to a large degree been neglected by anthropologists.

The aims of both disciplines have much in common. Both anthropology and the history of religions seek to interpret religious phenomena, to understand the meaning of religious beliefs and practices not only in themselves, but also from the point of view of the people who adhere to them. Interpretation is central to both disciplines. Anthropologists, however, point out that explanation is part of the general aim of the anthropological study of religion and, therefore, they do not see their task as purely descriptive. [223] Both the historian of

---

pologists (1967), his name does not often appear in anthropological circles. Some of his works do occasionally find a place in anthropological references and bibliographies, but this is not a common occurrence. For exceptions see Geertz, 1968; and Firth, 1973.

[222] Eliade, 1961a, p. 15.
[223] Beattie, 1959b, pp. 48 ff.

religions and the anthropologist expect to learn from the study of religions and cultures. Both claim that their studies can lead to greater self-understanding and self-knowledge. [224]

The attitudes towards the religions and cultures studied are shared by the historians of religions and anthropologists. Both reject in principle the "a priori" approach. Anthropologists have given up the attempt to give a categorical definition of religion and many historians of religions have followed suit. Neither scholar would consider it part of his task to judge the truth or falsehood of particular religious beliefs or of any religion. No judgment is passed and the attitude striven for is that of impartiality. Both anthropologists and historians of religions have exercised a major influence in the breaking down of prejudice, religious or cultural. [225]

One of the areas where the difference between anthropology and the history of religions is most apparent is in methodology. Both, of course, use the comparative and historical method; both aim at some kind of generalization and hence often start by formulating theories the applicability of which is put to the test. The need of studying religions in their cultural setting is admitted by both anthropologists and historians of religions. For both, the study of religions begins with the observation of data. Yet the data observed by the anthropologist have not always been the same kind of data available to the historian of religions. Because of the main area of anthropological study, namely, non-literate societies, anthropologists gathered data which one could label "folk religion". In order to collect this information, anthropologists had to develop a technique, that of fieldwork. Their training was geared to prepare them to observe societies face to face and to teach them how to get an inside view of a culture by direct personal contact with the people they were studying. Historians of religions have dedicated most of their efforts to the large civilizations which have a long literary history. Studying religions through texts, often a long and arduous task, has tended to make historians of religions typical "armchair" scholars. Contemporary conditions, however, are not likely to keep these two approaches apart. It seems that some historians of religions are already showing interest in the fieldwork method of anthropology. [226] The so-called primitive societies are

---

[224] Wach, 1947, pp. 4-5; Bohannan, 1953, pp. 10 and 14; Evans-Pritchard, 1951, p. 129.

[225] Little, 1958; Leiris, 1958; Shapiro, 1953; Hutchinson, 1969; Noss, 1974; Smart, 1969.

[226] White, C., 1967, pp. 161 ff.

changing and the modern anthropologist rarely studies a society which is not on the way to becoming literary. The anthropologist is usually faced with a large amount of literature about the society he has decided to study and has to become, for a while at least, an armchair scholar. [227]

Another difference between the two disciplines is that anthropologists have used such empirical methods as sampling, statistics and the like — methods which have not been used by historians of religions. The latter have had to have recourse to history and linguistics for many of their researches. One of the problems regarding the rapprochement between anthropology and the history of religions has been the methods pursued by the respective disciplines. Different procedures followed by the said disciplines for equally justifiable reasons may have led to different emphases, diverse theoretical assumptions and often apparently unreconcilable conclusions.

It is also possible that the word "empirical" is not used in exactly the same sense in both disciplines. For the anthropologist "empirical" denotes that his concern is limited to the study of those phenomena which are observable. When applied to the study of religion this implies that the attitudes and assumptions of the observer are influenced by the empirical method. The anthropologist assumes that his study of religion should not go beyond the verifiable, empirical data. He takes it for granted that he can study religious beliefs and practices without settling the issue of God or of the sacred. His tendency is to look at the human aspect of both beliefs and practices. This is probably one of the reasons why the anthropologist does not like to talk about religious experience. The historian of religions, on the other hand, assumes the existence of the sacred independent of man, and takes religious experience as the effect of the sacred on man. History of religions, in Wach's words, "is the story of man's understanding and appreciation of the fact that God has revealed himself to man." [228] The presence of the sacred and its manifestations are among the main assumptions of historians of religions. This attitude would be more evident in those scholars who approach the study of religions from a Christian standpoint. Such an approach can be described as an descending one, in the sense that it starts from God, or from the sacred or the divine. The anthropologist takes an as-

---

[227] The armchair method, once derided by anthropologists, is now considered useful. In fact anthropologists sometimes use it. Cf. Beattie, 1965, p. 58.

[228] Wach, 1958, p. 135.

cending path, starting from man himself. The historian of religions emphasizes the aspect that religions ultimately come into being because the sacred manifests itself to man. [229] The anthropologist looks at the other dimension, that religious beliefs and practices are the creations of man himself. The historian of religions, who directs his attention to the similarities in religious beliefs and experiences, will find it easier to see the sacred as a unifying principle, manifesting itself in diverse ways. The anthropologist, on the other hand, tends to be more aware of the many differences and thus finds it more plausible to ascribe the variety to man's creativity. Both views and approaches, though they may at times conflict, are complimentary. They represent two dimensions of the basic reality, that is, religious man; and they both can contribute to our understanding of man. The difficulty often lies in harmonizing the conclusions reached by the two approaches.

Anthropology and the history of religions have to face similar problems. The history of religions has been accused of attracting eccentric people to its ranks. [230] Anthropologists have often been rejected in their own society and they have been accused of romanticizing non-literate societies at the expense of Western civilization. [231] Both aim at understanding a society or religion from within, which is no easy task; hence they both feel the need to have their work evaluated by the people on whose society or religion they write. Another shared problem is that of objectivity. It is agreed that objectivity, like impartiality, is an ideal. A new problem has developed because the influence of Western technology and education has brought about an increased self-awareness on the part of those peoples studied by European scholars. The Western observer is always an outsider. The anthropologist may not be welcome because his presence may challenge native customs and beliefs. [232] The anthropologist and the historian of religions may also unintentionally suggest, to the people they are studying, Western attitudes of superiority in culture and religion. Finally, both scholars create new moral issues. The anthropologist has unwittingly often been the instrument of change, thereby raising ethical questions which may never have been experienced in the society he is studying. Anthropology is also directing serious questions

---

[229] See, for example, Zaehner, 1962, p. 28.
[230] Parrinder, 1962, p. 14.
[231] Braroe and Hicks, 1967, pp. 173 ff.
[232] Lévi-Strauss, 1967, p. 137.

to Western society itself. "The anthropologist's task," writes Paul Bohannan, "is in part to make members of his own culture ask—about their own institutions and ideas—questions they have never asked before." [233] In like manner, the historians of religions can create issues not only for believers in their own society, but also for the adherents of the religions they are studying. [234] The work of Christian historians of religions has made some theologians rewrite many of their statements dealing with non-Christian religions. [235]

The place of the history of religions in the academic world is still ambivalent, while anthropology stands well established among the social sciences. The history of religions aims at bridging the distance between these sciences and the normative disciplines of philosophy and theology. Thus another difference between anthropology and the history of religions is that the latter has been more influenced by philosophy and theology than has anthropology. Both anthropology and the history of religions are closely related to history, the aims and methods of which cannot be ignored.

EVALUATION OF ELIADE

The main reason why the works of the historian of religions can be evaluated by an anthropologist is due to the fact that the aims, attitudes, methods and problems of the two disciplines are sufficiently alike; both disciplines can therefore be related making an evaluation a feasible proposition. Also the two disciplines have a common origin and at first shared theories about the origin and nature of religion. Eliade is one of the few historians of religions who is more open to an anthropological evaluation because his principal concern has been the man of non-literate societies, an area which has been, and still is, the province of anthropology. Eliade's views on these cultures are based not on his own observations but on the field-work of anthropologists. Hence the question can be asked: does Eliade's view of non-literate man square with that of contemporary anthropology? Does his view of religious man in these societies take into account the researches of modern anthropologists?

Eliade constantly uses anthropological sources, and thus one can

---

[233] Bohannan, 1963, p. 10. Turner, V., 1969a, Douglas, 1970, and Mead, 1969, all raise provocative questions about contemporary Western culture.

[234] Zaehner, 1962, pp. 195-217. Zaehner's interpretation of Islamic texts would lead a Moslem believer to reconsider some of his basic assumptions.

[235] Schlette, 1966.

evaluate his use of these sources. More specifically, one can ask whether he uses his sources indiscriminately, or if he evaluates them, under what criteria does he do so? One can also ask whether he uses contemporary anthropological works judged significant by anthropologists themselves; whether he understands and interprets the sources he uses correctly; and whether he is selective in the choice of his sources and, if so, what norms does he use to select them? Historians of religions have in the past depended heavily on anthropological theory. Since much of the early theory on religion is today considered quite obsolete by anthropologists, one can ask whether and to what degree has Eliade abandoned the theories rejected by contemporary anthropology. One can also determine the influence, if any, of current anthropological theory on Eliade's views. Since the methods of both disciplines have many points of contact, one can also question whether Eliade adheres to those aspects of anthropological methodology which he accepts in principle.

There are a number of limitations in the attempt to evaluate Eliade from an anthropological standpoint. One cannot, for instance, evaluate Eliade's use and interpretation of the Indian scriptural texts. The work of anthropologists on Indian religions has been to a large degree restricted to folk religion. Similarly, Eliade incorporates in his works statements on the classical religions of Greece and Rome and on the ancient religions of the Middle East. Social and cultural anthropologists are not concerned with the religions of the past which lie in the province of archaeology. Eliade's views on these religions can best be judged by archaeologists, classical scholars and experts on the ancient civilizations of the East. One cannot fully determine the anthropological validity of Eliade's views on the great religions. The study of these religions by anthropologists is still in its infancy. Eliade has also made attempts to compare Christianity with other religions. Since, however, in-depth anthropological studies on Christianity are few and far between, an evaluation of Eliade's views on this matter is not possible.

This study is therefore limited in scope. It takes one aspect of Eliade's works, namely, his views on the religions of non-literate peoples and sees it in the light of contemporary anthropological studies. And since his views on religious man are substantiated by anthropological material, one can determine whether anthropological sources really support his picture of religious man. This evaluation, however, is by no means a full and exhaustive one. There is also room for a philosophical and theological evaluation of Eliade's works. One has also to admit of the possibility, and maybe also the desirability, of an evaluation of anthropological views of and approaches to religion from the standpoint of a historian of religions — an examination which lies outside the scope of this work. Since anthropology provides a lot of basic material for Eliade's reflections on religious man, an anthropological evaluation of his views seems to be one of the more pressing tasks.

CHAPTER TWO

ELIADE'S CONCEPT OF "RELIGIOUS MAN"

Primitive Man in Eliade's Works

The study of so-called "primitive" man occupies a prominent place in the works of Mircea Eliade. Archaic man's self-image is the theme not only of what he considers his most significant book, but also of most of his writings. [1] In contrast to some of his colleagues he has directed his attention to the works of anthropologists and ethnographers and his insights on religion are based on his studies of primitive man. He sees his pursuit as being essential to the historian of religions and he thus draws up cogent reasons why the study of ancient societies and their religions is necessary.

Eliade observes that the history of religions must include the study of the religions of pre-literate peoples because the discipline by nature encompasses all religions of mankind. [2] And he notes that the confrontation of primitive and modern cultures counts among the most significant events of the last few decades. [3] This encounter creates the need for dialogue which can only take place if we understand primitive religions. [4] Knowledge of traditional societies will enrich our own Western consciousness. It will lead to greater self-knowledge, for Western man will be able to see himself as other cultures see him. [5] This increase in self-knowledge is possible because some of the main constituents of religion, for instance, myths, are also a category of our thought. [6] Prehistoric cultures contain the sources of our own spiritual heritage. Thus they help us penetrate the history of the human spirit. [7] The result is that "there is this strange and reassuring fact that the change of spiritual perspective takes effect as a profound regeneration of our intimate being." [8]

---

[1] Eliade, 1959a, vii-ix.
[2] Eliade, 1969a, pp. 57-58.
[3] Eliade, 1960a, p. 7.
[4] Eliade, 1965b, p. 11. Cf. Eliade, 1959a, p. 159.
[5] Eliade, 1965b, p. 13; 1960a, pp. 10 & 232-33; 1961c, p. 878.
[6] Eliade, 1964b, p. 148.
[7] Eliade, 1960a, p. 244; 1961c, p. 877.
[8] Eliade, 1960a, p. 244.

The study of primitive cultures can, therefore, have beneficial intellectual results on our own civilization. It may lead us to uncover
new perspectives in European art; and it may also be an impetus
toward a renewal in philosophy, especially in the philosophy of symbolism. [9] Western philosophy has tended to draw its conclusions by
reflecting on the history of the West. This philosophical approach
Eliade criticizes as "dangerously close to 'provincializing' itself." [10]
The same danger applies to the whole European culture which has
ignored the great cultures of the East and traditional cultures. [11] By
taking into account primitive man "the cardinal problems of metaphysics could be renewed through a knowledge of archaic ontology." [12]
Eliade also suggests that the study of archaic religion is the best
starting point for the historian of religions, for primitive religion
still reflects a primordial or elementary stage. [13] Later religious developments can be better understood in the light of their antecedents.
Such remarks lead to the obvious question: What does Eliade mean
by the word "primitive"?

Eliade affirms that the term "primitive" is inadequate and misleading. [14] He suggests that a better term would be "preliterate" or
"archaic," but he still uses the word "primitive" for reasons of con-
venience. [15] Much of the material which Eliade labels primitive is
taken from the contemporary non-literate societies studied by anthropologists. These societies or peoples, together with cultures of the
past, Eliade refers to as primitive, archaic, ancient, traditional, premodern, exotic, anhistorical, and prehistoric. [16] They are considered
technologically poor and inferior and at times less complex when
compared to modern western culture. [17] By primitive one should not
imply an illogical mind, a primordial stupidity or a mental inferiority. [18]
Premodern man has a fully human mind. [19] Eliade considers the tribes
of South America and the remaining Australian aborigines as the

---

[9] Eliade, 1961c. pp. 867-77; 1965b, pp. 13-14.
[10] Eliade, 1959a, xii.
[11] Eliade, 1960a, pp. 8-9.
[12] Eliade, 1959a, xii.
[13] Eliade, 1963a, pp. 4-5; 1964b, p. 149; 1959b, p. 89.
[14] Eliade, 1969a, p. 57; 1967a, vi; cf. 1960a, p. 236.
[15] Eliade, 1967a, vi.
[16] Eliade, 1963a, pp. 12, 31, 98, 140, 144, & 191; 1960a, pp. 7, 44, & 61;
1959a, pp. 3, 32, 74, & 85; 1965a, p. 103; 1958b, p. 1; 1962b, p. 20.
[17] Eliade, 1960a, p. 163; 1965a, p. 103; 1946, p. 52.
[18] Eliade, 1963a, p. 12; 1969a, p. 33; 1958b, p. 126.
[19] Eliade, 1968c, p. 465.

best examples of archaic stages of culture and for this reason these societies have been the topic of his most recent studies. [20]

Primitive man is seen as being interested only in origins. [21] The exceptional value he attributes to the knowledge of the beginnings is the mental attitude typical of archaic man. [22] All renewal implies a return to the original events at the creation. [23] To primitive man "no being, no action that *means* anything has any effectiveness except insofar as the being has a heavenly prototype or the action reproduces a primeval cosmological one." [24] Cosmology, therefore, is foremost in the primitive's mind. His view of life and of the world forms a unity, an organic whole. [25] Another characteristic of traditional man is that his thoughts are expressed primarily in symbols. [26] Further, the archaic mind does not distinguish between myth and history and it also lacks the awareness of the meaning of the rites practiced so often. [27] Primitive man's behavior is definitely existential; [28] that is, his main religious beliefs and practices are always centered around the fundamental problems of human life. His life, however, seems to be one of perpetual fear. " 'Primitive' man lived in constant terror of finding out that the forces around him which he found so useful were worn out." [29]

Eliade's view of traditional man becomes clearer when he contrasts him with modern man. The crucial difference lies in the fact that modern man considers himself constituted by the whole history of humanity. [30] Preliterate man's view is ahistorical. [31] He sees himself indissolubly connected with the cosmos and the cosmic rhythms and considers himself the end product of a mythical history. [32] The difference between these two conflicting views is held to be so important that Eliade has dedicated his book, *Cosmos and History*, to its study. Another major difference lies in the fact that the primitive mind is

[20] Eliade, 1959a, p. 134. Confer also his articles on Australian religions and on South American High Gods cited in bibliography.
[21] Eliade, 1960a, p. 44; 1964c, p. 749.
[22] Eliade, 1963a, p. 76.
[23] Eliade, 1960a, p. 161.
[24] Eliade, 1958b, p. 273; cf. Eliade, 1965a, p. 59.
[25] Eliade, 1958b, pp. 189-90; 1963a, p. 31.
[26] Eliade, 1958b, p. 33.
[27] Eliade, 1958b, p. 396; 1960a, pp. 190 & 196.
[28] Eliade, 1960a, p. 196; 1960e, xx.
[29] Eliade, 1958b, p. 346.
[30] Eliade, 1959a, pp. 154 ff; 1963a, p. 13; 1965a, ix-xi.
[31] Eliade, 1959a, pp. 141 ff.
[32] Eliade, 1959a, vii.

not scientific. This theme is developed in *The Forge and the Crucible,* which sums up some of Eliade's earlier writings on the subject. [33]

Eliade insists that alchemy was not the fore-runner of modern science, for alchemy is impregnated with the traditional man's attitude to the cosmos, which looks upon the world as sacred. The cosmos became desanctified as a result of the triumph of the experimental sciences. [34] Modern man wishes to live in a desacralized world, [35] and, unlike primitive man, he is not capable of experiencing the sacred in his dealings with matter. There also seems to be a difference in their mental structure. "When we use the word 'because' and 'therefore,' the mind of the primitive man would phrase it perhaps as 'in the same way.' " [36] Eliade sees the man of exotic societies as being more overtly mythical than contemporary western man. Myth, however, does survive in modern societies in the form of prose narrative, especially the novel. [37] In some ways archaic man is better off than western man; he is more optimistic and his existence is not broken or alienated. [38] Primitive and modern man are alike in that the cultures of both have a coherent symbolism and an infantilized one existing side by side. [39] Eliade sees a definite similarity between traditional man and the modern artist. Both share the same attitude and desire of seeking the re-creation of the universe. [40]

Primitive man differs from modern man not only in his general mental outlook but also in his religious attitudes. Men of archaic societies, unlike contemporary men, live their organic life as a sacrament. [41] The outstanding reality is the sacred. "The archaic world knows nothing of 'profane' activities." [42] For primitive man there is no activity which is merely a profane skill. He thus "lives in a universe steeped in sacredness." [43] His great desire is to live in a sacred world or as close as possible to consecrated objects. [44] And again for him

---

[33] Eliade, 1938; 1955b; 1955c; 1955d. Cf. Eliade, 1968a and 1962a.
[34] Eliade, 1962a, p. 143.
[35] Eliade, 1965a, ix.
[36] Eliade, 1958b, p. 157.
[37] Eliade, 1964c, p. 748.
[38] Eliade, 1958b, p. 456.
[39] Eliade, 1958b, p. 445. By "infantalized" Eliade means an " 'easy' imitation of the archetype"; cf. Eliade, 1958b, p. 454.
[40] Eliade, 1964c, p. 748.
[41] Eliade, 1958b, p. 31.
[42] Eliade, 1959a, p. 27. Cf. Eliade, 1959a, p. 11.
[43] Eliade, 1958b, p. 331; 1962a, p. 143.
[44] Eliade, 1961a, p. 12.

nature is never purely "natural." [45] It is at the same time supernature, that is a "manifestation of sacred forces and figure of transcendental realities." [46] Extrahuman or supernatural models are the exemplars of primitive life. [47] Premodern man is thus seen as the religious man par excellence and, conversely, the religious man may be said to be a primitive. His real genius was almost exclusively on the religious plane. He undertakes to attain the religious ideal of humanity. [48] Irreligiosity is thus unknown among primitive societies.

Though the differences between primitive and modern man are numerous, Eliade nowhere denies the fundamental unity of mankind and as shown above he finds similarities between the two. It seems, however, that a greater continuity exists between the man of archaic societies and the mystic of the great religions who has kept his religiosity in a profane society. [49]

MYTH

Primitive and religious man's quest for origins is best exemplified in their mythology. "Myth narrates a sacred history; it relates an event that took place in primordial time, the fabled time of the 'beginnings.'" [50] Eliade considers myth to be always an account of a creation, in the sense that it takes one back to the very origins of the world. Admitting that myth is a complex cultural reality, hard to define, he looks upon it as the archaic man's attempt to describe the breakthrough of the supernatural into the world. The man of traditional societies clearly distinguishes between myths and fables. Only the former are considered true because they deal with sacred realities or with supernatural interventions in human affairs. [51] Myth is a paradigmatic model of what happened in the original past or, as he puts it elsewhere, it preserves and transmits the paradigms, exemplary models and archetypes. Myth unveils a mystery, it reveals a primordial event which is still recounted and repeated in the present. In other words prototype situations of men are expressed in mythological accounts. [52] Every human activity is therefore justified by reference to

---

45 Eliade, 1958b, p. 38.
46 Eliade, 1965a, xiv-xv.
47 Eliade, 1959a, p. 95.
48 Eliade, 1961a, pp. 165-66 & 187; 1967e, p. 504; 1959a, p. 86.
49 Eliade, 1957b, pp. 199-200.
50 Eliade, 1963a, p. 5. Cf. 1970, xii; 1973, p. 100.
51 Eliade, 1963a, pp. 5-6 and 9 ff.
52 Eliade, 1961a, pp. 95-96; 1960a, p. 32; 1963a, pp. 13 & 33.

a myth which relates the original deed, and the myth becomes an ideal, an example, towards which human actions should strive. [53] There is also a basic pattern in all mythology, a pattern in which opposite and contrary realities and statements are united harmoniously. Eliade refers to this model as the *coincidentia oppositorum*, which is a key concept in his works. "Myth reveals more profoundly than any rational experience ever could the actual structure of the divinity which transcends all attributes and reconciles all contraries." [54] There is in Eliade a tendency to oppose myth to reason for he explains that the decadence of mythology was due to rationalistic influences. But he is careful to note that "myth ... has its own particular 'logic,' its own intrinsic consistency," [55] and he observes that the most ancient philosophical speculation derives from mythology. [56]

The importance of myth in premodern societies cannot be overstressed. Myth is the very foundation of their social life and culture. [57] It is not a childish creation nor an aberrant production of an inferior mentality. On the contrary, it expresses for primitive man "a mode of being in the world." [58] For the man of traditional cultures myth constitutes the history of the acts of supernatural beings, a history looked upon as true and sacred. Since myth refers to creation, mythological accounts referring to an end to come are rare among primitives. [59] Preliterate man believes that knowledge of myth is also knowledge of the origin of things, and hence he claims that he can control and manipulate nature and human action. Recital of myths acquires a magical value. [60] Finally, for archaic man, myth is not only a system of knowledge but also a way of life. [61]

In contrast to prehistoric man, modern man is characterized by a disbelief in myths, a disbelief which was already present among the Greek philosophers. [62] Modern man is still in need of myths and there are clear residues of mythological behavior in contemporary modern societies. Myth tends to degenerate into an epic legend, a ballad, or a romance. The mythologies of early man have gradually

---

[53] Cf. Eliade, 1958b, pp. 416-417.
[54] Eliade, 1958b, p. 419.
[55] Eliade, 1958b, p. 428.
[56] Eliade, 1963a, p. 122 and pp. 150 ff. where he opposes myth to reason.
[57] Eliade, 1960a, p. 23.
[58] Eliade, 1960a, p. 24; cf. 1963a, pp. 3-4.
[59] Eliade, 1963a, p. 55.
[60] Eliade, 1963a, pp. 14-15.
[61] Eliade, 1963a, pp. 18-19.
[62] Eliade, 1963a, pp. 111-13.

become desacralized. Thus instead of possessing a sacred mythology, modern man has a secular and political one. These new secular myths, as well as some other characteristic features of western society, such as reading and visual entertainment, perform the same basic functions of myth in primitive society, even though they may have different meanings. [63]

For Eliade, myth has both a cultural and a religious function. On the cultural level, it provides models of all significant human actions. In doing so it bestows a meaning to the world and to human life. [64] Myth is also educational, in the sense that it does give an exemplar history; in other words, it is a history which can be repeated and therefore acquires meaning and value. It also expresses metaphysical and theological concepts. [65] On the religious plane "myths are the most effective means of awakening and maintaining consciousness of another world, a beyond, whether it be the divine world or the world of the Ancestors." [66] Myth also supplies man with models for enacting religious rites and with tools for deciphering divine messages. [67] It is also a reliable way by which man can project himself out of history and escape from the humdrum of profane time. Myth provides a way of resising the terror and dispair brought about by the tragic historical events. By living his myths traditional man can get away from chronological time and from historical conditions and transform himself into the primordial, sacred time of the beginnings. [68]

TIME

For Eliade, therefore, the concept of myth is closely linked with that of time and ritual. Myth directs man's attention towards the primordial atemporal moment, to the holy time which differs qualitatively from profane time. By narrating the myth archaic man abolishes profane time and forgets his human, unreal condition. Thus, for example, an Australian, listening to the recital of a myth "forgets, as it were, his particular situation and is projected into another world, in a universe which is no longer his poor little every-day universe." [69]

---

[63] Eliade, 1963a, pp. 190-91; 1958b, p. 431; 1960a, pp. 25-28 & 34; 1961a, p. 203 ff.
[64] Eliade, 1963a, pp. 2, 8 & 145; 1958b, p. 410; 1961a, p. 98.
[65] Eliade, 1958b, pp. 418 & 430.
[66] Eliade, 1963a, p. 139; cf. p. 145.
[67] Eliade, 1963a, p. 8; 1961a, p. 98 & 146.
[68] Eliade, 1963a, p. 18; 1960a, p. 34; 1973, pp. 100-101.
[69] Eliade, 1957b, p. 174.

In Eliade's view man is afraid of his own human predicament and he is constantly trying to find means of escaping it. What he calls the "terror of history" is a phenomenon common both to traditional and modern man, though it is much more apparent in the former. [70] Primitive man's experience of time differs radically from that of modern man; the main difference being that for preliterate man the change from temporal profane time to the sacred timeless origins is more easily achieved. [71]

Man's attitude to time is envisaged as a key problem. Three solutions, according to Eliade, can be attempted. The first is that of the ignorant man who lives in time and illusion; the second is the middle road, the one taken by the man who lives in human time while preserving an opening toward Great Time and never losing awareness of the unreality of historic time. Finally there is the solution of the yogin who, renouncing completely profane time, lives in sacred time. Primitives have chosen the middle road; the balance achieved in the myths. [72] The same attempt to avoid the "endless cycle of creation and destruction" inherent in all existence is seen as central not only in primitive religions but also in the religions of India. In the latter the concepts of renunciation and salvation are generally interpreted as endeavors to give up, break out of, and be delivered from the profane unreality and nonexistence of temporality. [73] Even Yoga is seen as a technique for escaping time, of freeing oneself from the chains of profane, meaningless history. The practitioner of Yoga is projected into a "mythical illud tempus" where reality can be conquered. [74] Though Eliade admits that Yoga is a unique Indian religious practice, he sees it as representing the archaic religious heritage. [75] Yoga has the same end as other religious practices, that is, "the exit from time and the abolition of time." [76] Likewise, shamanism is envisaged in the same light.

> While preparing for his ecstasy and during it, the shaman abolishes the present human condition and, for the time being, recovers the situation as it was at the beginning. Friendships with animals, knowledge of their language, transformation into an animal are so many signs that the shaman has re-established the "paradisal" situation lost at the dawn of time. [77]

---

[70] Eliade, 1964c, p. 748; 1963a, pp. 137 & 192.
[71] Eliade, 1958b, p. 388.
[72] Eliade, 1975b, pp. 182 & 200.
[73] Eliade, 1957b, pp. 175 ff; 1969c, p. 67.
[74] Eliade, 1957b, pp. 195 ff; 1958a, pp. 67-68; 1954a, p. 65.
[75] Eliade, 1958a, p. 339; 1954a, p. 68.
[76] Eliade, 1954b, p. 83; cf. 1969c, p. 67-79; 1958a, pp. 99 & 223.
[77] Eliade, 1964a, p. 99.

Shamanic initiation as well as many of the shamanistic performances are considered as symbols of the abolition of profane time and of the return to the mythical, sacred time of the past. [78]

RITE

Freedom from time is achieved not only by the recitation of the myth, but also and especially by a ritual repetition of the sacred action outlined in the myth itself. It is in the rite that the imitation of the sacred, by external gestures takes place and that primitive man acts out his desire to transcend the human condition. [79] For archaic man, entering into a ritual is leaving chronological time and going into the sacred beginnings when times stood still. Ritual also transports man into a sacred place, the center of the world. Eliade's views on ritual are developed in his *Rites and Symbols of Initiation*. Initiation ceremonies are seen as consisting of "a body of rites and oral teachings whose purpose is to produce a decisive alteration in the religious and social status of the person to be initiated." [80] The rites are intended to produce a fundamental change in man's existential situation. They re-enact in dramatized form man's death to the profane condition and his birth to eternal, mythical time. Rejecting the explanation that initiation is a social rite of passage from adolescence to maturity, he insists again and again that its essence lies in the endeavor to bring about a complete change in man's ontological status. [81] Initiation rites are important in the life of primitive man because they reintegrate the sacred time of the beginnings of things; they introduce a dialogue between men and supernatural beings and they re-create the universe. [82] The entrance rites to secret societies, shamanistic initiatory practices and Yoga are interpreted as initiation ceremonies having the same essential meaning and significance. [83] Eliade detects the survival of initiatory motifs and a structural pattern in rites peculiar to masons and blacksmiths, especially in Eastern Europe, in the ceremonial of the medieval guilds, in more or less military youth organizations and in other public festivals. [84] All these rites have the same end in view: namely, they aim to recapture the sacred time by denying human pro-

---

[78] Eliade, 1964a, pp. 94, 103, 132, 144, 171, 322 & 486.
[79] Eliade, 1959a, p. 35.
[80] Eliade, 1965a, x; cf. Eliade 1965c, p. 2.
[81] Eliade, 1965a, xii; 1961a, p. 187; 1960a, pp. 192 ff; 1965c, p. 2.
[82] Eliade, 1965a, p. 6.
[83] Eliade, 1965a, pp. 2 & 106-107; 1958a, pp. 5 ff. & 165 ff.; 1963b, p. 128.
[84] Eliade, 1965a, pp. 122-23.

fane time and by recreating in dramatic form this passage from the human condition to the eternal bliss. The symbolic passage from death to life is central to these rites.

Myth and rite are thus an effort on man's part to return to his blissful origins, the primordial, paradisial life before he was burdened by historical time and circumstances. But such a return is never fully achieved. The escape from time is acquired only for a moment or for a relatively brief period. The function of myths and rites, therefore, is partly thwarted. Myth and ritual can thus be seen more as symbols pointing to a desired end, than a fully effective means of realizing the end. The study of symbolism, therefore, acquires some importance in the writings of Eliade.

SYMBOL

Eliade approves of the intensified study of symbolism which owes its origin to the perspectives of depth psychology, modern art, ethnology, linguistics and philosophy. [85] Admitting that all man's activities involve symbolism, he nevertheless insists that the symbol is a specifically religious mode of cognition. [86] Because man is a temporal, earthbound being, he cannot have a direct access to the sacred which is transcendent. Man's knowledge of the sacred is, therefore, not completely a result of man's endeavors; it is not initially the end product of man's rationalistic reasonings. Man knows the sacred because the sacred reveals itself to mankind—hence the concepts of hierophany, kratophany and other types of revelation with which Eliade deals at some length. [87] All these revelations are conveyed to man in the idiom of the symbol. Hence Eliade can speak of the hierophanies being converted into symbols and of symbols becoming prolongations of the hierophanies. [88] In other words, the symbol is the way in which the holy is made manifest to man; the manner in which man can arrive at some knowledge of the sacred and the transcendent. For the "sacred is always made known through some thing." [89] The sky, for instance, is a symbol through which the sacred immediately unveils itself to man. Eliade therefore states: "The transcendence of God is

---

[85] Eliade, 1969c, pp. 9 ff.; 1965a, pp. 9 ff. & 189-90; 1959b, pp. 86-87.

[86] Eliade, 1959b, p. 95; 1969c, p. 9.

[87] For Eliade a hierophany is anything that manifests the sacred; a kratophany is the manifestation of the sacred as power. See Eliade, 1958b, pp. 10 ff. where he elaborates on all these theophanies.

[88] Cf. Eliade, 1958b, pp. 39 & 446-48; 1961a, p. 11.

[89] Eliade, 1958b, p. 26.

directly revealed in the inaccessibility, infinity, eternity and creative power [rain] of the sky." [90] And again he writes: "The sky is a direct and abiding revelation." [91]

Symbols and images are ways of expressing more than can be conveyed by human words; they impart information which is often difficult, if not impossible, to express. They are signs of transcendent reality, giving a "clear view of the modalities of the sacred." [92] Symbols can therefore be called an "autonomous form of revelation." [93] The symbol has a uniqueness about it because it brings to light a sacred and cosmological reality which no other manifestation is capable of revealing. Symbols play an important part in man's religious life and they convey to man a deeper meaning than ordinary knowledge. [94]

Eliade does not oppose symbolic thinking with rational or conceptual thought. But he distinguishes between symbol and concept. He affirms that primitive man was not just a "rational" animal, but also a "homo symbolicus." [95] Symbolic thinking is a coherent system and symbols have their own logic and metaphysics.

> Obviously, the metaphysical concepts of the archaic world were not always formulated in theoretical language; but the symbol, the myth, the rite, express, on different planes and through means proper to them, a complex system of coherent affirmations about the ultimate reality of things, a system that can be regarded as constituting a metaphysics. [96]

Eliade also alludes to the logical structure of symbolism; he writes:

> There is a logic of the symbol. Certain groups of symbols, at least, prove to be coherent, logically connected with one another; in a word, they can be systematically formulated, translated into rational terms. [97]

There are, however, important differences between concepts and symbols. The latter are acts of the whole man, the former are specifically acts of man's intelligence or reasoning powers. Hence, symbols "speak to the whole human being and not only to the intelligence." [98] All

---

[90] Eliade, 1958b, p. 40; cf. p. 99.
[91] Eliade, 1958b, p. 111.
[92] Eliade, 1969c, p. 17; 1958b, pp. 4 & 452.
[93] Eliade, 1958b, p. 448.
[94] Eliade, 1961a, pp. 130 & 211; 1958b, p. 447; 1969c, p. 71.
[95] Eliade, 1959b, p. 95.
[96] Eliade, 1959a, p. 3; cf. 1958b, p. 445. In his study of South American High Gods, 1971a, p. 266, he affirms that the archaic religions of South America reveal a "theoretical coherence".
[97] Eliade, 1969c, p. 37; cf. 1958b, pp. 8 & 453 ff.
[98] Eliade, 1961a, p. 129.

religious phenomena involve man in his totality; they are not just the work of the intellect or of the imagination. [99] While rationalization and systematization are prominent in conceptual thinking, they are less so in symbolic thinking. Emotion and intuition are more evident in symbolic thought. Similarly, while consciousness necessarily plays a leading role in rationalization and conceptualization, the unconscious has an equally important place in the process of symbolization. "Symbols address themselves not only to the awakened consciousness, but to the totality of the psychic life." [100] Symbols also seem to emphasize man's social nature. They are collective archetypes and form a popular memory. [101] Myths are common property of a society and ritual is an action which men perform as a group. It is because of religious symbolism that man does not feel himself isolated in the cosmos. [102] Conceptualization, on the other hand, stresses man's individuality. It demands reflection, an act which man carries out alone. Concepts also seem to be more abstract, almost one step further removed from reality than the symbols. Hence Eliade can write:

> Finally, it is necessary to underline the *existential value* of religious symbolism; that is, the fact that a symbol always aims at a *reality or a situation in which human existence is engaged*. It is above all this existential dimension that marks off and distinguishes symbols from concepts. Symbols still keep contact with the profound sources of life; they express, one might say, the "spiritual as lived." [103]

The symbol has suffered the same fate as myth. It has greatly degenerated in Western society. "The life of modern man is swarming with half-forgotten myths, decaying hierophanies and secularized symbols." [104] Symbols have fallen into the state of "superstition and economic-cum-aesthetic value"—a condition common in modern societies. [105] They have lost their religious meaning and have only social or artistic value. They have become more rationalized, degraded and infantilized. [106] Inferior symbolism is found also in traditional societies, but it is much more rampant in our own. Archaic man still possesses the primal symbols, such as the moon, the stars, the sun, and so on.

---

[99] Eliade, 1958b, p. 56; 1960a, p. 16.
[100] Eliade, 1959b, p. 106.
[101] Cf. Eliade, 1959a, pp. 37-46.
[102] Eliade, 1959b, p. 103; 1960a, p. 16.
[103] Eliade, 1959b, p. 102.
[104] Eliade, 1969c, p. 18.
[105] Eliade, 1958b, pp. 446 ff.
[106] Eliade, 1958b, pp. 444-45.

For this reason he is more aware of the reality of the sacred. Modern man, living in an artificially created environment has created a deeper chasm between himself and the holy. Primitive man's life is, therefore, a more integrated one. "Thanks chiefly to his symbols, *the real existence* of primitive man was not the broken and alienated existence lived by civilized man today." [107] There is, however, still some hope for modern man because the degraded images and symbols which he still possesses, can be the point of departure for his spiritual revival. [108]

The function of the symbol is basically a religious one. It transforms "a thing or an action into *something other* than that thing or action appears in the eyes of profane experience." [109] Symbols serve to reveal a sacred or cosmological reality, to effect a permanent solidarity between man and the sacred. [110] Symbols are never univocal; they are multivalent or polyvalent, insofar as they disclose many senses or meanings at the same time. [111] The function of symbolism is therefore one of unification. Symbols state contraditions in a unified system; in others words, *the coincidentia oppositorum* takes place on a symbolic level.

> Perhaps the most important function of religious symbolism ... is its capacity for expressing paradoxical situations, or certain structures of ultimate reality, otherwise quite inexpressible. [112]

PRINCIPAL THEMES

There is a basic pattern in Eliade's works which underlies the concept of myth, ritual, time and symbol. This pattern of closely related ideas is threefold in nature. First, it involves the nature of the sacred and its relationship with the profane. Secondly, it is dominated by the theme of death and resurrection. And finally, it takes the position that man has in the course of history degenerated spiritually.

The sacred is seen as "pre-eminently the real." [113] It is a powerful, efficacious force, the source of all life and energy. The sacred is the "wholly other," the transcendent, a reality which does not belong to our world even though it is manifested in and through it. It is also essentially ambivalent. The sacred attracts and repels at the same

---

[107] Eliade, 1958b, p. 456.
[108] Eliade, 1969c, p. 18.
[109] Eliade, 1959b, p. 445; 1959b, p. 98.
[110] Eliade, 1958b, p. 447.
[111] Eliade, 1958b, p. 450; 1969c, p. 14; 1959b, p. 99.
[112] Eliade, 1959b, p. 101; cf. 1958b, pp. 451-52.
[113] Eliade, 1961a, p. 28.

time; it is the cause of both life and death; it is both useful and dangerous, accessible and inaccessible. [114] Thus, there is an inherent opposition within the concept of the sacred. The opposition it not only internal but also external, in the sense that the sacred is contrasted to the profane. Eliade accepts Roger Caillois' definition of the sacred as that which is opposite to and totally different from the profane. [115] The two concepts—sacred and profane—are two different levels of reality which are opposed to one other. Primitive man's behavior is

> governed by belief in an absolute reality opposed to the profane world of "unrealities"; in the last analysis, the latter does not constitute a "world," properly speaking; it is the "unreal" *par excellence*, the uncreated, the non-existence: the void. [116]

The polarity between the sacred and the profane is both archaic and universal. [117]

This dualism is reflected in the relationship between myth and history. Myth is sacred history; it relates the origin of man and his cultures by reference to the acts of supernatural beings at the dawn of creation. [118] History, on the other hand, deals with temporary profane reality. Myth is the real, the meaningful, and the holy; history is the unreal, the meaningless, and the sinful. [119] The fullness of reality present at the beginning contains no trace of history. Myth aims at doing away with history. "The man of archaic cultures tolerates 'history' with difficulty and attempts periodically to abolish it." [120] There is a tendency, especially in preliterate societies, for historical figures to be transported into the plane of mythology. [121] For archaic man history coincides with myth. [122] This anti-historical attitude is evident in religious phenomena, for instance, in shamanism and yoga, in religious beliefs and in messianic creeds. [123] Great historical pressures were endured without despair or suicide because of

---

[114] Eliade, 1958a, pp. 152 & 284; 1960a, p. 18; 1961a, p. 11; 1958b, pp. 13-16, 370-71 & 384.
[115] Eliade, 1958b, xiv, pp. 12 ff., 447 & 459; 1961a, p. 10; 1960a, p. 130; 1958a, pp. 96 & 100.
[116] Eliade, 1959a, p. 92.
[117] Eliade, 1958a, p. 96.
[118] Eliade, 1965a, x-xi; 1963a, pp. 5 & 18-19.
[119] Eliade, 1958b, p. 401; 1959a, pp. 34-35; 1963a, p. 2.
[120] Eliade, 1959a, p. 36; cf. p. 76.
[121] Eliade, 1964a, pp. 355 & 362; 1959a, pp. 42-43.
[122] Eliade, 1958b, p. 396.
[123] Eliade, 1958a, pp. 67-68, 223 & 339-40; 1959a, p. 111.

these mythological structures. [124] Traditional man is saved from the "terror of history" because of the mythological archetypes which are repeated and recreated in the rituals.

There is likewise a great dichotomy between sacred time and profane time. The former is momentary, an eternal presence, the latter has duration, a past as well as a future. Profane time, unlike sacred time, is not renewable. "The time of the event that the ritual commemorates or re-enacts is made *present*, represented, so to speak, however far back it may have been in ordinary reckoning." [125] There is a great tendency in all societies to bring back this mythical time of the beginnings, a return effected by every rite, including the orgies which take place on New Year festivals. [126] Thus, referring to the Australian Aborigines, Eliade writes:

> This is why the initiation ceremonies are so important in the lives of the aborigines; by performing them, they reintegrate the sacred time of the beginning of things, they commune with the presence of Baiamai and other mythical beings, and finally, they regenerate the world... [127]

This nostalgia for a regeneration of time is universal.

> We thus find in man at every level, the same longing to destroy profane time and live in sacred time. Further, we see the desire and hope of regenerating time as a whole, of being able to live—"humanly," "historically"—in eternity, by transforming successive time into a single eternal moment. [128]

Such an attitude toward time is part of primitive ontology. Primitive man maintains that his acts are real only insofar as they repeat the paradigmatic gestures of the past and that only through this repetition can there be an abolition of profane time. This interpretation of archaic man's attitude to time is most forcibly put in *Cosmos and History*, where we read:

> This refusal to preserve the memory of the past, even of the immediate past, seems to us to betoken a particular anthropology. We refer to archaic man's refusal to accept himself as a historical being, his refusal to grant value to memory and hence to the unusual events... that in fact constitute concrete duration. [129]

The same pattern emerges when Eliade deals with sacred and profane place. The former is significantly the real, the meaningful, the latter

---

[124] Eliade, 1959a, pp. 151 ff.
[125] Eliade, 1958b, p. 392; cf. pp. 388 ff.; 1961a, pp. 68-69.
[126] Eliade, 1958b, pp. 394-95 & 399.
[127] Eliade, 1965a, p. 6.
[128] Eliade, 1958b, p. 407.
[129] Eliade, 1959a, p. 85; cf. p. 35.

is the structureless, the formless and the inconsistent. [130] A consecration of a locality involves a transformation of profane space. Temples and shrines were believed to be copies of primeval archetypes. [131] The center is held to be pre-eminently the zone of the sacred, and themes of a sacred mountain situated in the center of the world are obvious signs of a mythical return to creation. [132] Ritual thus becomes the ideal means for providing both a time and a place for man to transform himself from the profane unreality of everyday existence into the sacred reality of the eternal beginnings. In ritual, time is here and now wiped out. [133]

The passage from the profane to the sacred is experienced by man as a death to ordinary, unreal life and a rebirth or resurrection to the real, divine existence. Eliade sees this attempt on man's part to make this transition especially in initiation rites. During these rites the novice goes through a symbolic representation, like seclusion and circumcision, and a symbolic rebirth to a new life. He becomes a new man by re-living the ancient cosmology.

> Everywhere we have found the symbolism of death as the ground of all spiritual birth—that is of regeneration. In all these contexts death signifies the surpassing of the profane, non-sanctified condition, the condition of the "natural man," ignorant of religion and blind to the spiritual. The mystery of initiation discloses to the neophite, little by little, the true dimension of existence; by introducing him to the sacred, the mystery obliges him to assume the responsibilities of a man. [134]

The same initiatory pattern is found in secret cults, though here the emphasis lies in the new birth. [135] Moreover shamanistic experiences cannot be understood unless one sees them as initiation techniques. The shaman re-enacts ritually the symbolic death and resurrection before he is accepted as a religious specialist. [136] "It is only this initiatory death and rebirth that consecrates a shaman." [137] In his trances he descends into hell and ascends to heaven, thereby re-enacting the symbolic death and resurrection. [138] Yoga also is essentially an

---

[130] Eliade, 1961a, p. 20.
[131] Eliade, 1958b, pp. 396-72.
[132] Eliade, 1959a, pp. 12 ff., & 17 ff.
[133] Eliade, 1959a, p. 35; 1961a, p. 68; cf. 1958b, p. 32.
[134] Eliade, 1960a, p. 200; cf. 1965a, pp. 13-14, 29, 34, 91 & 135; 1961a, pp. 191-92 & 197 ff.
[135] Eliade, 1965a, pp. 5 & 41-80.
[136] Eliade, 1964a, pp. 45, 53 ff., 64 & 84.
[137] Eliade, 1964a, p. 76.
[138] Eliade, 1969c, pp. 164-66.

ecstatic experience whose structure is initiatory. The yogin begins by forsaking the profane world, dying to his family and his society, and attempts to pass beyond the human condition to achieve a rebirth to another mode of being. [139] Other ceremonies and symbols dramatically portray the same pattern. Thus, for example, New Year ceremonies state the primeval passage from chaos to cosmos and thereby regenerate the whole world. Every ritual of the cosmogony is preceded by a symbolic retrogression to chaos. And death and rebirth lie at the very heart of aquatic symbolism; [140] in other words, whenever water is used ritually, it expresses the participants' desire to die and to rise again renewed. .

The endeavor to pass from the profane to the sacred, to die in order to be reborn on a higher level of existence, is more apparent in primitive man than in modern man. The latter is seen as spiritually inferior to the former. Primitive man considers himself as constituted ultimately by supernatural beings at the beginning of time. Modern man looks upon himself as constituted by history. Modern man makes himself. He rejects the sacred and the transcendent.

> Modern nonreligious man assumes a new existential situation; he regards himself solely as the subject and agent of history, and he refuses all appeal to transcendence. In other words, he accepts no model for humanity outside the human condition as it can be seen in its various historical situations. Man *makes himself*, and he only makes himself completely in proportion as he desacralizes himself and the world. The sacred is the prime obstacle to his freedom. He will become himself only when he is totally demysticized. [141]

Modern man still has a terror of history and like primitive man he tries to find an escape from time. Myths still persist in his life. But the answer to his problems is given in secular terms. [142] He still has vestiges of the religiousness of early man, but demythologization and desacralization, which have a long history, have now reached alarming proportions. [143] While archaic man looked upon all activities as being sacred, the man of contemporary, Western culture has removed the sacred element from his life and world. Even in symbolism one can detect the loss of the sense of the sacred. This change in man's image of himself was made possible by scientific thought. [144]

---

[139] Eliade, 1958a, pp. 5-6, 165, 227, 272-73, 310, 323-24 & 362 ff.

[140] For the New Year ceremonies confer Eliade, 1959a, pp. 53-54 & 62 ff. See Eliade, 1965a, xiii, for the rituals of cosmogony and Eliade, 1958b, pp. 196 ff. for the symbolism of water.

[141] Eliade, 1961a, p. 203; cf. 1965a, xiv; 1959a, pp. 141-44 & 154-162.

[142] Eliade, 1961a, pp. 204-205.

[143] Eliade, 1963a, pp. 111-13; 1960a, pp. 29 & 233 ff.; 1961a, pp. 107-12.

[144] Eliade, 1959a, pp. 28-29; 1961a, pp. 13 & 50-51; 1969c, p. 147; 1964a, p. 456.

RELIGIOUS MAN

Eliade's themes on the sacred and the profane and on religious degeneration are also important because they help define religion and religious man. It is interesting to note that nowhere does Eliade give a precise definition of religion or discuss the problem at any length. He maintains that in order to define religion one must have possession of those pure expressions of it which were present at the very beginning. But the evidence for the origin and early stages of religion is wanting. [145] Eliade, therefore, prefers to talk about religious life, religious experience and especially religious man. So much so that even in his book, *The Sacred and the Profane*, which he subtitles, "The Nature of Religion," the topic discussed is religious man rather than religion. On finds, however, in his writings, a number of statements which bring out what he considers as the constitutive elements of religion. Religion is a revelation of the sacred. It deals with meta-empirical reality. [146] It is the "corpus of historical technique and rituals" which provides man with the means of keeping in touch with his mythical past. [147] And its function is to awaken and sustain the consciousness of another world. [148] Religion is also a philosophy of life. It offers the paradigmatic solution to every existential crisis. Paradox is woven into the very structure of religion. The divine reality is experienced ambivalently, and religion aims at presenting a synthesis, a *coincidentia oppositorum*. [149]

Religion is not just a social or psychological fact. It cannot, therefore, be explained by social, historical, or psychological functions, for these miss the "irreducible element" in religion, namely, the holy. [150] The relation between religion and culture is thus viewed with caution. "Religious forms are non-temporal; they are not necessarily bound to time. We have no proof that religious structures are created by certain types of civilization or by certain historic moments." [151] Religious reality transcends the plane of history, even though different religious experiences can be explained by differences in culture. [152]

---

[145] Eliade, 1958b, p. 1; 1967e, pp. 498-505.

[146] Eliade, 1960a, p. 18; 1959b, p. 95.

[147] Eliade, 1967b, pp. 211-12.

[148] Eliade, 1960c, p. 366.

[149] Eliade, 1965b, pp. 82 ff., 122 ff. & 206-207; 1958b, pp. 419 ff.; 1961a, pp. 156 & 210; 1960a, pp. 17-18; 1961d, p. 383.

[150] Eliade, 1958b, xiii.

[151] Eliade, 1960a, p. 178.

[152] Eliade, 1961a, p. 17; 1960a, p. 178.

There is an element of unity in all religions, a unity which is of greater moment than the differences. [153]

Like myth, ritual and symbol, religion has also degenerated since ancient times. [154] Such degeneration is evident in some traditional societies. The best example of this retrogression, repeated in many of Eliade's works, is the case of the so-called "otiose god." These are divinities which have been pushed to the periphery of religious life where they are frequently ignored. Eliade goes as far as to compare the phenomenon of the otiose god to the death of god theology in Western culture, a movement which started with Nietzsche. [155]

The sacred is also at the center of religious life and experience. Religious life is the experience of the kratophanies, hierophanies and theophanies which affect the whole of man's life. It demands the awareness of the sacred and profane dichotomy and it stirs the depths of man's being. [156] On the level of this genuine experience nature is never purely natural. "For those who have a religious experience all nature is capable of revealing itself as cosmic sacrality. The cosmos in its entirety becomes a hierophany." [157] The same experience is one of re-entering the mythical paradise of the beginnings. It is found stronger among shamans, the mystics of primitive societies. [158]

For Eliade, faith is the new dimension, acquired through religious experience, and it is found mainly in Judaism and Christianity. [159] In a passage which is crucial to the understanding of Eliade's own theology of religions, he thus writes on Abraham's sacrifice:

> Whereas, for the entire Paleo-Semitic world, such a sacrifice, despite its religious function, was only custom, a rite whose meaning was perfectly intelligible, in Abraham's case it is an act of faith. He does not understand why the sacrifice is demanded of him; nevertheless he performs it because it was the Lord who demanded it. By this act, which is apparently absurd, Abraham initiates a new religious experience, faith. All others (the whole Oriental world) continue to move in an economy of the sacred that will be transcended by Abraham and his successors. To employ Kierkegaard's terminology, their sacrifices belonged to the "general"; that is, they were based upon archaic theophanies that were concerned only with the circulation of sacred energy in the cosmos... These were acts whose justification lay in themselves; they entered into a logical and coherent system: what had

---

[153] Eliade, 1961a, pp. 17 & 62-63.

[154] Eliade, 1960a, p. 137.

[155] Eliade, 1958b, pp. 43 ff.; 1960a, pp. 134-37; 1963a, pp. 93-98; 1961a, pp. 121-25; 1967a, pp. 5-6; 1969a, pp. 47 ff. & 155; 1971a, p. 238.

[156] Eliade, 1958b, p. 126; 1960a, p. 17.

[157] Eliade, 1961a, p. 12; cf. 1958b, p. 425.

[158] Eliade, 1960a, pp. 44 & 64-68; 1964a, pp. 265-66.

[159] Eliade, 1959a, pp. 108-109.

belonged to God must be returned to him. For Abraham, Isaac was a *gift* from the Lord and not the product of a direct and material conception. Between God and Abraham yawned an abyss; there was a fundamental break in continuity. Abraham's religious act inaugurates a new religious dimension: God reveals himself as personal, as a "totally distinct" existence that ordains, bestows, demands, without any rational (that is, general and forseeable) justification, and for which all is possible. This new religious dimension renders "faith" possible in the Judaeo-Christian sense. [160]

For Eliade, therefore, faith, as understood in Christian theology, cannot be applied to all religious men. The common factor among all religious men is the desire for being. Since the profane is unreal, religious man tries to live as long as possible near his gods, the sacred supernatural beings, to whom he owes his origin. In other words, he wants to inhabit a sacred universe. This desire "is in fact equivalent to his desire to take up his abode in objective reality, not to let himself be paralyzed by the never-ceasing relativity of purely subjective experience." [161]

Sacred space thus acquires importance in the life of religious man. He expresses the dichotomy between the space that is sacred and the lifeless space of the secular world in his ritual. [162] And he, consequently, always seeks to fix his abode at the center of the world, a center represented by shrines and temples and conceived as an organized cosmos. [163] Just as religious man alternates his existence between sacred and profane space, so also he lives in two kinds of time. He experiences intervals of time that are sacred. For him profane duration can be periodically stopped. [164] Through sacred time, as well as through sacred space, religious man re-actualizes the cosmogony and re-enters the time of origins where authentic existence came into being. Religious man thus attempts to live in the continual presence of the sacred past. [165]

Religious man is essentially mythical. He is "above all a man paralyzed by the myth of the eternal return." [166] His greatest hope is to re-create the mythical events. "The more religious man is, the more paradigmatic models does he possess to guide his attitudes and actions." [167] He, therefore, assumes a humanity that has a transhuman,

---

[160] Eliade, 1959a, pp. 109-110; the same idea is repeated on pp. 159-62.
[161] Eliade, 1961a, p. 28; cf. pp. 13, 64-65, 87, 91 & 106.
[162] Eliade, 1961a, p. 20.
[163] Eliade, 1961a, pp. 22, 43-44 & 65.
[164] Eliade, 1961a, pp. 70-71 & 104.
[165] Eliade, 1961a, pp. 81 & 88-89; 1963a, p. 92; 1959a, p. 86.
[166] Eliade, 1961a, p. 93.
[167] Eliade, 1961a, p. 96; cf. p. 106.

transcendant model. The mythical gods are the models of his actions, and since the gods are always living and vibrant with life and energy, death becomes but another modality of human existence. Also, by desiring and trying to live with his gods, religious man escapes the unreality of the meaningless change inherent in profane space and time. [168]

Religious man's view of the universe is unique. For him nature has always a religious value and the supernatural is closely linked with the natural. He is led to the former by reflecting on the latter. In other words, for religious man "the world always presents a supernatural valence." [169] The world speaks to religious man of his gods and of their doings. His view of the universe is cosmic. He is completely open to the whole world; that is, he communes with his gods and he shares in the sanctity of the universe. This openess enables him to know himself as he really is, a religious creature sharing in the life of the sacred or divine. [170] Such an attitude does not imply that religious man is shirking his responsibility. Rather, his responsibility is "on the cosmic plane in contradistinction to the moral, social, or historical responsibilities that are alone regarded as valid in modern civilizations." [171] Religious man has therefore a completely different attitude to life, to the world, and to man than non-religious man. Religious man is not defined by the historical or cultural context in which he lives. This image of religious man is central in Eliade's thought. He writes:

> Religious man assumes a particular and characteristic mode of existence in the world and, despite the great number of historic-religious forms, this characteristic form is always recognizable. Whatever the historical context in which he is placed, *homo religiosus* always believes that there is an absolute reality, *the sacred*, which transcends this world but manifests itself in this world, thereby sanctifying it and making it real. He further believes that life has a sacred origin and that human existence realizes all of its potentialities in proportion as it is religious—i.e., participates in reality. [172]

For religious man, therefore, it is only the spiritual, non-material world which possesses the fulness of being. The present worldly condition acquires its meaning and value only with reference to the other worldly dimension. It is the fulness of being, the ultimate reality, for which religious man strives.

---

[168] Eliade, 1961a, pp. 99-100 & 148; 1959b, p. 459.
[169] Eliade, 1961a, p. 138, cf. pp. 116-118 & 150.
[170] Eliade, 1961a, pp. 146, 165-167, 169-170 & 172.
[171] Eliade, 1961a, p. 93.
[172] Eliade, 1961a, p. 202.

CHAPTER THREE

"RELIGIOUS MAN" IN CONTEMPORARY ANTHROPOLOGY

PRIMITIVE MAN IN ANTHROPOLOGY

The anthropologists' concern for the study of man and his religions, has, like Eliade's, been directed mainly to so-called primitive, or non-literate, cultures. And ever since anthropologists began to dedicate more of their scholarly endeavor to the study of non-literate societies, they have had to face the question of whether their attempts were really worthwhile. With the rise of specialization non-literate societies often became the exclusive or main concern of many anthropologists, thereby giving them a certain priority in the study of man. And even today some still ask whether anthropologists have overrated the importance of non-literate cultures since these comprise a small, and perhaps insignificant, minority of the world population. [1] In anthropological literature, however, one comes across justifications for the study of non-literate societies and cogent reasons in support of the momentous place they should have in the study of mankind.

Non-literate societies, which have attracted the attention of many of the influential scholars of the Western world, [2] are studied not only because they are interesting in themselves, but also because no scientific endeavor should neglect them. It is the nature of science to obtain and extend knowledge. Science suffers no unknown territory to remain unexplored. The fact that non-literate societies are different from our's and present new frontiers in human knowledge suffices to establish their place in the academic world. Since non-literate cultures are becoming extinct the need to intensify their study is even more urgent. For when a society vanishes, a door closes, locking out unique knowledge. [3] Non-literate peoples are also a laboratory in which one may study the diversity of human institutions. In spite of the fact that

---

[1] Evans-Pritchard, 1965b, pp. 1-2, complains of this attitude which is common among theologians, historians of religions and other scholars. For a typical example questioning the importance of primitive religions, see Smith, W. C., 1959, pp. 37-38.

[2] Such as Spencer, Durkheim, Bergson, Darwin, Marx and Freud. Cf. Evans-Pritchard, 1965b, p. 1.

[3] Nadel, 1951, p. 2; Evans-Pritchard, 1951, p. 9; Lévi-Strauss, 1966, p. 125; 1967, p. 135.

they are much smaller in size, and less widespread in their influence than the great civilizations, they are still vastly more representative of human culture. They provide a whole range of human behavior patterns making possible the discovery of the fundamental principles of cultural and social systems. Social life in general cannot be understood unless the greatest diversity of social institutions is taken into account. [4]

Another common reason advanced for the study of non-literate societies is that they can be seen as complete units. Consequently, the relationships between the various cultural traits and social institutions can be more readily detected. Studying non-literate peoples can thus be seen as a useful, if not necessary, step to the study and understanding of the more complex societies. [5] Non-literate societies provide an excellent starting point because it is easier to observe a culture other than one's own. The student finds it less exacting to be objective when he directs his analysis to cultures which are foreign to his own background. [6] Moreover, since non-literate cultures are now being transformed, they offer us an opportunity to study social change, making possible the understanding of cultural processes. The study of these cultures is, therefore, relevant to the understanding of the great civilizations which are today also caught up in the process of change. Anthropologists have also observed that non-literate cultures do leave their impact on the great civilizations. The former do not just vanish; they are usually incorporated into a larger unit. Hence the study of non-literate peoples is also useful because it may help us understand ourselves better. Non-literate peoples have something positive to offer us; they do not merely provide some scholars with a harmless academic pastime. [7]

Most of the reasons given to support the study of non-literate cultures apply also to the study of their religions. Unlike some of the great religions, in particular Judaism, Christianity, and Islam in the West, and Buddhism, Hinduism, and Jainism in the East, the religions of non-literate peoples are largely historically unrelated. Knowl-

[4] See Benedict, 1934, p. 17; Evans-Pritchard, 1965b, p. 1; Pelto, 1966, p. 5; Lisitsky, 1956, p. 15.

[5] Evans-Pritchard, 1951, pp. 8-9; Pelto, 1966, p. 5; Lisitzky, 1956, p. 15; Dozier, 1955, p. 232; Linton, 1944, p. 12; Lienhardt, G., 1966, p. 2.

[6] Evans-Pritchard, 1951, p. 9. One should note, however, that this argument by itself is not convincing. One could gain the same objectivity by studying the great civilizations of the past or contemporary Asian cultures.

[7] Lévi-Strauss, 1966, p. 125; Beattie, 1964, p. 4; Bohannan, 1963, p. 10; Tax, 1964b, p. 253; Berndt and Berndt, 1967, p. 145.

edge of the latter, therefore, provides the student with the large number of specimens needed if he is to embark on the task of understanding religion in general. Those scholars whose main preoccupation is to outline the nature of religion cannot make much headway without some consideration of the religions of non-literate peoples. The study of these religions may also cast light on philosophical and theological problems, for example, on the difference between natural and revealed religion, which have occupied the attention of students of religion for centuries. [8]

One of the most common terms used to describe non-literate societies is the word "primitive." In the 19th and early 20th centuries, "primitive" implied early in time and simple in structure. Contrary to its etymology, it acquired a pejorative sense, and was used to mean inferior, backward, savage, uncivilized and rude. The use of the word "primitive" to refer to contemporary non-literate peoples has been under question for over half a century. There is an increasing awareness among anthropologists that the term "primitive" is unsatisfactory and inadequate. [9] It is thus agreed that, if used at all, "primitive" should not carry a derogatory connotation, nor should it denote mental inferiority. [10] Most anthropologists would prefer to abandon the word altogether. Those who still favor its use insist that the meaning attached to it should be more carefully determined. [11] In actual fact the word "primitive" is gradually becoming less common in anthropology. [12] As Ashley Montagu puts it:

> The word primitive is not only confusing and damaging, but obfuscating, corresponding to nothing in reality, and obstructive of progress in understanding the meaning of the great variability presented by man in all his manifold variety. [13]

---

[8] Evans-Pritchard, 1965b, p. 2; cf. Benedict, 1934, p. 17.

[9] Lévi-Strauss, 1967, pp. 42-43; Keesing, 1958, pp. 44-46; Jacobs, 1964, p. 8; Montagu, 1968b, pp. 151-52; Dozier, 1955, p. 230.

[10] Pelto, 1966, p. 5, note 2; Goode, 1951, p. 24; Langness, 1965, p. 32, note 1; Diamond, 1963, pp. 104-107.

[11] Diamond, 1963, pp. 104 ff.

[12] The word "primitive" is nowadays often dropped from text-book titles and course descriptions. The text-books of the 1950's and 1960's still use the word frequently with varied and imprecise meanings and emphases. Many authors give their own definition of the word "primitive," coupled with an apology for its use. Some explain that they still use the word because it is difficult to supplant it or to replace it with a better term. The text-books of the early 1970s seem to have outgrown the need to discuss the word "primitive." If they use it at all, they take it for granted that it refers to non-literate societies which have a simpler technology than Western culture.

[13] Montagu, 1968a, viii.

When anthropologists use the word "primitive" they do so to refer to "peoples living in small-scale societies with a simple material culture and lacking (written) literature." [14] Attempts have been made to find a more suitable term and many alternatives have been tried without success. [15] The term non-literate, in spite of its deficiencies, has become quite common in anthropology. It has definite positive qualities, carrying no derogatory implications and bearing a more solid foundation in objective phenomena. Moreover, it concentrates on an important criterion namely, the presence of a writing technique, which underlies some of the major differences between literate and non-literate cultures. [16]

While there is general agreement among anthropologists about the meaning and use of the word "primitive," it is still debated whether and to what degree contemporary non-literate societies represent an earlier, prehistoric human condition. It would seem that a large number of anthropologists are wary of comparing non-literate cultures with prehistoric ones; and much less would they be inclined to deduce the cultural forms of the latter from the former. Non-literate peoples of today, it is claimed, have a long history, and have therefore undergone changes. [17] Since this history is unknown and probably unknowable, it is difficult to determine to what extent and in what respects contemporary-literate peoples represent an earlier phase in the development of mankind. Others, evolutionists in particular, maintain that the social and religious life of prehistoric man can be deduced from the social and religious behavior of non-literate cultures. [18] Still others restrict the similarity to technology or to material culture. [19] It has to be admitted that some comparisons between the material cultures of pre-

---

[14] Evans-Pritchard, 1965b, p. 18; 1951, p. 8; Titiev, 1963, p. 386; Norbeck, 1961, p. 9.

[15] Cf. Mair, 1965, p. 11; Beattie, 1964, pp. 4-5. A typical example of an unsuccessful word is "exotic." It has been used, among others, by Nadel, 1951, p. 7; Bohannan, 1963, pp. 7, 12; and Lienhardt, G., 1966, p. 3. The word, however, has not become common in anthropological usage.

[16] Berndt, C., 1960, pp. 7 ff.; Goody and Watt, 1962, *passim*; Malefijt, 1968, pp. 4-5, note; For some of the deficiencies of the term "non-literate," see Herskovits, 1948, pp. 74-75, and Keesing, 1958, p. 45.

[17] Boas, 1940, p. 633; Brown, I. C., 1963, p. 7; Lévi-Strauss, 1961, p. 39; 1967, p. 42; Lowie, 1924, ix-x; Evans-Pritchard, 1951, p. 7; Pinney, 1968, p. 10; Keesing, 1958, p. 45; Tokarev, 1966, p. 8.

[18] This is the view, in particular, of those who postulate "unilineal evolution," like White, L., 1959, and Childe, 1951. Cf. Service, 1962, pp. 8 ff. For a discussion of this viewpoint see Steward, 1955, p. 3 ff.

[19] Lisitzky, 1956, p. 15.

historic man and of contemporary non-literate peoples is possible; for instance, similarities exist between prehistoric stone-age cultures and the few non-literate societies of today who still use stone tools. Possibly some aspects of the life-styles of one can be validly deduced from the other. But identification on the level of values, beliefs, and personal relations are less easy to make. When they are made they are necessarily based on scientifically undemonstrable assumptions and remain in the realm of untestable theories. It is extremely doubtful, therefore, whether one can call any contemporary non-literate culture a replica of a prehistoric one. [20]

It is necessary to outline some of the differences between non-literate and Western cultures because until quite recently most anthropologists, having their cultural roots in the West, have tried to define non-literate societies by drawing attention to those elements which differentiate them from Western culture. [21] Though all societies have a technology, Western culture possesses a more complicated technological machinery. In like manner, the economy and politics of Western societies are highly elaborate when compared to those of non-literate societies. And again, Western culture with its emphasis on formal education and on specialization of labor and social function stands in sharp contrast to simpler methods in non-literate cultures. In some respects, however, non-literate cultures may be more complex; as, for instance, in the case of kinship relations; moreover, the languages of peoples without writing are often far from simple in structure. Non-literate peoples do not have a systematic art, science, or theology. Nevertheless, like all societies, many possess a developed art form, a genuine quest for knowledge for its own sake and elaborate religious thought. [22] Western societies contain within themselves a great diversity; non-literate ones are more homogeneous and non-pluralistic. It is also probable that, at least in the last few centuries, Western societies have changed at a faster pace than non-literate ones, although it has to be stressed that the latter are at present going through a rapid process of cultural and religious change. There are also great differences between non-literate cultures themselves; for example, in type of government, in religious beliefs and practices, and in economic transactions.

---

[20] Montagu, 1962a, pp. 4-5, is much more definite on this issue. Cf. Benedict, 1934, p. 18.
[21] Piddington, 1950, p. 5; Pinney, 1968, p. 10; Evans-Pritchard, 1951, p. 6.
[22] Gunther, 1968, pp. 76-114; Lévi-Strauss, 1962, pp. 1 ff.; Brown, I. C., 1963, p. 120.

These differences are frequently much greater than those between Western societies. [23]

The difference between non-literate and Western culture is fundamentally one of technology and its implications, one of these latter being a more impersonal attitude in the West. In some instances non-literate societies are superior to Western ones. Non-literate peoples seem less alienated than Western man and certain forms of crime are more rampant in Western societies. [24] In other instances, however, Western societies are definitely superior, as in the knowledge of and control over nature. Generally speaking, therefore, both types of societies have advantages and disadvantages, shortcomings, and good points. Cultural differences in themselves cannot be easily evaluated. [25] In like manner, the anthropologist does not approach the study of the religions of non-literate peoples with the assumption that Christianity or any other religion is culturally superior. It is thus just as naive to talk of spiritual degeneration or progress as it is to talk without qualification of general human progress. [26]

Differences between societies cannot be explained by saying that they are made up of different kinds of people. Non-literate man is not looked upon as fundamentally different from the man of Western culture. The mentality and logical make-up of all peoples are the same, irrespective of which culture they belong to. [27] This is not to deny, however, that non-literate societies differ from Western ones in many respects, including religious matters. Religious values seem to permeate most aspects of non-literate cultures. [28] Men of these cultures do not make a dichotomy between church and state and their religious life is less organized than that of Western man. Finally, the phenomenon of irreligiosity, now so common in Western societies, is very rare in non-literate ones.

---

[23] For a typical example of the great variety of governments and politics in non-literate societies, see Mair, 1962.

[24] Lévi-Strauss, 1963, pp. 365-366; Montagu, 1962a, pp. 2-3; Diamond, 1963, pp. 136, 143; Goody and Watt, 1962, pp. 334-335.

[25] Montagu, 1968b, pp. 154 ff.

[26] Progress is not always an unmixed blessing. Even the invention of writing may have had some disastrous consequences. Cf. Lévi-Strauss, 1961, pp. 28-31.

[27] Mair, 1965, p. 3; Diamond, 1963, p. 141. Lévy-Bruhl's theory of primitive mentality has been abandoned by anthropologists; Cf. Evans-Pritchard, 1965b, pp. 78-99; Bohannan, 1963, pp. 320-326.

[28] Cf. Turner, V., 1967, p. 181.

MYTH

In the understanding of religious man myth plays a crucial part. For religious beliefs and attitudes are reflected and expressed in mythology more than in any other aspect of a people's way of life. Myth is no doubt an integral part of religion. [29] It is therefore not surprising that in recent studies on religion anthropologists have concentrated rather heavily on myth.

One of the main difficulties in the study of mythology is due to the fact that, whereas in Western culture a clear distinction is made between myth and folklore, this distinction cannot easily be applied to non-literate cultures. Some authors have reported that the peoples they have studied do in fact make distinctions between myth, folklore, traditional tales, and the like, but this seems to be a rare occurrence rather than the norm. [30] Myth can be defined as a narrative well-known among the members of a particular society or among at least a group or groups within that society, which explains the origins of natural and social phenomena and the interrelationship among men, between man and his deities and between man and his universe. [31] Folklore, on the other hand, refers as a rule to all the knowledge of a society which is transmitted by word of mouth but which contains no reference to an invisible world or to deities. Though in anthropological literature myth and folklore are at times used interchangeably, myth is seen as the primary religious phenomenon. [32] Other problems, besides the definitional one, beset the student of mythology. The themes and content of myths vary so much that classification does not often help the student to simplify his study of mythology. Besides, different and contradictory accounts often occur in the same tradition — a problem inherent also in the Bible. [33] Myths can be owned by different social groups. [34] And when a scholar starts on the task of comparing myths cross-culturally, the differences are as glaring as the similarities. It

---

[29] Berndt and Berndt, 1964, pp. 217-250; Lessa, 1966, p. 30; Firth, 1960, p. 284.

[30] Cf. Evans-Pritchard, 1967, pp. 31-32; Greenway, 1965, p. 32. For accounts of societies where native distinctions have been recorded, see Malinowski, 1926, pp. 102 ff.; Nadel, 1954a, p. 56; Barton, 1955, pp. 2-3; Scorza, 1972. For a review of some contemporary studies on myth and folklore, see Dorson, 1973.

[31] Cf. Turner, V., 1968b, p. 576; King, A. R., 1964, p. 45.

[32] Bascom, 1968, pp. 496 ff. Bascom maintains that in non-literate societies folklore is virtually identical with culture.

[33] Lessa, 1966, p. 6; Lienhardt, G., 1960, pp. 171 ff.; Wilson 1959, pp. 7 ff.; A typical example from the Bible is the Book of Genesis which gives two creation accounts in chapter one and chapter two respectively.

[34] Firth, 1951, pp. 171 ff.

has become a truism in anthropology that mythological accounts cannot be taken at their face value and that, no matter how bizarre and incongruous the stories may be, they point to deeper realities about man himself. Exegesis, therefore, is essential for the understanding and interpreting of a myth. [35] Thus, to give one example, the role played by animals in myths has to be analyzed in relation to the meaning the particular animal portrays in the society in question. For animals often represent culturally idealized types. [36]

A large number of anthropological studies on myth deal with its functional value and with its relations to various aspects of man's social and cultural life. The function of myth has been described as that of a unifying device or cohesive force for society, or of a storehouse for adjustive responses; in other words, its function is to discharge the emotions in socially accepted ways. [37] Myth provides an explanation of the ordered phenomena of nature. It can have specific group functions, supplying the society with a charter for belief and authority. Myth not only justifies religious beliefs and values, but also "tends to sustain some system of authority and the distinction of power and status this implies." [38] Myth also expresses basic human feeling towards the world. Some have seen it as a system of education into the total reality system of a society. [39]

Many cultural items can be reflected in a people's mythology. Myths may describe those physical characteristics of man which are considered normal, or it can even demonstrate the types of disease prevalent in a society and the form of family life accepted as ideal. The material culture as well as the orientations, norms, beliefs and ideals of a society are frequently expressed in the language of myth. Sometimes much can be learned about the physical environment of a particular society by a careful reading of their mythology. This knowledge about culture can be unrecognized by its carriers. [40]

Myth, however, is never a complete replica or reflection of a people's culture. It can also contradict culture and it may contain exaggerated

---

[35] Lessa, 1966, p. 48.

[36] Horner, 1966, p. 154; Douglas, 1957, pp. 231 ff.

[37] Radcliff-Brown, 1922, pp. 46 ff.; Kluckhohn, 1942, pp. 65, 70; Mair, 1965, p. 230; Geiser, 1973.

[38] Beattie, 1960, p. 11. Cf. Beattie, 1965, pp. 160-161; Lienhardt, G., 1966, p. 73; Firth, 1951, p. 180; Greenway, 1965, p. 6; Kluckhohn and Leighton, 1962, p. 194; Malinowski, 1926, pp. 100-101, 116-117; Bourdillon, 1972.

[39] Horner, 1966, p. 145.

[40] Lessa, 1966, p. 22; Spencer, R. F., 1966, pp. 278 ff.; Hart and Hart, 1966, p. 84; Lévi-Strauss, 1958b, pp. 7-13.

and inverted features of real life. Some myths have little or no connection with the social structure. [41] And not all myths represent a harmonious unity of social life; some, on the contrary, can be devisive and highly argumentative, expressing and not solving social-psychological conflicts of a particular social structure or of certain distributions of power within society. [42]

Anthropologists have turned away from sweeping generalizations about myth and have admitted that myth is multidimensional and that the part it plays in a people's way of life may vary from society to society. They have tended to concentrate on particular societies, avoiding comparisons and shunning attempts to reach universally applicable statements on mythology. One exception to this trend is the work of Claude Lévi-Strauss, whose structural analysis of myth has already left a lasting impact on anthropology. [43] In spite of the fact that his writings tend to be somewhat obscure and his method hotly debated, some of his less philosophical assumptions and conclusions have become largely accepted in anthropological literature. [44] Many anthropologists have applied his method to diverse cultures, and one of his most ardent followers, Edmund Leach, has examined the Bible along the lines suggested by him. [45] Lévi-Strauss looks upon myth as a clue to the mechanism of the human thought. Myth is a mental category, intrinsic to the workings of the human mind. Like language, which he takes as his model, myth has its own logic and is as rigorous as any scientific endeavor. Man is thus a myth-making creature and this process of myth-creation works mainly on the unconscious level. The primary task of myth is to tackle and solve the contradictions and problems of life. [46]

For anthropologists, therefore, myth is never seen as just a story of literary and thematic interest. It is part and parcel of man's make-up, making him aware of his roots in society and giving him a tool to

---

[41] Lessa, 1966, pp. 23-26; Fischer, 1966a, p. 127; Mair, 1965, p. 230; Turner, V., 1968b, p. 581; Middleton, 1954, p. 53.
[42] Fischer, 1966a, p. 129; Firth, 1951, pp. 174 ff.; Leach, 1964a, pp. 184 ff.; Gluckman, 1952, makes similar observations on ritual.
[43] See Lévi-Strauss, 1958a, 1958b, 1960, 1962, 1964.
[44] For discussions on Lévi-Strauss's views and method, cf. Burridge, 1964; Douglas, 1964; Yulman, 1964a; Turner, T., 1969; Bharati, 1972, pp. 248-249. For a simpler exposition of his views see Bourdillon, 1968; Malefijt, 1968, pp. 182-184. A popular account of Lévi-Strauss's achievements and ideas appeared in The New York Times Magazine section for January 28, 1968, pp. 28 ff.
[45] See Ames, 1964; Yulman, 1964b; Colby, 1966; Khare, 1967; Robinson and Joiner, 1968; Leach, 1961, 1962, 1966a, 1968d.
[46] Lévi-Straus, 1958a, p. 229; cf. Greenway, 1966, x; Fischer, 1966a, pp. 120 ff.

face human existence. [47] While there are many myths of origins, it has
to be emphasized that mythological interest in origins is not universal.
In like manner the explanatory quality in myth, though common, is not
part of the very nature of myth. Myth frequently deals not only with
the past, but, perhaps mainly, with the present. [48] In other words, myth
does not only try to give an explanation of how things were at the
beginning, but also attempts to account for contemporary happenings.
The present state of affairs of a particular society is a key element in
the understanding of a culture's mythological tradition. John Beattie
expressed the view of many anthropologists when he wrote:

> What interests us most about myths is the way in which they express
> attitudes and beliefs current at the present time. Mythologies always em-
> body systems of values, and judgments about what is considered good and
> proper by the people who have the myth. [49]

Myth grapples with contemporary problems and adapts itself to the
ever-changing social and cultural situation. Myth is therefore plastic
and subject to modification. [50] Since myth is constantly being created,
it has to be looked upon as essentially man-made, stemming from
man's concious and/or unconscious effort to overcome the problems of
life. Myth is thus true or real because it is a dramatic embodiment of
certain facts about man and about society; for it depicts the worldview of a society and expresses often in religious language man's
solutions to the problems that are peculiar to him as a reasoning creature. [51]

Many peoples believe that their myths relate events which happened
in the past. Hence the relation between myth and history has to be
questioned. Myths can contain, or have firm foundation in, historical
facts and one reason for studying mythology is that it could possibly
teach us what happened in the prehistoric age. [52] Yet it is debatable
whether the distinction between myth and history is applicable to non-
literate societies. Some anthropologists have argued that history, in our
meaning of the term, is a consequence of literacy and hence it has no
replica in non-literate cultures. For the latter scholars myth and history

---

[47] Lévi-Strauss, 1964, p. 27.
[48] Krige and Krige, 1954, p. 60; Greenway, 1965, p. 32. See also Middleton,
1954, and Burridge, 1957.
[49] Beattie, 1960, p. 11.
[50] Berndt, R., 1966, pp. 195 ff.; Firth, 1960, pp. 228 ff.; Burridge, 1960, p. 33;
Butt, 1960, pp. 377 ff.
[51] Burridge, 1960, pp. 250, 253; Fischer, 1966a, p. 125.
[52] Fischer, 1966a, p. 124; Greenway, 1966, p. x; Wilson, 1959, p. 51.

merge into one. [53] Even when a myth purports to relate what happened in the past it is necessarily molded into forms that are dependent upon existing social relationships and therefore must be largely a projection of the present into the past. Studies of the concept of the past in non-literate societies are rare in anthropological literature. The difficulty often encountered in dealing with the relation between myth and history is probably due to the fact that one is inclined to ask to what degree can they be substantiated by scientific evidence. Myth and history, however, differ primarily in character. As Evans-Pritchard aptly describes it:

> [Myth] is not concerned so much with a succession of events as with the moral significance of situations, and is hence often allegorical or symbolical in form. It is not incapsulated as history is, but is a re-enactment fusing present and past. It tends to be timeless, placed in thought beyond, or above, historical time; and when it is firmly placed in historical time, it is also nevertheless, timeless in that it could have happened at any time, the archetypal not being bound to time or space. Then the very improbabilities, even absurdities, in many myths are not to be taken, as in an historical record, literally and hence as naivety and credulity, but are of the essence of myth which, just because the events lie outside human experience, demands an act of will and of imagination. [54]

Myth, therefore, does not aim at historical reconstruction. It is more a religious commentary on the beliefs and values of a society.

TIME

The problem of the relationship between myth and history is important because it brings into focus the question of time. In particular one has to ask whether religious man's view of time is unique or not. The main anthropological concern is the study of systems of time-reckoning. [55] Cosmic, human, and social cycles are at the root of all time measurement. [56] Social cycles seem to vary much more than cosmic and human ones for the simple reason that societies differ. In most non-literate societies it is the annual sequence of economic and/or social activities which provides the measurement of time. [57] Sequence and duration form part of the system of time measurement in all societies. The cyclical and linear patterns of time are also universal and

---

[53] Firth, 1951, p. 181. Cf., Goody and Watt, 1962, pp. 310-11; Middleton, 1960, pp. 180, 235; Gorman, 1973.
[54] Evans-Pritchard, 1961, p. 179.
[55] Pocock, 1964, p. 304.
[56] Goody, 1968, pp. 23 ff.; Berndt and Berndt, 1967, p. 188.
[57] Leach, 1963b, p. 133; Morey, 1971.

can exist in harmony. [58] But the emphasis varies, and among non-literate peoples the cyclical pattern frequently predominates. In many of these societies the equivalent of our concept of time is absent. Time-perspective is not exactly the same as in Western culture. [59] There is some justification in looking on the Western concept of time as a consequence of the invention of writing, and hence its application to non-literate societies has to be made, if at all, with great caution. Written documents contribute to the formation and development of a linear concept of time. [60]

The rise of economic specialization, the development of technology and the growth of an educational system are all influential in the formation of the concept of time. Accurate time measurement is a necessary accompaniment of these developments. In non-literate societies, however, one does not find the same social, economic, and technological pressures leading to the formation of minutely measured sequence of events. In these cultures one cannot, and in fact does not, speak of time saved, wasted and gained. People in these societies may never "experience the same feeling of fighting against time, of having to coordinate activities with an abstract passage of time, since their points of reference are mainly the activities themselves, which are generally of a leisurely and routine character. " [61] Non-literate societies have no device for indicating time in the distant past with any accuracy similar to the dating processes of the great civilizations. Even genealogies are not a device for doing so. [62] Thus while all societies are aware of the repetitive and sequential elements of life, not all have worked out a system of precise time-measurement. And while we certainly cannot say that non-literate peoples do not have a sense of time, applying to them the Western concept of time presents some insurmountable problems.

Religious motivations do play a part in the ordering of human events. Not only do religious cyclical rituals form a prominent part in the lives of many peoples, but they also may influence and regulate their social activities. [63] Just as people measure time by relating social and econo-

---

[58] Cf. Goody and Watt, 1962.

[59] Berndt and Berndt, 1964, p. 432; cf. Geertz. 1960, p. 39; Barden, 1973; Tierney, 1973a.

[60] Cf. Goody and Watt, 1962.

[61] Evans-Pritchard, 1939, p. 208.

[62] Goody, 1968, p. 39; Bohannan, 1953, pp. 328-29; Evans-Pritchard, 1939, pp. 211 ff.

[63] Bohannan, 1963, p. 322.

mic activities, so also they measure it by relating ritual or religious activities. There is some ground for making a distinction between religious and non-religious time. The former can be described as the time when religious rites take place. Since it is of the very nature of ritual to be repetitive, religious time is by nature timeless and unchangeable. Past, present, and future are united in one action and often they are not distinguished in the ritual process. This explains why religious rites are always thought of as originating in the mythological era which is independent of the constantly changing human condition. What happened in the mythological era sets a precedent for human behavior and can be indefinitely repeated. [64] Non-religious time, on the other hand, has an element of finality about it. It is never completely unchangeable. Some anthropologists have argued that religious and non-religious time patterns are based upon two different kinds of experience which are logically distinct and even contradictory; namely, the notion of repetition and non-repetition. Some natural phenomena occur repeatedly, but life-change itself is irreversible. Religion may be seen as a means of uniting the two aspects of time under one category. [65] In ordinary daily life, however, the dichotomy does not seem to play an important role. Many societies base the weekly division of time on economic grounds, while the rest-day, when present, is given a religious origin and significance. [66] In experience itself the dichotomy is not always sharply marked. One recent writer on African religions has summarized the native concept of time without using the customary dichotomies of sacred and profane time, cyclical and linear time, and religious and non-religious time. [67] From the scanty anthropological writings on time one can conclude that religious considerations are nearly always present in the concept that non-literate peoples have of time. It is, however, extremely doubtful one can say that the religious conception of time is unique.

RITUAL

Closely related to myth is the concept of ritual. Anthropologists have largely abandoned the so-called "ritual view of myth" which looked on myth as a later evolutionary development that came into being as an explanation of ritual behavior. [68] Myth and ritual are considered to be

---

[64] Berndt and Berndt, 1967, pp. 187-188; Reichard, 1950, vol. 1, pp. 24, 158.
[65] Leach, 1963b, p. 125.
[66] Goody, 1968, p. 34.
[67] Mbiti, 1970, pp. 19-36.
[68] Kluckhohn, 1942, pp. 54-59; Malefijt, 1968, pp. 187-188; Lessa, 1961, pp.

complementary to each other. Both have been assigned similar social and psychological functions and both are held to be closely related to other aspects of culture. Moreover, myth and ritual have a common basis in the religious beliefs of a people. [69]

While ethologists have reached agreement on the definition of ritualization in animals, anthropologists are still debating the problem of how best to define ritual in man. [70] One approach insists that rituals include all magical and communicative behavior. The emphasis thus lies in the behavioral act itself — a position very close to the ethological viewpoint. [71] Another way of looking at ritual is to see it as a means of, or procedure for, understanding the occult, or the sphere of the spiritual world. The emphasis now shifts from the ritual act itself to the meaning it points to. [72] Anthropological studies on religion often describe ritual as a "prescribed formal behavior for occasions not given over to technological routine, having reference to beliefs in mystical beings or powers. " [73] Ritual is thus seen as an essentially non-empirical behavior, having no practical utility. [74] It is therefore a magical or religious act and should be distinguished from ceremony. Ritual is the action of a religious man who believes it is efficacious and communicative with the spiritual world. [75] Such a definition of ritual may be narrow, but it does have nonetheless the advantage of enabling the student to concentrate his efforts on understanding what is probably the most elaborate and complicated form of meaningful stereotyped behavior.

Like myth, ritual has also sociological and psychological functions. [76] Ritual behavior can often have the effects of reducing the anxiety of many people in a group. Rituals can function as cathartic devices, seeking to dissipate certain anti-social tendencies. They can heighten the

---

450 ff. Some anthropologists still maintain a ritual view of myth; cf. Leach, 1968a; Wallace, 1966, pp. 216 ff.

[69] Cf. Lessa, 1966, p. 30; Spiro, 1964b, p. 103; Malefijt, 1968, pp. 188-89.

[70] Turner, V., 1969b, p. 7.

[71] Leach, 1968a, 523 ff.; cf. also 1966b.

[72] Fortes, 1966; cf. 1962, pp. 78, 83 ff.

[73] Turner, V., 1957, p. 20. Cf. Wilson, 1957, p. 9.

[74] Beattie, 1959a, p. 144; Nadel, 1954b, pp. 99 ff.; Fortes, 1962, p. 66. Rappaport, 1967, pp. 1 ff., agrees that rituals involve non-empirical or supernatural beings, but he maintains that some rituals do have a practical and useful result. Cf. Turner, D. H., 1972, who describes ritual without reference to empirical results.

[75] Wilson, 1957, pp. 9-10. For a broader definition of ritual, see Goody, 1961, p. 159.

[76] Kluckhohn, 1942, p. 57; Parvathamma, 1972.

emotions as well as canalize them. [77] "Ritual adapts and periodically readapts the individual to the basic condition and axiomatic value of human life." [78] Both myth and ritual give some fixity to the ideal pattern of cultures and both are important means through which the culture of a society is transmitted. Ritual can be a means of compelling outward conformity to an approved system of communication or of inculcating the total values of the traditional way of life. [79] Both ritual and myth can act as a brake upon the speed of culture change. [80] Certain types of rituals, for instance divinatory rites, can also perform a legal function, supplying the society with a decision making procedure. [81]

Ritual can be seen under many aspects. It is an efficacious form of communication not only between man and the gods and spirits he believes in, but also between men. [82] It also communicates knowledge of culture to the observer. Thus, for example, sacrifice can be seen as a form of exchange between man and his gods. The human actor presents gifts which are accepted by the spirit or by the god. Once the sacrifice has been made, subsequent events are interpreted in the light of this transaction. Ritual can also serve to reaffirm social status. It is a characteristic of all kinds of rituals that participants adopt insignia, like special clothing or body painting, which emphasize in an exaggerated way the formal social distinction that separate individuals from one another. Ritual reminds the congregation just where each member stands in relation to each other and in relation to a larger system. [83] Ritual can also pass on valuable knowledge about the society as a whole. The frequency, size and the quality of sacrifices in a given culture are largely determined by its economic resources. [84] Ritual behavior, therefore, seems to point beyond itself. It lays bare aspects of a people's social life, and it reveals the cultural values and religious beliefs of a society. Anthropologists writing on ritual have concentrated either on relating ritual and social relations or on the ideological structure of the rites. [85]

Two typical examples of how anthropologists have dealt with ritual

---

[77] Wilson, 1957, pp. 227, 232; 1959, p. 217; Gluckman, 1962, pp. 34 ff.
[78] Turner, V., 1957, p. 46.
[79] Wilson, 1957, pp. 226-227.
[80] Kluckhohn, 1942, pp. 61-62.
[81] Park, G. K., 1963, pp. 233 ff.
[82] Cf. Malefijt, 1968, p. 209; Firth, 1973, pp. 174 ff. Paine, 1972, notices the significance of ritual as communication among the Reindeer Lapps.
[83] Leach, 1968a, p. 524; Srinivas, 1952, *passim*.
[84] Firth, 1963b, p. 15; Malefijt, 1968, pp. 213-214.
[85] Turner, V., 1965, pp. 155 ff.

are ancestor cults initiation rites. In several African cultures one of the most distinguishing marks of their religions is the cult of ancestors. Such cults, it has been repeatedly pointed out, cannot be understood unless one is aware of the pattern of family relations in the society under investigation and of the filial duties and respects demanded by tradition. [86] A society's social life may be almost wholly organized by reference to relations of descent and kinship. The duties, rights, privileges, and abilities of a person are often defined only in the light of genealogical knowledge. This is the fundamental sociological reason why the cult towards ancestors can become the hallmark of a people's religious life. Ancestor cult has, therefore, been described as the ritualization of filial piety; it is the transportation of the social and religious relationships between parents and children into ritual drama. There are, of course, deeper symbolic elements involved. Beliefs in afterlife, in the relationship between living and dead, are portrayed in ancestral rites. These rites stand for a whole range of human relations and ideals.

> Yet there is a common element in what is often rather misleadingly called "ancestor-worship." Whatever the nature of the offering, or the reason behind it, it does perpetuate the memory of the dead; and it does acknowledge that the living and the dead belong to a single community, wider than that of the living alone. And this is not simply a pious belief. There obviously is continuity, biological and cultural, between the living and the dead. We are partly formed by the past, even the distant past. Sacrificial offerings for ancestors symbolically recognize this. Further, those who remember their dead together, and share the same dead, also of necessity emphasize their living relationships among themselves: commemoration of the ancestor is affirmation of the range of relationships he created among the living, a holding together of all those who count him important in their past. [87]

Initiation rites have been a popular topic in anthropological literature. Most anthropologists see in these rites an emphasis on the social transition to the full tribal life. Specific details of the rites have been related to elements in the social structure. The rites have been declared to be a "status dramatization," thereby implying that the way a society looks upon the statuses and roles of life is necessary for understanding initiation rituals. Or again, these rites can be considered as means whereby meaningful control and clear demarcation of statuses are maintained. They have also been explained as a means of providing a

---

[86] See Beidelman, 1964, Bradbury, 1960, 1963; Colson, 1954; Faron, 1961; Fortes, 1959, 1960, 1961; Winter, 1956. The title "ancestor-worship," often given to these rites, is misleading. In many cases there is no worship in the strict meaning of the term; cf. Geertz, 1960, p. 76; Kuper, 1964, p. 60.

[87] Lienhardt, G., 1966, p. 144.

system of educating members into the tradition of a society. [88] These rites, however, by opening the door to full adulthood, also introduce the initiate into the religious life of a society. The rites are filled with religious symbols. The symbolism of death on many levels is often clearly portrayed. [89] But the values and beliefs expressed and dramatized in these rites are not univocal nor unidimensional. [90] The changes which these rites symbolically display and effect are both of a moral and of a social nature. Many rituals have a religious depth not easily fathomed by looking at the observational data. [91]

SYMBOL

Since ritual tells us much about a people's religious and cultural situation some anthropologists have remarked that the main question to ask in the study of ritual is not what it does, or what is it believed to do, but rather what does ritual say. [92] Ritual, like myth, is therefore, seen as highly symbolical.

> Rituals in tribal societies are not thus mere congregations at which people pray: they are built out of the very texture of social relations, each person having to perform symbolic actions, or undergo symbolic operations, which emphasize his role in relation to the other participants in the ceremony. Hence to understand the ritual, the anthropologist has to trace its symbolic actions and apparatus through a major range of social activities and other customs and complexes of symbols. [93]

The study of ritual and myth as symbolic systems has been one of the major concerns of anthropological studies on religion for the last decade.

Symbolism has frequently been taken to be a distinctive characteristic of man. [94] In the study of symbolism it is useful to distinguish between sign and symbol. [95] Signs in general give information about

---

[88] Cf. Gennep, 1908; Goffman, 1959; Young, 1965; Richards, 1956; Norbeck, Walker and Cohn, 1962; Mendelson, 1965; Cohen, 1964; Beidelman, 1965; Allen, M. R., 1967.

[89] Turner, V., 1962b, p. 167; cf. *Idem*, 1964c, *passim*.

[90] Turner, V., 1962b, p. 171; Berndt and Berndt, 1967, pp. 58 ff.; Wilson, 1957, pp. 86 ff.; Beidelman, 1965, *passim*; Firth, 1973, pp. 181-186.

[91] Turner, V., 1962b, pp. 171-172.

[92] Beattie, 1966, p. 61; cf. Lamphere, 1969, *passim*.

[93] Gluckman, 1962, p. 42.

[94] White, L., 1949, 1962; Aranguren, 1974, pp. 11 ff. Firth, 1973, who has written one of the more impressive manuals on symbolism, states that symbolization is a universal human process.

[95] This is one of the most common distinctions used. A second distinction takes sign as universal mode of communication and subdivides it into signal and symbol. Still another approach divides sign into index, signal, icon and symbol. We

some state of affairs; they convey, as traffic lights do, specific messages. Symbols, on the other hand, are vehicles of meaning, intentionally or conventionally ascribed to. They convey or contain an understanding which no direct specific message can have or do.

> A symbol is thus definable in relation to something else that is called its referent, object or designatum... a symbol points to a referent; pictures the referent's meaning; is an instrument for comprehending a referent; is a part which represents the whole, or is a surrogate for the whole, serving to recall to mind an absent referent. [96]

Symbols stand not for things or objects, but rather for ideals, values and abstract notions. They point to something which exists, or is believed to exist, but the referent is either in itself incomprehensible or is not fully comprehended by the human understanding. Symbolism is thus an expressive form of communication, conveying an important message which cannot be said directly. Symbols imply meaning which cannot be derived immediately from the context of experience because they refer to another order of reality. [97]

Symbols perform, first of all, the function of language. They are the channel through which beliefs and attitudes are passed on from one generation to the next. [98] Since symbols refer to deeply felt values, they carry a strong emotional overtone. [99] They are thus an outlet for human emotion. Symbols are not necessarily the result of well-thought out procedures, though perhaps in Western culture they tend to be more so. [100] Even though symbolism has been described as "a tool of thinking," [101] it seems clear that symbols are not always set up by some arbitray decision. In fact they are often the result of a historical process, and they can survive even when the conditions favoring their creation cease to exist. Symbols, therefore, do not always function consciously or rationally. Many symbols, for instance, dress, serve the group with the effective mechanism for maintaining group consciousness and for integrating the values of a sectarian society. [102] Symbols tend to strengthen the culture and preserve its identity.

---

follow here the simpler distinction between sign and symbol. Cf. Smith, E., 1952, pp. 31 ff.; Beattie, 1964, pp. 69 ff.; Firth, 1973, pp. 74-75. See also Langer, 1957, pp. 53 ff.; Thass-Thienemann, 1968, pp. 18-25.

[96] Smith, E., 1952, p. 13.
[97] Beattie, 1964, p. 71; Lévi-Strauss, 1963, p. 200; Sapir, 1937, p. 493.
[98] Hostetler, 1964, pp. 12-13; Firth, 1973, pp. 79-82.
[99] Smith, E., 1952, p. 14; Firth, 1973, p. 49.
[100] Hostetler, 1964, p. 19.
[101] Thass-Thienemann, 1968, p. 24.
[102] Hostetler, 1964, p. 12; cf. Firth, 1973, pp. 83 ff.

To the believer, symbols are often a means of procuring a desired effect. [103] They not only indicate the inner changes of moral and social status but they are also believed to bring them about. Symbolic ritual may also effect psychosomatic changes. [104] There is an intrinsic relation between the symbol and what it stands for. [105] The symbol and its referent are frequently identified; people behave toward the symbol as if it were the thing symbolized. Hence the result for which the symbol stands is often considered to be a direct effect of the symbolic action. Yet people do not always believe that the symbol alone suffices to bring about the desired results. [106] Hunting rituals, to give but one example, stand for the desired end, that is, the procurement of food through the aid of the gods and the spirits. But the rites are accompanied or followed by the actual hunt for which innumerable weapons have been invented. Symbolic action, heretofore, often functions as a complement to and preparation for practical or technical action. [107]

The fact that symbols frequently function below the level of consciousness does not mean that they are unreasonable or without logic. Symbols run according to rules and can be very neatly structured. They clearly involve unconscious projection mechanisms, but they could also be partly organized by conscious conceptual thought and deliberately articulated into an elaborate system. [108] The structural analysis of myth and ritual is based on the logic of symbolic representation and attempts to evoke the meaning of religious beliefs and rituals by an analysis of the positional framework of symbols. This approach emphasizes the fact that symbols often form a structured pattern, that is, the meaning of a particular symbol is related to other symbols which form a cluster or an ordered mosaic. The meaning of the symbol can be more fully grasped if seen as a part of a complex system of interrelated ideas. Most of the structural studies have presented symbols as being basically binary; they are considered as made up of two sets of opposite ideas so neatly interrelated and enmeshed that they can be represented in diagrammatic form. [109] While not all anthropologists would agree that this approach provides the true key to the understanding of symbols, few would doubt that it can make at least some contribution to

---

[103] Lienhardt, G., 1960, p. 291.
[104] Turner, V., 1969b, p. 14; 1962b, p. 171.
[105] Evans-Pritchard, 1953a, pp. 1-2.
[106] Lienhardt, G., 1960, pp. 283, 291.
[107] Lienhardt, G., 1960, p. 283.
[108] Turner, V., 1969b, p. 14.
[109] Turner, V., 1962b, p. 125; 1969b, pp. 12-13.

our understanding of symbolic man. Symbols, which can be conceived as forming the smallest unit of ritual, can be multivalent, that is, they can express different motivations. They can also be multivocal, possessing different cognitive and ideological "components indissociable from man's conceptual, linguistic and other cultural capacities." [110] A symbol can, therefore, possess many meanings at the same time. The structure of symbols can be further complicated because different symbols can stand for a common idea and the same symbolic pattern can be repeated in different ritual situations. [111] Some symbols play a dominant part in the ritual context, thus forming the main interpretative key. [112]

The study of symbolism takes place on three different levels. [113] There is first the ethnographic level. This describes the external form and observable characteristics of symbolic situations. The objects used as symbols, the place where the symbolic representation takes place, and the words and actions that accompany it are recorded. Few anthropologists stop at this level, for it seems that this level of investigation by itself does not lead to an understanding of the symbols used. In symbolism what is important is not the object itself but the ideas behind it — a fact sufficiently illustrated by particular symbolic studies.[114] This leads to the exegetical level. Here one asks what the people involved in the symbolic behavior say about their own symbols. This level stresses conscious symbolism. Information of this sort may be elicited both from the religious specialist and from the layman. A myth can be an exegesis of a particular symbolic ritual, but many societies give detailed non-mythical interpretation to their own symbols. It is possible, as one anthropologist has suggested, that culture contact may be largely the cause of exegetical (oral and written) literature of a society. [115] The work of some anthropologists along this line brings out clearly the need for this level of anthropological investigation. [116]

Anthropological studies on symbolism, however, do not and cannot stop here. The explanatory level, that of contextual analysis, is a

---

[110] Turner, V., 1969b, pp. 8-9.
[111] Wilson, 1954, pp. 229, 234.
[112] Turner, V., 1969b, pp. 12 ff.; *Idem*, 1963.
[113] Turner, V., 1957, pp. 21 ff.
[114] See for instance the following articles on the symbolism of the left and right hands: Wieschoff, 1938; Needham, 1960, 1967; Beidelman, 1961; Rigby, 1966; Beattie, 1968.
[115] Turner, V., 1969b, pp. 11-12.
[116] One should particularly take note of the works of Turner, V., Wilson, and Richards. Cf. Lienhardt, G., 1960, pp. 252 ff.

necessary scientific requirement. It is not a valid principle in social
science that nothing can be imputed to a people under study unless it
is consciously present in the mind of every one of them. There are
levels of awareness of symbolic meanings within the same cultural
milieu. Different categories of people in the same culture may regard
their ritual symbols differently. It is also an established fact in social
science that people are also motivated by an unconscious process and
that, therefore, the meaning of the symbols may be unknown to them.
There is a deeper symbolism which is so embedded in the ritual action
that its meaning is neither obvious nor explicit. [117] Moreover, the observer can see the rites in their total cultural and social setting and can
thus perceive more easily the interconnections between symbols and
their importance in the religious life of the society. It is an accepted
maxim in anthropology that the meaning of a symbol makes sense only
in its cultural context. [118] Symbols often stand for a very complex set
of social relationships, implying a moral and not just a utilitarian significance. [119] Such social symbolism is rarely recognized explicitly. The
clues to the understanding of symbols lie in everyday situations. The
ideas people have of property, their ideals of manhood, and their concept of cleanliness often point to the interpretation of their symbolic
rites. [120] Symbols may have a different meaning, or none at all, outside their cultural context. [121] The images men use, and the objects
which represent their values and religious concepts are often determined by the physical and cultural environment. [122] To treat symbolic
objects outside their cultural background can have disasterous consequences. [123]

Symbolism is a necessary constituent of religion. Religious beliefs
habitually express themselves in symbolic form. The symbol has been
called the "natural language of religion." [124] Religious symbolism,

---

[117] Evans-Pritchard, 1953a, p. 3.

[118] This, of course, is also recognized by those anthropologists who follow
Lévi-Strauss' structural approach.

[119] Evans-Pritchard, 1953a, pp. 4-11.

[120] Douglas, 1955, p. 385.

[121] Berndt and Berndt, 1967, p. 80.

[122] Wilson, 1957, p. 10.

[123] A typical example of this is Morris and Morris, 1966, pp. 2-21. The authors
deal with sacred apes, but by the end of the chapter the reader still does not
know why apes were chosen by certain peoples to represent their gods and
heroes.

[124] Smith, E., 1952, p. 18. Some anthropologists, for example Bharati, 1972,
p. 262, are not happy with what they call "symbol talk," which interposes symbols
where actors do not see any. Bharati thinks this is symbolic reductionism. Firth,

like all symbolic elements in life, has a tendency to run wild. [125] This explains why religious symbolism is often hard to understand. Yet symbolism is not only a phenomenon restricted to the world of religion. Social and political symbolism often flourish in a society. It is not only religious man who can be called a symbolic being. Besides, there is an interplay between religious and social symbolism. Social and environmental objects and symbols at times provide the raw material for religious symbolism, and ordinary social life can be experienced through symbolic notions and values which are essentially religious. [126] Religious symbolism cannot, therefore, be studied in isolation from the rest of culture.

MAGIC, WITCHCRAFT AND SORCERY

Myth, ritual and symbol, though integral to religion, often figure prominently in other aspects of a people's way of life. In non-literate societies beliefs and practices concerning magic, witchcraft and sorcery may contain an elaborate mythology, depend on ritual procedures believed to be effective, and be highly symbolical in character. The student of religious myth, ritual and symbol is, therefore, led to the study of magic and witchcraft and their relation to religion. [127]

Anthropological studies of witchcraft in the last four decades or so, can be classified under two headings: functional and social or cultural. The former concentrate on the positive and negative effects of these practices, both on the psychological and on the sociological level; the latter tend to related witch beliefs to the social structure and to underline the ideological patterns involved. [128] Though these studies do not

---

however, 1973, p. 15, points out that the anthropologist is also concerned with the ways in which ordinary people "consciously interpret what they do as having symbolic meaning."

[125] Whitehead, 1958, p. 61.

[126] Hostetler, 1964, p. 12; Smith, E., 1952, p. 17; Douglas, 1955, pp. 391-396.

[127] For an introduction to the study of witchcraft in non-literate societies see Marwick, 1967, and Mair, 1969a. The problem of the relationship between magic and religion and explicit anthropological attempts to deal with it will be discussed in Chapter V. Magic, witchcraft and sorcery are here used to denote a system of beliefs and practices. The three can, and have been, carefully distinguished; cf. Middleton and Winter, 1963, pp. 1 ff.

[128] See Kennedy, 1967; Mair, 1969a, pp. 119-121; Middleton and Winter, 1963, pp. 1 ff. For typical functional studies, cf. Krige, 1947 and Kluckhohn, 1944. Nash, 1973, states that the sociological and psychological functions are now integrated. For studies relating witch beliefs to society, cf. Evans-Pritchard, 1929; Nadel, 1952; Wilson, 1951; Marwick, 1965 and Glover, 1972. In the last few years there seems to have been a decline in sociological studies of witchcraft; cf. Marwick, 1972. Among the best monographs dealing with the ideology

always outline explicitly the similarities between witchcraft and religious beliefs and practices, the links between the two are manifold and apparent. Both have been assigned similar social and/or psychological functions. [129] They are both intimately related to society. Social relations are frequently enacted or expressed in both magical and religious beliefs. Like religion, witchcraft has not only social implications, but also legal, political and economic ones. All these beliefs and practices, though not always necessarily related to the social structure, can be better understood if seen in their cultural context. [130]

Religion and witchcraft, moreover, both form part of a consistent worldview of a people. Witchcraft may also form the part of a people's conception of the universe as a moral order. Since some links between morality and religion are universal, it is impossible to consider the moral impact of a religion without taking into account the moral implications of witchcraft. [131] Both religion and witchcraft are very personalistic, involving the moral relations between the individuals of a society. One of the most common conclusions one can draw from anthropological studies, no matter what emphasis the particular author cares to make, is that witchcraft and the like can be understood only in relation to the concept of evil. [132] They, therefore, indicate a philosophical framework of a society which, just as all societies do, has to face and cope with the universal problem of evil in general and of evil men in particular. This philosophical attitude is part of the mentality of a people and also lies at the basis of religious beliefs and values which often deal with what is considered as pre-eminently the good. Further, beliefs in witchcraft are attempts to deal with the problem of human suffering and "some explanation of undeserved suffering is a necessary part of the conception of a spiritual (religious) world which supports the order of society. " [133] Both witchcraft and religion deal fundamentally with some of the main problems of daily living. Other

---

behind witch beliefs are Evans-Pritchard, 1937, and Temples, 1959; see also Saler, 1964, and Middleton, 1955.

[129] The classical example is Malinowski, 1925, *passim*. Cf. Marwick, 1967, Lowie, 1963, and Kluckhohn and Leighton, 1962, p. 178-252.

[130] The relationship between religion and culture will be discussed in Chapter V.

[131] Mair, 1964, p. 185; Marwick, 1963, p. 124. For the anthropological treatment of morality and religion, cf. Furer-Haimendorf, 1967, and Edel and Edel, 1968.

[132] Mair, 1969a, pp. 8-13. Most of the monographs already referred to bring out this point clearly.

[133] Mair, 1964, p. 186; cf. Crawford, 1967, pp. 73 ff.

attempts to get to the bottom of the philosophy underlying witchcraft beliefs show how directly relevant is the study of witchcraft in understanding some religious beliefs. Thus, in Temple's classical study on Bantu philosophy, magic is seen as a philosophy of force acting through the whole universe. [134] This philosophy would have immediate repercussions on religious beliefs dealing with the action of the gods or spirits on mankind and also with the way people can commune with their deities.

There can also be direct links between religious beliefs, like the concept of God, and the notion of witchcraft. [135] Some anthropologists have suggested that "beliefs in witchcraft are part of the corpus of beliefs that we commonly call religious." [136] Finally, it has to be stressed that concepts like religion and witchcraft are Western concepts and they are not indigenous to non-literate societies. [137] In general, anthropologists have held that magic implies the belief that men may directly affect nature and one another, while religion involves the appeal to divine powers by various forms of prayer. [138] Consequently, though the link between witchcraft and religion is not a necessary one, a full understanding of religion in most non-literate societies cannot be reached without taking into account the problem of magic, witchcraft, and sorcery. [139]

ETHNOMEDICINE

One of the areas in which religious and magical notions are most visible is in the explanation and treatment of illness. So much so that anthropologists, past and present, have often remarked that medicine in non-literate societies seems to be to a very large degree magically or religiously oriented. Medicine at times appears to be part of the religion of a people or clearly related to it. [140] Religion, medicine, and

---

[134] Temples, 1959; Wax, 1968.

[135] Mair, 1964, p. 187.

[136] Mair, 1964, p. 186.

[137] Wax, 1968, pp. 224 ff.

[138] Middleton, 1967, pp. ix-x.

[139] Light can be shed on the matter by comparing witchcraft in both literate and non-literate societies. Such attempts are still in their infancy. Cf. Mair, 1969a, pp. 222-241; Malefijt, 1968, pp. 286-289; Marwick, 1963; and Parrinder, 1963. One should also note that Evans-Pritchard, 1937, did in fact discuss witchcraft without direct involvement in religious matters. Yet, as a rule, in African cultures at least, a nexus between religion and witchcraft exists. Cf. Crawford, 1967, p. 73.

[140] Cf. Nadel, 1954b, pp. 132-162; Murphy, 1958, chapter III; Ackerknecht, 1946, p. 468; Hughes, 1968, p. 89; Wilson, 1957, p. 3; Field, 1937; Fabrega, 1972.

morality are found in many cultures to be bound together in the behavioral act or event. Healing procedures, for example, may be governed by the same principles and modes of classification as their religious rites and moral concepts.[141] Disease may be looked upon as being caused by witchcraft or sorcery or as being the result of possession by evil spirits. And in those cultures where ancestor cult is a dominant feature serious human illnesses may be seen as sent by the ancestors because of a break of the moral or social code. [142] Certain attitudes to illness are sometimes directly linked with social, religious, and moral principles. [143] Diseases may be generally attributed to non-human or non-empirical causes, such as the loss of soul or the intrusion of a disease-causing object.

Writers on ethnomedicine have frequently remarked that among non-literate societies not all diseases are explained by magical or religious influences. Many ordinary illnesses are taken for granted and no appeal is made to explain them by recurrence to the spiritual order. This latter order is brought in to explain certain types of illnesses or to answer philosophical question relating to disease, which are usually not answered by empirical methods. [144] Similarly, not all treatment of disease is based on religious or magical practices. Empirical procedures have been recorded for many societies and some estimate that in non-literate cultures between twenty-five to fifty per cent of their medicine is effective. [145]

Magical rites often become the key element in the diagnosis of a disease and in the application of a cure. [146] The fact that ritual attention is given only to certain types of illness suggests that the concept of disease contains philosophical and spiritual values which form part of the cultural heritage of a society. [147] The nature of human personality, of human relationships and of the power of spiritual forces are often evident in the way a people react to illness. [148] So also, the curer, or

---

[141] Hughes, 1968, p. 88; Turner, V., 1964d, p. 300. Cf. Malefijt, 1968. pp. 246 ff.

[142] Metzger and Williams, 1963, p. 298; Turner, V., 1964d, pp. 301-302; Glick, 1967, p. 32; Price-Williams, 1962, p. 123; Bidney, 1963, p. 143; Stanley and Freed, 1964, pp. 295 ff.

[143] Lieban, 1962, pp. 306 ff.

[144] Obeyesekere, 1969, p. 174; Levy, 1969, p. 221; Cf. Glick, 1967, pp. 31 ff.; Peck, 1968, pp. 78 ff., 84-85; Hughes, 1968, pp. 87-88; Mike, 1973, pp. 77 ff.; Seijas, 1973, pp. 544-545.

[145] Hughes, 1968, p. 90; Malefijt, 1968, pp. 246-248.

[146] Turner, V., 1964d, p. 343; Rubel, 1960, p. 797.

[147] Cf. Levy, 1969, p. 221.

[148] Read, 1948, p. 171.

the medicine man, together with his technique, may be given a religious role. His skill is at times considered a gift of the gods, or his refusal to undertake a cure may be taken as a sign that spiritual punishment may soon come down upon him. [149] The study of folk medicine has important theoretical implications for the persistent question arises between a magico-religious outlook as opposed to the scientific viewpoint; both are harmoniously united in a fairly logical system of medicine. [150] It may also lead us to determine where exactly non-empirical dimensions enter into the explanation and treatment of human illness. [151] The study of ethnomedicine is thus important because it shows how religious and magical beliefs and practices are an effective means by which many peoples approach and grapple with one of the main problems of life.

RELIGIOUS CHANGE

Another area of research in anthropology is the study of cultural and religious change. Few are those non-literate societies who have not come into contact with one of the great civilizations and who have not been greatly influenced especially by Western technology. The consequent rise of religious and political movements has become a major phenomenon in the lives of non-literate peoples. [152]

The attempts by anthropologists to go beyond the description of the features of such movements and the chronicle of their main events have been extremely varied. Some, opting for a kind of psychological explanation, have concluded that the movements give the participants refuge and consolation in time of difficulty; [153] others have theorized that they provide symbolically a way of dealing with problems which cannot be solved in a more empirical manner; [154] still others have maintained that they are a native attempt to seek satisfaction in an imaginative projection. [155] Some anthropologists have looked upon

---

[149] Metzger and Williams, 1963, pp. 217, 232. Cf. Turner, V., 1964d.

[150] Hughes, 1968, p. 90; Ackerknecht, 1946, p. 492. For the relation between Western medicine and folk-medicine, see Leach, 1949, pp. 162 ff., and Glick, 1967, pp. 31 ff.

[151] Frake, 1961.

[152] For a general introduction to these movements, also called, "nativistic cults," "millenarian cults," "cargo cults," etc., cf. Worsley, 1957; Mair, 1959; Wallace, 1956; Linton, 1943. For more detailed studies of particular movements, see Sundkler, 1961; Burridge, 1960.

[153] Allan, 1951.

[154] Beattie, 1966, pp. 70 ff. Schwartz, 1973, sees the Cargo cults of Melanesia as a reaction to culture contact.

[155] Firth, 1951, pp. 110-113; cf. idem 1955a, pp. 130-131.

these movements as rooted in "deprivation," in the psychological make-up of individuals, or in the psychological reaction to cultural inade-quacy. [156] Others have sought a historical or ethnographic explanation, showing why movements of this nature arose in certain situations and historical periods. Here, religious movements are seen as essentially social. At times the emphasis has been placed on the intellectual and philosophical tradition out of which the movements took their depar-ture. [157] Economic and political problems caused by European influ-ence have also been considered as the basic cause which triggered them off. Less common among antropologists, though by no means absent, are attempts to give a Marxist or Hegelian explanation. [158] One of the most recent attempts to go beyond these explanations is that of Bur-ridge who writes:

> Essentially, millenarian activities repeat in a variety of idiom the process whereby an animal became man, a moral being aware of his morality... The main theme is moral regeneration, the generation of new moralities, the creation of a new man defined in relation to more highly differentiated criteria. [159]

These movements are mainly preoccupied with the ordering and re-ordering of "power." They seek the means for transforming man and his culture. Their salvific or redemptive element is conceived in terms of worldly goods and achievements.

These anthropological approaches vary not only in emphasis but also in perspective. Though they cannot be easily harmonized, they all seem to point to a few similar general conclusions. Anthropological descrip-tions and explanations of religious activities bring into focus the fact that the study of culture change in general is necessary for an under-standing of religion and religious man. Since change never occurs solely in the religious sphere, but is accompanied by parallel develop-ments in political, economic, and social fields, the study of these move-ments may lead to a better understanding of the relation between religion and culture. These movements show how religious beliefs and values affect the totality of man's life and how political and economic upheavals have repercussions on the religious plane. Religion emerges as a dynamic reality, every changing and adapting itself to face up to

---

[156] Kaminsky, 1962, p. 216; Thrupp, 1962, p. 26; Aberle, 1962; Bruijn, 1951, pp. 9-10.

[157] Stanner, 1958, pp. 1 ff.; Burridge, 1960. For attempts to explain similar movements in literate societies, see, for example, Hobsbawn, 1959.

[158] Cf. Burridge, 1969, pp. 130-140.

[159] Burridge, 1969, pp. 142-143.

the new conditions of human life. The ideologies of a society in process emerge even more forcefully. Religious ideals, new and old, become more open to observation; the values which sustain man's hope become more evident. For religious movements are not just concerned with solving an immediate problem; nor are they a lamentation of a bygone happier state of affairs. They also turn man's gaze to the future.

Another line of approach, still largely unexplored, is the place of the leaders of these movements in the religious life of the people. Whether these movements are fundamentally religious or not, it is an established fact that their leaders more often than not assume a religious role or have one ascribed to them by their adherents. The leader of the movement frequently becomes the religious man par excellence in the eyes of those who follow him. Perhaps the study of religious movements presents one of the most fertile areas for exploring the concept of religious man.

NEW DIRECTIONS FOR THE STUDY OF RELIGION AND RELIGIOUS MAN

Recent developments in anthropological method may herald a new era in the study of religion. Though the application of these new techniques to religion has been sporadic, one can already detect some trends which religious studies might take.

This new theoretical orientation is usually referred to as Cognitive Anthropology, or ethnoscience, or the new ethnography. Culture is here viewed as a cognitive organization of material phenomena, a way of knowing and ordering the world around us. It is an ideal, normative system. [160] The ethnographer's task is to discover how different peoples organize and use their cultures. [161] Insisting that there are logical organizing principles underlying human behavior, the ethnographer's task is to unearth and understand them. Hence there are two main questions which cognitive anthropology seeks to answer. Firstly, what are the significant phenomena for a particular group of people who share a common culture? Secondly, how are these phenomena organized by them? The whole endeavor is to avoid imposing on an alien culture a pre-conceived order, and to elicit its semantic categories. In other words, one asks, what is the conceptual system of a particular people? [162] The data of cognitive anthropology are the

[160] Wallace, 1968, p. 537; Cf. Conklin, 1968, pp. 172 ff. For a review of the present state of ethnoscience see Werner, 1972.
[161] For some examples confer Berlin, Breedlove and Raven, 1966, and Conklin, 1955, 1962.
[162] Frake, 1962, pp. 28, 38; Tyler, 1968, p. 3.

mental phenomena which are operative in man's grasp of the environment. What it seeks to describe is not material culture but rather those perceptions, beliefs and values which are standardized, repetitive and conventional in a society. [163] As one anthropologist expressed it: "Cognitive anthropology entails an ethnographic technique which describes cultures from the inside out rather than from the outside in." [164]

In the past anthropologists have often studied other societies from the viewpoint of their own (that is, the anthropologists') culture. The questions they asked and the problems they examined were taken from Western culture. The new ethnography would insist that even the very questions asked have to come from the culture of the people under investigation. [165] What is of significance or of importance to the student may be quite trivial to the alien culture and vice versa. One cannot assume that a system of classification is universal and applicable to all cultures. [166] The results of this approach should raise the standards of reliability, validity and exhaustiveness in ethnography, as studies along this line on kinship, folk taxonomies and color classification have already shown. [167] The method is suitable to describe anything people talk about, be it kinsmen, plants or gods. Kinship studies following this method have been found easier because greater attention to kinship has been given in the last few decades, while anthropological studies of religious beliefs and practices have generally lagged behind. [168] The student who attempts to describe a religion using the new ethnographic method will be delving into new fields. [169] The prospects, however, are promising and worth the effort for in the field of religion, more perhaps than in any other field, the ethnographer has approached alien religions with a stereotypic set of definitions and questions which are an obvious product of the West.

The new ethnography consequently lays great stress on the study of the language of the society. Cognitive anthropology has in fact been greatly influenced by linguistics. Language and culture are considered to be intimately related; the former is seen as an essential and integral part of the latter. [170] Language interpenetrates with human experience.

---

[163] Wallace, 1968, pp. 539-540.

[164] Tyler, 1968, p. 20.

[165] Frake, 1964, p. 132.

[166] Sturtevant, 1964, p. 105.

[167] Sturtevant, 1964, p. 132. Though such studies do raise the problem of cultural relativity, this observation still holds good.

[168] Frake, 1964, p. 143; Sturtevant, 1964, pp. 102-103.

[169] Frake, 1965.

[170] Wallace, 1968, p. 536; Hymes, 1964, pp. 2-17; Cf. Goodenough, 1964, pp. 36 ff.; Bright, 1968, pp. 18 ff.

The interests and emphases of a people on such aspects of culture as technology, social organization, religion, and folklore are reflected and revealed in their language. [171] Even morality may be manifested in the linguistic usage. [172] It is through language that one often understands the values, emotions, and beliefs of a particular society. [173] Light can be shed on ways of thought by a consideration of what certain words mean. [174]

Language not only reflects culture, but also to some degree affects it. Language may determine the sensory perceptions and the habitual modes of thought; it may influence the logical make up of the people who speak it. [175] The way people look at their social problems may be linguistically determined; in fact, language may even denote different worldviews. [176] The only way an anthropologist can hope to understand another culture is by acquiring a mastery of its language. The problems involved, therefore, in any ethnographic work deal not merely with the translation of words, but more so with translation of ideas, values and beliefs. When one has to give an account of an alien religion the problems become even more acute. Thus, for instance, translating the names of deities and titles attributed to them may prove to be a hazardous task. [177] The relation between religion and language is just as intimate as that of any other aspect of one's culture and language. Phenomena such as glossolalia are sufficient proof of this. [178] Even in Western culture one can clearly see this link; Indo-European language patterns have played an influential role in shaping Western theology. [179] Language can be inextricably linked with various religious attitudes and beliefs. Some anthropologists have seen such a close relation between religion and language that they have remarked that changing one's language involves changing one's religion. [180] This deeper understanding of the relation of language to culture in general

---

[171] Hoijer, 1953, pp. 554 ff.; cf. Nida, 1954, pp. 210-213; Kerman, 1972, p. 335-339. For a specific example relating differences in language to diverse social conditions, see Fischer, 1966b.

[172] Nadel, 1954a, pp. 55-57.

[173] Colby, 1966; Cf. Greenberg, 1964, p. 31.

[174] Evans-Pritchard, 1956b, p. 331.

[175] Hoijer, 1953, pp. 558-559; Cf. Gleason, 1962, p. 215; Lotz, 1964, pp. 182-184.

[176] Goodenough, 1964, p. 30; Hymes, 1964, p. 6.

[177] Nida, 1964, pp. 91 ff.; Cf. Idem, 1954, pp. 198-223, where he applies the same method to the Bible.

[178] Cf. Carlyle, 1956.

[179] Gleason, 1962, pp. 212 ff.

[180] Hostetler, 1964.

and to religion in particular might lend new insights into the understanding of religious beliefs and values, thus opening the way to a better clarification of what religious man is.

RELIGIOUS MAN

The study of religious man has not been the preoccupation of antropology. The main thrust in anthropological literature has been the study of religious beliefs and practices. Even when religious specialists and mystics are studied, the stress has been on the social and/or psychological significance of their position rather than on the religious dimension that they present to the community. [181] Religion, for the anthropologist, is the belief in supernatural powers, beings, and forces; supernatural in the sense that they lie beyond empirical investigation and verification. [182] While most anthropologists who have gone into the problem of defining religion in some detail tend to avoid the use of the term "supernatural," the word is still well entrenched in anthropological literature. [183] Abandoning the earlier quest for the origin and development of religion, anthropologists have sought to understand the values and beliefs of particular religions, relating them to other aspects of man's individual and social life. [184]

Religion is seen as a creation of man through which he copes with certain problems of human life. It is a quest on man's part. Religious man is, therefore, the person who does make use of religious beliefs and practices to counteract the difficulties of life. He is the one who adheres strongly to religious views of the universe, to religious explanations of life-crises and to religious statements about man and his nature. Religious man sees himself related not only to the universe and

---

[181] See Firth, 1950, p. 295; Malefijt, 1968, pp. 228-245.

[182] Cf., for instance, Malefijt, 1968, pp. 9-12; Norbeck, 1961, pp. 32 ff.; Spiro, 1967, *passim*. Many of the contributors to the series, Case Studies in Anthropology, ed. by George and Louise Spindler, describe religion in terms of the supernatural.

[183] The way in which anthropologists have studied the problem of defining religion will be dealt with in Chapter V.

[184] Cf. Norbeck, 1964, and Evans-Pritchard, 1965b, who state that the study of the origins and development of religion is no longer an important preoccupation in anthropology. Some attempts, however, to draw up new theories have been made in the 1960s; cf. Swanson, 1960; Murray, 1963; Bellah, 1964; Mandelbaum, 1966; and Wallace, 1966, pp. 216 ff. Bellah's article seems to be the most well-known attempt to discuss religious evolution. His basic assumptions, however, are still those of the 19th century anthropologists and he makes no endeavor to answer the critique which contemporary anthropologists have put forward against theories of the origin and development of religion.

to his fellow men, but also to another world of unperceived forces and spirits. The view of religious man is not limited to empirical reality but goes beyond it. This does not mean that religious man sees an opposition between the world of empirical reality and that of spiritual beings; on the contrary, the two worlds are believed to be closely related, often influencing each other.

Three approaches to religious man predominate in anthropology today. The first trend contrasts religious man with scientific man by pointing out that the former believes in a spiritual world, the latter does not. The emphasis here lies not in opposing religious and scientific views, but in focusing on different attitudes and mental orientations which become apparent when man approaches the problem of human existence. Thus while religious myth dramatises the universe, the scientific activity analyses it. Ritual is not an operation guided by trial and error based on observation; it is rather a symbolic action and dramatic performance. Religious man is therefore engaged in an artistic behavior by which he symbolizes and thus counteracts the problems of life. [185]

Another approach avoids the contrast between scientific and religious man. Man is seen as essentially theory building, that is, his main concern is to try to explain the working principles of one's everyday world by discovering constant principles that underlie the apparent chaos and flux of sensory experience. [186] The search for explanation and prediction is one of the determining characteristics of man. Now, both explanation and prediction figure prominently in scientific and religious views of the world. To give one example, Robin Horton argues that the reference to microscopic entities in modern science can be paralleled to the references to gods and spirits in religious beliefs. [187] Leaving aside the criterion of verification, he points out that just as science portrays various levels of abstraction, so does religion. In other words the difference between religious and scientific man does not lie in their approach to the universe nor in the type of explanation they propose. Rather, the difference lies in the explanatory models used. Western man uses things or objects as models, non-literate man prefers people. The reason for this preference is due to the fact that in non-literate societies the activities of people present the

---

[185] Beattie, 1966.

[186] Horton is the main proponent of this view; Cf. Horton, 1964; Cf. *Idem*, 1962a. Jarvie would support this position for he holds that Cargo-Cults are a type of explanatory theory, an interpretation which Beattie vigorously opposes; Cf. Jarvie, 1963; Beattie, 1966, p. 71; Agassi and Jarvie, 1973.

[187] Horton, 1962a, pp. 207 ff.

most markedly ordered and regulated area of their experience, whereas their control of nature is not sufficiently developed to be ordered and predictable. The opposite is true of Western societies.

One final attempt to explain the problem has been to see religious beliefs and ritual as an attempt to deal with the question of a transcendent being who is by nature paradoxical and difficult to grasp. Religious man would thus be the person who has a sense of dependence on this transcendent being and who is constantly engaged in trying to overcome the inherent difficulty of expressing the relation he experiences with the divine transcendence. [188] This aspiration of man is held to be universal. Differences in religious beliefs and practices are then related to the social order; that is, religions express in different cultural idioms the basic experience of man, which is his relation to a transcendent being. [189]

These attempts to describe religious man are not easily reconcilable and they are obviously based on the initial assumptions made on the meaning and definition of religion. In spite, however, of these widely divergent views, there seems to emerge a few common points shared by most. The human dimension of religion is the focal point in anthropological studies, and hence the basic social conditions and human states are given prominence. Religious man, like all men, is faced with the problems of life, which include his social milieu as well as his own inner psychological states. The distinguishing characteristic of religious man seems to be that he attempts to solve these problems by going beyond the world itself and by postulating another order of reality with which he believes he is personally related and involved.

---

[188] Turner, V., 1962c. This view seems to be also held by Evans-Pritchard, 1965a and Lienhardt, G., 1960.
[189] Cf. Evans-Pritchard, 1953b.

CHAPTER FOUR

AN ANTHROPOLOGICAL CRITIQUE OF ELIADE'S VIEWS ON "RELIGIOUS MAN"

VALIDITY OF AN ANTHROPOLOGICAL EVALUATION

The image of religious man in contemporary anthropology presents a marked contrast to Eliade's views. Historians of religions in general, and Eliade in particular, are not likely to accept favorably an anthropological critique of their fundamental conclusions on religion and religious man. No comprehensive attempt has been made by any anthropologist to evaluate Eliade's works. The occasional reviews of Eliade's books by anthropologists do not exhibit much understanding of his method, nor depth in anthropological and historical perspective. It is consequently not surprising that Mac Linscott Ricketts, who has tried to refute the anthropological critique of Eliade, has produced an impassioned defense of the master. [1] Ricketts' aim of bridging the communications gap between anthropology and the history of religions is praiseworthy, but it is doubtful whether his response will have the desired effect. The lack of understanding between the history of religion and anthropology is mutual and reciprocal. The task of evaluating Eliade's works from an anthropological point of view is not an easy one. It is fraught with many problems which perhaps only those scholars who have been trained in both disciplines can hope to overcome. One has to assume that the methodological approaches to, and conclusions about, religion of both disciplines are not immune from critique, even though the critique attempted below concentrates on the anthropological side of the coin.

One of the main problems which historians of religions and religionists in general have with anthropological works on religion is that they appear to be reductionistic. In fact, the social sciences have all been charged with reductionism. [2] In other words, these sciences, is is claimed,

---

[1] Ricketts, 1973.

[2] This charge could possibly be reversed. An anthropologist would argue that to see religious elements in all human actions and to explain human behavior and experience always in religious terms would be equally reductionistic. Bharati, 1972, p. 262, must have had this observation in mind when he accused some anthropologists of symbolic reductionism.

tend to explain away religious beliefs and practices and see them only as psychological, social or cultural manifestations. [3] The charge of reductionism, common among historians of religions, has been one of Eliade's main reasons for rejecting anthropological methodology. [4]

There are some good reasons for this accusation. Early anthropology did not look favorably on religion. Besides, many anthropologists, past and present, have been inclined to be non-believers or anti-religious in their attitude. [5] Some contemporary anthropologists betray an open hostility to religious beliefs. [6] Such a tendency has in fact been recognized by anthropologists themselves. [7] One must, however, hasten to add that Geoffrey Parrinder, in stating that the "anthropologist is the most subtle foe of religion today," [8] has taken an extreme position among historians of religions. Given this general attitude among many historians of religions, one is not surprised to find that the theoretical formulations of anthropology, as well as its methodology, have been neglected by Eliade. Historians of religions generally look on the social sciences as merely descriptive disciplines which supply them with religious data for examination and consideration.

Such a view of the social sciences is, however, untenable; and the charge of reductionism has been overplayed because of a partial misunderstanding of the empirical method. The reductionistic tendency, one must note, is partly the result or consequence of the empirical approach. The empirical scientist limits his area of inquiry to those data which are verifiable by empirically testable methods. He cannot examine religious beliefs apart from the persons who adhere to them. Thus, for instance, in studying beliefs in God, gods and spirits, the anthropologist cannot direct his investigations towards them as if the gods and spirits were objective, because empirically they are not so.

---

[3] Rasmussen, 1968, p. 139.

[4] Eliade, 1967e, p. 502; 1969a, pp. 66-67; Maquire, 1960, pp. 8-9; Malandra, 1967, p. 23.

[5] Evans-Pritchard, 1959a, pp. 161ff.

[6] Leach, 1968c, is one of the more extreme examples. This short essay can only be described as insolent. Lévi-Strauss betrays a similar attitude by his refusal to deal with religious matters directly. See also Firth, 1951, p. 247, who says that rational evidence leads one to hold that belief in gods and spirits is illusory.

[7] Evans-Pritchard, 1959a, passim; 1965b, pp. 14-16; Turner, V., 1969a, p. 4; Horton, 1962b, p. 139. Spiro, 1964a, p. 1, admits that anthropologists have used religion as "the handmaiden for the understanding of a variety of other socio-cultural phenomena."

[8] Parrinder, 1962, p. 2.

Once the student has understood this basic orientation of the social sciences, his fears of reductionism should be greatly assuaged.

Anthropology, like the other social sciences, cannot be reduced to a descriptive discipline. Pure description, as has already been pointed out, [9] is not possible. Any attempt to describe includes some effort to explain. No scientific study can stop with the collection or description of data. [10] The task of understanding cannot be achieved by a purely descriptive method. This becomes more obvious when one deals with foreign cultures. Anthropology has, therefore, used a number of explanatory models in order to make intelligible the customs it has encountered in field research. Four types of explanation are found in anthropological literature: (1) explanation in terms of antecedent events or efficient causes; (2) explanation in terms of mediating factors; (3) explanation in terms of ends or purposes; and (4) explanation in terms of general laws or principles. [11] The first type of explanation is historical. Largely due to the fact that the history of non-literate peoples is often unknown or hard to explore, it has received the least attention by anthropologists. [12] The second type of explanation seeks to draw out the meaning of customs and values in terms of their interconnectedness. Objects, events and values are often interrelated or correlated. Though such relations may not be evident at first sight, once discovered, the object under study appears under a new light. The third kind of explanation is teleological and it has been often used in functional studies. Here one sees events, social relations and so on, as contributing, consciously or not, to an end or purpose, for example, the maintenance of order in society or the satisfaction of human psychological needs. The final type of explanation sees its object within a larger framework, as pertaining to a class. The particular is here understood in terms of the general. This assumes the general principle is already applicable and meaningful in its own right.

These types of explanation are not restricted to anthropological usage. Some of them, in particular the last two types mentioned above, are common in philosophy and theology. Theoretical formulations form part of all the social sciences. [13] It is in fact difficult to see how under-

---

[9] Cf. Chapter I, pp. 9-10.

[10] Schwartz and Ewald, 1968, pp. 32-33.

[11] I rely here mainly on Beattie, 1959b, which is an excellent treatment on the matter. For a lengthier and more thorough discussion, see Brown, R., 1963.

[12] For some recent attempts to draw up histories of non-literate societies, see Lewis, I. M., 1968.

[13] Cf. Brown, R., 1963, especially, pp. 165ff.

standing can proceed without some explanatory device on the lines suggested above. Explanation gives meaning, renders the unintelligible meaningful. It elucidates otherwise obscure data. To explain does not necessarily mean to dilute or to whittle down. "To seek an explanation of religious practices and of the whole religious orientation in terms of the historical and material situations is not to sap human existence of religious meaning. " [14] Anthropological explanation, or any kind of explanation for that matter, is, therefore, not necessarily reductionistic. True enough, explanations offered by different disciplines are often incompatible and at times openly contradictory; but the different ex-planations can at times support one another, making the object of inquiry more meaningful. [15]

The accusation of reductionism is further weakened by the fact that anthropological writers, no matter what their personal views on religion are, have never denied the importance of religious beliefs and practices for maintaining, enhancing and transforming human cultures. [16] More-over, not all anthropological works on religion fall under the label of reductionism, as Eliade himself admits. [17] Finally, one may note that the main sources on the religions of non-literate societies are anthro-pological works. No matter how reductionistic they might be, they cannot be ignored by the historian of religions who embarks on the study of the religions of non-literate cultures.

ELIADE'S AIMS, METHODS AND SOURCES

Before drawing up an extensive critique of Eliade's picture of reli-gious man it is necessary to investigate his aims and method and to evaluate his use of the anthropological sources upon which he bases his conclusions.

AIMS

Like historians of religions and phenomenologists in general, Eliade's primary concern is to understand beliefs and practices and to construct

---

[14] Malandra, 1967, p. 69.

[15] Kluckhohn, 1944, is a typical example of an attempt to unite psychological and sociological explanations. The debatable point in anthropology is whether to model explanation on the natural sciences or on history. See Nadel, 1951, pp. 191ff., Brown, R., 1963 and Homans, 1967.

[16] Turner, V., 1969a, p. 4; Malefijt, 1968, *passim*.

[17] Eliade, 1967e, p. 502.

an image of religious man in the light of this understanding. [18] His approach is definitely sympathetic and he rightly emphasizes the need for mutual dialogue between believers of different religious convictions. [19] There is, however, serious doubt whether one can call his approach impartial. His treatment of Christianity gives the impression that he assumes from the start the uniqueness of the Christian faith. [20] Though he states that he has neither "the responsibility nor the competence" to be a theologian, he nevertheless affirms that man is by nature a Christian, quoting the Christian adage: "Homo naturaliter Christianus. " [21] His objective of understanding is also marred by the fact that he leaves out Islam and the Chinese religious tradition from his considerations. [22] Since he asserts that the concern of the historian of religions is the "entire religious history of humanity," [23] the omission of even two important religious traditions not only brings into question his thoroughness, but also makes it obvious that his explicit goals have not been reached.

Together with most historians of religions Eliade has abandoned the search for the origin of religion. Nowhere in his writings do we come across attempts to outline stages of religious development or to classify religions into neat categories. Here Eliade has been influenced by contemporary anthropology which has largely given up these broader pursuits of origin, development and classification. [24] Eliade, however, does diverge from his own aims by propounding a theory of religious degradation along the lines of Andrew Lang and Wilhelm Schmidt. [25]

The two principal aims of Eliade are integration and generalization.

---

[18] Cf. Chapter I, pp. 24 ff.

[19] Cf. Chapter II, p. 45.

[20] Eliade, 1958b, p. 30, note 1; 1959a, p. 137; 1960a, pp. 29, 152-154; 1961a, pp. 72, 92, 111-112; 1963a, pp. 64-65; 1965a, p. 137; 1969c, p. 161.

[21] Eliade, 1969c, pp. 157-158; cf. also Eliade, 1969 c., pp. 67-68. The reference to the Christian adage occurs in Eliade 1960a, p. 31. The more common form of the saying is "anima naturaliter christiana"; cf. Rahner, 1969, p. 303; Bilaniuk, 1967, p. 545. Reno, 1972, p. 154, observes that Eliade assumes a progressional view of hierophanies "for essentially theological reasons." Ricketts, 1973, pp. 27-28, makes an unconvincing attempt to defend Eliade on this point. It has to be granted, however, that Leach's critique is extreme and unwarranted.

[22] One should note, however, that in his religious, anthology Eliade, 1967a, includes selections from the Islamic and Chinese traditions. But these traditions have not been incorporated in the rest of Eliade's works.

[23] Eliade, 1965a, p. 1.

[24] Cf. Chapter II, p. 62 and Chapter III, p. 96. See also Eliade, 1969a, pp. 27-28.

[25] This theory is discussed briefly later in this chapter.

He writes:

> What principally concerns us now is to integrate the researches of the orientalists, ethnologists, depth psychologists and historians of religion in order to arrive at a total knowledge of man. [26]

He complains that neglect of generalization has led to "a progressive loss of creativity and an accompanying loss of interpretative cultural synthesis in favor of fragmentic, analytical research." [27] The goal of integrating religous research done in different disciplines is certainly desirable, yet nowhere does Eliade investigate the problem of integrating in concrete all these researches. The various scientific disciplines which have contributed to the study of religion follow different methodologies and emphasize different aspects of religious man, making integration a herculean task. [28] One cannot embark on this kind of integration before one studies and compares the methods involved. [29] This is hardly achieved by explicitly ignoring the methodologies of the disciplines from which data are drawn, as does Eliade. [30] His grand aim of integration has, therefore, remained unfulfilled.

Eliade has certainly been more successful with his scope of generalization. Most of his works, in particular those which pursue a single theme, are explicit endeavors to draw up general and universal characteristics of religious behavior and experience; his works probably contain the most comprehensive generalizations of religious man in contemporary literature. Generalization, a common enterprise in many sciences, is a valid procedure of the historian of religions.

METHOD

In anthropological literature one encounters two procedures aimed directly or indirectly at generalization. One approach starts from hypotheses or theories, often formulated from intensive studies of one or several societies. These theories are then applied to other cultures

---

[26] Eliade, 1965b, p. 12.

[27] Eliade, 1969a, pp. 58-59.

[28] Park, W. Z., 1965, pp. 1305-1306, goes as far to say that the results of ethnology, psychology and sociology are not comparable. This is an exaggeration since the said disciplines have borrowed concepts and methods from one another.

[29] This procedure has been followed in Chapter I. The view put forward here is that the integration of disciplines has to take place somewhat along the lines suggested in Chapter I.

[30] Eliade, 1964a, xi; 1960a, pp. 209-210.

with the intention of testing their applicability. [31] The second approach, more common in anthropology, emphasizes the study of individual cultures or societies and attempts to reach conclusions of a general nature by induction. [32] Eliade opts for the first approach; but it is difficult to detect in his writings any explicit scientific methodology.

Two typical examples of how he uses this method can be seen in his interpretation of initiation rites and of the belief in a high god in non-literate societies. In the first case [33] Eliade makes a fairly intensive study of a few Australian tribes and then backs up his conclusions by random and scanty reference from elsewhere. There is no guiding principle in the selection of data. He does not test his hypothesis that initiation rituals bring about an ontological change in the status of the novices. Leaving aside the consideration that Eliade does not distinguish between initiation and puberty rites, it is an ethnographic fact that not all societies hold initiation rituals. [34] Some hold them only for girls, other only for boys, and still others for both sexes, or not at all. Not all initiation rites are accompanied by ordeals or mutilations; the latter are, in fact, a rare occurance both in male and female initiations. Again, not all those societies who hold initiation rites reveal tribal secrets or mysteries, or teach sacred lore, in connection with the rites. [35] Likewise, the display of death and rebirth motifs, though common, is by no means universal. [36] Thus, when Eliade states that death to the profane condition and resurrection to a new world is "documented in every kind of initiation," [37] or that "circumcision is extremely widespread, we

[31] Typical examples are the attempts by anthropologists to apply Lévi-Strauss's theory of myth to particular societies; see Chapter III, p. 74, footnote 45. Lévi-Strauss himself follows this method in his book *The Raw and the Cooked,* where he starts with an intensive study of a few culturally related tribes. Another example is Whiting, 1950.

[32] This has been the orientation of British anthropologists. Evans-Pritchard suggests that this is the best approach to the study of religion; cf. Evans-Pritchard, 1959b, pp. 8-9. This topic is discussed in Chapter V.

[33] Eliade, 1965a.

[34] Data referred to in this section are based on Robert Textor's summary of the *Human Relations Area Files,* Textor, 1967, and on the references quoted in Chapter III, especially under footnote 88. One should note in particular the charts given by Young, 1965, pp. 165-177.

[35] The *Human Relations Area Files* lists 12 societies where important secrets are revealed in connection with male initiation rites and 11 where no such links exist. No conclusions can be drawn from about 351 societies because the ethnographic reports on this point are incomplete or doubtful. Cf. Textor, 1967, par. 375.

[36] Malefijt, 1968, pp. 192-193.

[37] Eliade, 1965a, p. 19. This general statement, like so many others, is not backed up by ethnographic references.

might also say universal," [38] or again, that the initiation rites for girls
are individual, and those for men collective, [39] the anthropologist's
answer is that such statements are factually wrong. In the same book,
Rites and Symbols of Initiation, we read that rites for entrance into
secret societies correspond in every way to tribal initiation. [40] However, the *Human Relations Area Files* specify that only nine cultures
where the existence of secret societies has been recorded have been
studied in detail. Consequently, in a large number of cases the data
about these societies is extremely scanty. [41] There is, therefore, no
other alternative but to doubt the sweeping generalization on the relations between initiation rites and secret societies till more data on the
latter have been amassed.

A second example of Eliade's tendency towards generalization can
be seen in the way he treats the problem of the belief in a high god in
non-literate societies. The main ethnographic facts underlying this hypothesis are the reports that in many cultures there is a definite belief in
a creator god, but that very few rites, if any, are performed in worship.
Such gods, who receive no public worship in organized rites, have been
called otiose, or inactive gods. From these basic data Eliade has constructed an elaborate and highly generalized description of the history
and structure of the high god, a description which Charles Long has
accurately summarized in six stages:

> 1) He (i.e., the high god) is a being who created the world; 2) his
> symbolism is related to the sky and thus he always represents transcen-
> dence, power and wisdom; 3) after the creation of the world, the high
> god becomes deus otiosus, removed from the world he has created; 4) in his
> place are substituted the dramatic deities of fertility and creativity; 5) the
> high god is not completely forgotten, but he is no longer a part of the life of
> man and the world; 6) he is called upon and remembered in moments of
> strife or catastrophe when the basic structure of the world is threatened and
> when no help can be gained from the deities of fertility and creativity. [42]

Eliade repeats this same view unchanged throughout many of his works
without ever asking to what degree do the general statements on the

---

[38] Eliade, 1965a, p. 42. Eighty-three cultures are listed by the *Human Relations
Area Files* as performing male genital multilations; two hundred and forty-two
cultures do not perform any multilations. Cf. Textor, 1967, par 377.

[39] Eliade, 1965a, p. 42. One should note that accurate accounts of female initiation rites are rarer in anthropological sources. See Textor, 1967, pars. 380ff.

[40] Eliade, 1965a, p. 75.

[41] See Textor, 1967, par. 471.

[42] Long, 1969, p. 144.

high god correspond to the ethnographic reports amassed in the last few decades. [43]

Since general statements must be meaningful in themselves, the meaning of "otiose god" must be determined. Several questions have to be asked: is the high god considered inactive from the point of view of the people who profess belief in him, or is he otiose from the standpoint of the historian of religions' own religious tenets? One must also determine whether the fact that no public worship is offered to the high god necessarily implies that he does not play an important role in the religious life of the people who claim him as their creator. Such questions raise the issue of the viability of the concept "otiose god." [44] Eliade does not offer answerss to the above mentioned questions; on the contrary, he ignores them. Further, Eliade's description of the high god contains a number of ethnographic statements which can be tested by empirical research. The most important of these statements are: (1) belief in a creator high god is universal in non-literate societies; (2) the otiose god is now an almost universal feature of these societies; and (3) the high god is always a sky god; that is, the sky is always used as the main symbol of the high god's attributes. [45] A glance at the ethnographic evidence, however, shows that none of these general statement can be supported as they stand. According to the *Human Relations Area Files* there are one hunderd and fifty six cultures where belief in a high god has been recorded, one hunderd and four cultures where this belief is absent and one hundred and forty societies which have to be excluded from consideration because of scanty evidence. [46] While the existence of belief in a creator high god in non-literate societies was rightly vindicated by Wilhelm Schmidt, it still remains true that there are many examples where this belief is absent. Turning now to the activity of the high god, out of the one hundred and fifty six cases where belief in him is present, more than half of them give clear indication that the god is considered active rather than otiose. The activity of the high god is in many cases involvement in human morality, in other words, he is conceived as punishing the bad and rewarding the good. This implies that he is involved in daily human affairs. Several

---

[43] Eliade, 1958b, pp. 43ff.; 1960a, pp. 134-137; 1961a, pp. 121-125; 1963a, pp. 93-98; 1964a, p. 188; 1966, pp. 128-129; 1967a, pp. 5-6; 1969a, p. 155.

[44] For a debate on this see Horton, 1962b, O'Connell, 1962 and Shelton, 1964 and 1965. Cf. Edel, 1957, p. 160.

[45] See Eliade, 1958b, pp. 38ff.

[46] See Textor, 1967, par. 426ff.

reports indicate that the name or names of the high god are often on the lips of ordinary people and that the god is prayed to privately, even if no rites are offered him. Some cases of organized public worship of the high gods have also been recorded. [47] Since detailed descriptions of the concept of god are few, the statement that the sky is universally used as a symbol of the high god remains an unproved assumption. [48] Only further ethnographic research can solve the problem.

Most of the statements that Eliade makes on the high god are thus not supported by the incomplete ethnographic evidence at hand. His claims that the creator high god became an otiose god cannot be proved or disproved. The degradation of the concept of God could be true, but it could just as well be false. We have no way of putting the theory to the test and settling the issue with finality. Therefore, Eliade's generalizations on the high god and his demise are based mainly on assumptions, some of which are impervious to empirical verification, others clearly contradict ethnographic reports.

Finally, many of Eliade's generalizations are elusive and difficult to understand. He writes:

> To the primitive, a lunar symbol (an amulet or iconographic sign) does not merely contain in itself all the lunar forces at work on the level of the cosmos—but actually, by the power of the ritual involved, places the wearer himself at the center of those forces, increasing his vitality, making him more real, and guaranteeing him a happier state after his death. [49]

Or again:

> To the primitive mind, the intuition of the cosmic destiny of the moon was equivalent to the first step, the foundation of an anthropology. [50]

We are reminded of numerous "primitive" or mythical intuitions and of similar operations of the supposedly "primitive" mind, [51] but we are

---

[47] Cf. Smith, E., 1966, pp. 92, 186ff., 228-229, 261-262, 280-281, where African concepts of God and man's relationship to him are outlined. The book contains two examples of organized worship of the high god, Smith, E., 1966, pp. 230 and 253. Smith's collection of essays is used by Eliade who selects a few passages for incorporation into his religious anthology, Eliade, 1967a. The data referred to in this footnote are, however, ignored by Eliade.

[48] Evans-Pritchard's study on the Nuer is a typical case of a people who use the sky as a multi-dimensional symbol of God; cf. Evans-Pritchard, 1956a, pp. 1-27. There are, however, few books on the religions of non-literate societies comparable to his meticulous descriptions of the concept of God of these people.

[49] Eliade, 1958b, p. 156.

[50] Eliade, 1958b, p. 158.

[51] See, for instance, Eliade, 1958b, p. 245.

never told what a primitive intuition is and how we arrive at the conclusion that a certain statement constitutes a primitive intuition. Many of Eliade's generalizations, asserted so confidently, are not workable hypotheses. As one anthropologist has accurately observed, there "is enough detailed ethnography now in print to support and to contradict almost any generalization about human society." [52]

Eliade could have avoided unwarranted generalizations had he followed his own warning that "it is unwise to make hasty generalizations," [53] and used the historical or the comparative method. We find, however, no evidence that he has consulted historical methodology or that he has used the comparative method carefully. [54]

Another major defect in Eliade's writings is that his method has not been influenced by some of the fundamental orientations of history. Historians, in agreement with anthropologists, admit that, since their task is not only to record events but also to explain them, they have to rely on generalizations. [55] But particular generalizations are means and not ends in themselves. They have to be referred to factual data, to be explored and tested for possible error. This problem is an acute one especially for the student of ancient history. As one historian, referring to ancient history, has remarked:

> In no field of history does new specific information appear more constantly to upset old concepts and to enlarge our view of the area. [56]

And again:

> What he [that is, the ancient historian] writes today will not be the whole story ten years from now and may even need drastic alteration purely on the factual level. [57]

---

[52] Lienhardt, P., 1960, p. 1092.

[53] Eliade, 1958b, p. 24.

[54] The only instance where Eliade seems to follow to some degree the historical method is in his *Yoga: Immortality and Freedom* where he treats the Indian scriptures in historical order. In general, Eliade gives the impression that he has accepted the cultural historical method of W. Schmidt; see, for example, Eliade, 1960a, pp. 176ff., 201; 1965a, p. 44 and 1961a, p. 145. Recently, however, he seems slightly hesitant; cf. Eliade 1969a, pp. 24-25. One book, *Shamanism: Archaic Techniques of Ecstacy*, shows little influence of Schmidt's methodology. Few anthropologists today would accept Schmidt's historical reconstructions; cf. Evans-Pritchard, 1965b, pp. 103-104; Bharati, 1972, p. 231.

[55] White, M., 1965, p. 3; cf. Cantor and Schneider, 1967, p. 19. For a lengthy and scholarly discussion on the problem of generalization in history see Gottschalk, 1963. For some of the general problems of historical knowledge, problems shared in common with anthropologists, confer Zogorin, 1959.

[56] Starr, 1963, p. 6.

[57] Starr, 1963, p. 7.

These observations can be applied without hesitation to the religious data on non-literate societies. The advance in anthropological methodology has changed not just the approach to the data, but also some of the data themselves. For new techniques have brought to light new data and disproved older data, thus forcing anthropologists to abandon some of their more common concepts.

In history, as in the natural and social sciences, [58] generalizations are looked upon as hypotheses for which both positive and negative proofs are applied. These hypotheses can also be tested by the use of correlations. [59] Historians do not hesitate to reject a hypothesis when it is in contradiction with established facts—established at times by other disciplines. [60] Even those historians who look more favorably than others on generalizations are aware that the testing of hypotheses is imperative. Popper, for example, while accusing those writers who shun or disparage the technique of generalization as succumbing to the error of historicism, still affirms that the "function of observation and experiment is the more modest one of helping us to test our theories and to eliminate those which do not stand up to tests." [61]

Historians also warn against the danger of selecting facts which support an assumed generalization while omitting facts which negate it.

> The duty of the historian to respect his facts is not exhausted by the obligation to see that his facts are accurate. He must also seek to bring into the picture all known and knowable facts relevant, in one sense or another, to the theme on which he is engaged and to the interpretation proposed. [62]

Nowhere in Eliade's writings can we detect any attempt on his part to take into account these simple methodological procedures so common in history. [63]

Historians of religions themselves admit that the comparative method has been used in their discipline somewhat unsatisfactorily. [64] Its use by Eliade is equally defective. Data from multiple religions and from

---

[58] For a discussion of the scientific formulation of hypotheses in the social and historical disciplines see Social Science Research Council, 1954.

[59] Starr, 1963, pp. 10-11.

[60] Toynbee, 1965, pp. 19-20.

[61] Popper, 1957, p. 98.

[62] Carr, 1967, p. 32.

[63] One is thus inclined to conclude that Eliade, by calling himself a historian of religions is usurping the name of a well-established discipline without accepting its basic method. This can lead to nothing else but confusion.

[64] Cf. Adams, 1965, pp. 55 and 90; Parrinder, 1962, p. 14.

different historical periods are collected and grouped together in typical
Frazerian style. Eliade is aware that Frazer's method has now been
abandoned, and he is also familiar with some of the anthropological
critique levelled at the British anthropologist. He goes as far as to call
Frazer's method "confusionistic." [65] But his admiration for the man
and his voluminous literary production does not seem to have dimin-
ished over the years. In Eliade's writings Frazer holds a prominent place.
In *Patterns in Comparative Religion* there are over eighty references
to Frazer's works, by far the largest number of references to a single
author in that book. More recently, Frazer's encyclopedic approach is
labelled a "splendid tradition." [66] In spite of the fact that some historians of religions have defended Eliade against the charge of following
the Frazerian comparative method, it can hardly be disputed that in
many of his works Eliade, adopts the method so conspicuously followed
in *The Golden Bough.* [67] Frazer's voluminous reading enabled him to
support practically every statement he made by references to half-a-
dozen tribes, thereby making his theories look extremely impressive. [68]
Eliade's *Patterns in Comparative Religion* does exactly the same thing,
with the difference that his aims are obviously not similar to those of
Frazer. We find in Eliade no attempt to compare, in other words to
draw up similarities and differences. There seems to be an implicit
assumption that differences are not very significant. Here Eliade
ignores the repeated insistence of his colleagues that differences must
also be taken into consideration. [69] What Eliade compares most of the
time is the outward manifestations of things rather than their meanings.
Images are collected in great abundance under pre-arranged labels because they portray an exterior likeness, while they may possibly have

---

[65] Eliade, 1963a, p. 42; 1969c, p. 175. Cf. also, 1969a, pp. 14 and 54-55.

[66] Eliade, 1969a, p. 30.

[67] The following writers have accused Eliade of following Frazer's method:
Lessa, 1959a, pp. 122-123; Raglan, 1959, p. 3; Frye, 1959, pp. 426-427 and Altizer,
1963, p. 41. Luyster, 1966, pp. 240ff. makes an impassioned attempt to defend
Eliade, but he misses the main point. Anthropologists do not complain that Eliade,
like Frazer, draws up an elaborate theory of religious evolution. Their objection
is that Eliade, like Frazer, lumps religious beliefs and practices together in a
comparative way which ignores the differences and the cultural and historical
situations. Ricketts, 1973, pp. 29-30 is equally emotional in his defence of this
accusation against Eliade, but he contributes no objective factors to enlighten the
reader.

[68] Fox, 1967, pp. 85-86 has labelled this approach a disease.

[69] Cf. Streng, 1969, Foreword; Smith, W. C., 1964, p. 78; Lanternari, 1962,
pp. 53 and 69.

meant something quite different to the groups that used them. [70]

One of the most glaring examples of this method is Eliade's treatment of shamanistic initiation. In *Rites and Symbols of Initiation* he interprets initiation rites, rites of entrance in secret societies and shamanistic initiation as part of a larger complex, namely, initiation into a higher order of reality. But shamans are first of all religious specialists and comparing them with other religious specialists would seem to be the first logical step in an ordered and meaningful comparative approach. [71] It seems obvious to the student who goes beyond the observation of outward rites, that there are important differences between shamanistic initiation rites and other initiation rituals. The latter emphasize primarily the individual's new status, be it social, religious or both; the novice acquires membership in the society's cultural and religious life, a membership which he or she shares in common with others on an equal basis. Shamanistic initiation, on the other hand, does precisely the opposite: it gives the shaman a new identity, a status which differs from that of his fellow men. While initiation rituals incorporate the novice in the life of the tribe, shamanistic initiations set the shaman apart from his community, for by initiation he acquires new powers which no one else has. While in those societies which perform initiation rites all young members are initiated by custom at a time decided upon by the elders, shamanistic initiation is restricted to a few individuals who have already given adequate proof of their ability to be shamans. Vocation, in one form or another, is often the reason why a man or a woman becomes a shaman; this is obviously not the case in initiation rites. [72] The purpose of these initiation rituals contains important different elements which are crucial to the understanding of shamanism.

Another flaw in Eliade's comparison between the various initiation rites is the fact that he omits patent correlations. He seems to have forgotten that in many of those societies where shamanism is an important aspect in a society's religious life, initiation rites are not

---

[70] Haynes, 1965, p. 804. Allen, D., 1972, p. 185, observes that Eliade reads into specific religious data all kinds of sophisticated universal structures and meanings.

[71] Cf. Malefijt, 1968, pp. 288 ff. *The International Encyclopedia of the Social Sciences* does not have a separate article on shamanism; shamans are treated under the essay on Religious Specialists; cf. Turner, V. 1968a.

[72] These observations can be made by careful reading of Eliade's work on initiation and shamanism, Eliade, 1964a and 1965a. For anthropological literature on initiation rites, see Chapter III, footnote 88.

performed. [73] Such correlations must be taken into account; to ignore them can only lead to misunderstanding the importance of religious beliefs and practices and ultimately to a distorted picture of religious man.

The identification of the otiose god, already referred to, with Nietzsche's proclamation that God is dead is one of the more extreme examples of Eliade's comparative method. [74] It is an accepted fact that religious unbelief is much less common in non-literate societies than in Western culture. Even in those societies where the high god can be called inactive, we still do not detect a higher incidence of unbelief. Eliade's own view is that other religious beliefs and practices take the place of the high god. The events, if one may call them so, are totally different in meaning. Far from being similar, the otiose god and Nietzsche's death of God portray two religious worlds which are completely apart. It is only a superficial comparison which concludes that they are similar or identical. [75]

Eliade's comparisons follow, on principle, a methodology which is highly tenuous. He assures us that

> From a methodological point of view, the reconstruction of an initiatory scenario on the basis of a few fragmentary documents and with the aid of ingenious comparisons is a perfectly valid procedure. [76]

This methodology implies that comparisons depend very much on the ingenuity of the writer. But should not the similarities and differences suggest themselves from the data? [77] Is not comparison only possible when there are enough facts to make it? [78] To follow Eliade's procedure is to preclude any attempt to achieve objectivity. Imagination and intuition may be useful tools in the hands of a historian of religions, but they must be contained by objective criteria. The charge that in

---

[73] See Levin and Potapov, 1964, *passim*. For detailed study of one society where shamanism is an important aspect of religious life, while initiation is absent, see Oswalt, 1967.

[74] Eliade, 1969a, pp. 47-48. For Eliade, the death of God in Nietzsche and the degeneration of the high god to an otiose god are the same. The consequences, however, are different.

[75] Eliade does point out one difference between the otiose god and Nietzsche's death of God, but the difference is not central to the problem. Had Eliade compared Nietzsche's death of God with the death of God theology of the second half of the 1960's, he would have seen how out of place is his alleged similarity between Nietzsche and non-literate peoples.

[76] Eliade, 1965a, p. 104.

[77] Brandon, 1962, p. 4.

[78] Bouquet, 1956, p. 21; cf. Streng, 1969, p. 9.

Eliade's works there are "precipitate comparisons and identifications" is not restricted to anthropological literature. [79]

It seems clear, therefore, that Eliade is not following a method which one could describe as scientific or empirical. Disavowing the procedure of the social sciences, he insists that there is room for another approach, namely the phenomenological method, which insists that religious phenomena must be seen and studied as religious. [80] Phenomenologists assume that religious manifestations must be understood in their own right, apart from the historical and cultural situation. Eliade follows this path throughout; nowhere does he give the historical and/or cultural situation of the beliefs and rites he examines because he does not apparently think this is necessary. [81] The basic problem here is to determine more specifically what does studying religious beliefs and practices as religious mean? Yet Eliade, apparently contradicting himself, admits that "account must be taken of cultural individuality," [82] and that different cultures do affect religion. [83] He even goes so far as to say that

> for the student of religion "history" means primarily that all religious phenomena are conditioned. A pure religious phenomenon does not exist. A religious phenomenon is also a social, an economic, a psychological phenomenon, and, of course, a historical one, because it takes place in historical time and it is conditioned by everything that had happened before. [84]

Such statements, echoed by several historians of religions, [85] are contrary to the actual procedure of Eliade in treating religious beliefs and practices apart from their cultural environment. Had Eliade started his investigations by an attempt to grasp religious data firstly in their cultural and social environment, he would have avoided many of his ill-conceived comparisons. For religious beliefs, values and symbols make sense only when seen in the total context of a cultural milieu. One can, for instance, appreciate religious symbols and grasp their significance only after having taken the cultural situation into consideration. Often, the cultural and social context is the reason why a certain object has been chosen or has become a religious symbol; Indian's

---

[79] Schlette, 1966, p. 53.

[80] Eliade, 1960a, pp. 207-210; 1964a, p. xi. Cf. Pettazzoni, 1954, p. 216. Streng, 1969, p. 42.

[81] Eliade, 1963a, p. 42.

[82] Eliade, 1965b, p. 56.

[83] Eliade, 1963a, pp. 42-47.

[84] Eliade, 1969a, p. 52.

[85] Brandon, 1962, pp. 2ff.; Ashby, 1965, p. 30; Streng, 1969, p. 9.

sacred cow is an excellent case in point. [86] Having thus arrived at the meaning of symbols and beliefs, then one can start making profitable cross-cultural comparisons. In this way one can go beyond comparing outward manifestations of religions and relate meanings and values.

Some scholars have interpreted Eliade's phenomenological method as a re-structuring of phenomena, [87] implying that such re-structuring is possible only after having detached beliefs from their cultural background. But such re-structuring or re-ordering, if it is to boast of any validity, must be based on some objective criteria; otherwise any student can re-order the "phenomena" according to a subjective norm of his own choosing. [88] In Eliade's method no objective criteria are given, nor any explicit attempt is made to draw them up.

Eliade's phenomenological method presents, moreover, insurmountable difficulties to the understanding of religious beliefs and practices because some of the key concepts are far from clear. The term "phenomenon" seems to include both subjective and objective dimensions. "Reality," another important word, used very frequently by Eliade, is made to do some very hard work, as one anthropologist complained. [89] Its use seems to be restricted to the spiritual order, while the material world tends to be equated with what is unreal and illusory. As this same anthropologist observes:

> He [Eliade] tries to create a way of thought or feeling in which distinction between subject and object, the self and the non-self, what is "inside" the mind and what is "outside," are regarded as less relevant than in our own philosophic tradition. [90]

And Altizer, though his understanding of Eliade may leave much to be desired, [91] has made the accurate remark that "one can sense in Eliade the Eastern Christian hostility to the rational spirit of Western theology." [92]

Finally, the "sacred" or the "holy," among others of those constantly recurring words, refers to a non-empirical realm or datum and are, therefore, not subject to empirical investigation. Eliade speaks of

---

[86] Cf. for instance, Harris, 1966.

[87] Rasmussen, 1968.

[88] This is one of the main objections put forward against Lévi-Strauss' analysis of myth. He has not developed criteria objective enough to break down the myth into its smallest components.

[89] Lienhardt, G., 1958, p. 416.

[90] Lienhardt, G., 1958, p. 416.

[91] Ricketts, 1967, pp. 40ff.

[92] Altizer, 1963, p. 37.

countless manifestations, called hierophanies, kratophanies and so on, and yet there is no way to determine with any precision what these manifestations consist of, and who decides in a particular instance that such a manifestation occurs.

In conclusion, therefore, the claim that Eliade's method is scientific and empirical, a claim supported by several historians of religions, [93] cannot be substantiated by concrete evidence. "Unscientific zeal," as one of Eliade's most ardent supporters has remarked, [94] seems to be one of the main hallmarks of his approach. Eliade's unspecified method is not rigorous enough; it deals with religious matters which lie beyond empirical verification; and it is mainly deductive, based on adhered to metaphysical assumptions. [95]

SOURCES

While Eliade can bypass anthropological methodology, he cannot do without its literature. Anthropological and ethnographic sources appear throughout Eliade's works, and what he says on religious beliefs and practices of non-literate societies and the conclusions he draws on religious man can be examined only after the way he uses these sources has been previously examined. [96] It is assumed that it belongs to the scholars within a particular discipline to pass judgment on its own literature. In other words, the evaluation of the good and inferior sources in anthropology is determined by contemporary anthropologists and not by scholars in other academic fields.

In general, there are three main critiques which can be levelled at the way Eliade uses his sources. First, he does not distinguish between primary and secondary sources. [97] Many anthropological writings on non-literate societies are secondary sources, though most ethnographic works can be regarded as primary sources. The distinction between primary and secondary sources is important because secondary sources are more interpretative and necessarily selective. To use secondary sources well one must be aware of individual prejudices, interests and influences.

---

[93] Streng, 1969, p. 9; Bolle, 1967, p. 95.

[94] Luyster, 1966, p. 243.

[95] Lessa, 1959a, pp. 122-123; 1959b, pp. 1146-1147; Saler, 1967, pp. 262-263.

[96] It is not possible to evaluate every reference Eliade makes to anthropological sources. Here we select those sources which are very closely linked with some of Eliade's main themes.

[97] For a good treatment of the distinction between primary and secondary sources and how they ought to be used, see Cantor and Schneider, 1967, pp. 39-105.

Secondly, Eliade makes, as a rule, no attempt to evaluate the sources he cites; when he does evaluate, he is not always right from an anthropological standpoint. It has to be emphasized that not all ethnograpic reporting is of the same academic standard; neither are all anthropological writings on religion of the same value. A typical example of a poorly evaluated book by Eliade is Robert Lowie's book *Primitive Religion*. [98] This book is still often quoted by historians of religions of non-literate societies. [99] Eliade thinks very highly of it. [100] Written almost a half a century ago, Lowie's book was an excellent one in that it abandoned the then common approach of drawing up elaborate evolutionary schemes and of placing the religions of these people as the lowest form of religion. But in the light of advances made since that time the book is inferior with very little depth to it. It is based mainly on the study of four American Indian tribes. The anthropologist who drew up the biographical essay on Robert Lowie for the *International Encyclopedia of the Social Sciences* does not mention the book, not even in the bibliography of Lowie's works. [101] Again, it is a recognized fact in anthropology that some of the best monographs on religion have been produced by British anthropologists. These sources have been largely neglected by Eliade; when, however, he does mention them, it is clear that they have left no impact on what Eliade says about the religions of non-literate societies. Sometimes one doubts whether Eliade has grasped their significance. [102]

Another example of Eliade's uncritical use of sources is that of the anthropological material in his first article on Australian religions. [103] This article discusses at some length the high god theory in Australian tribes and relies heavily on older anthropological works on the subject. But anthropologists today tend to regard these older sources as very questionable, because what was written about the high god at the turn of the last century was often dictated by the emotional debate as to whether the concept of god is "primitive" or not. Consequently, contem-

---

[98] Lowie, 1924.

[99] Cf. for example, Adams, 1965, p. 24; Burtt, 1957, p. 487; Noss, 1974, p. 31.

[100] Eliade, 1969a, p. 27.

[101] Cf. Driver, 1968. Note, however, that this critique of Lowie's book on religion does not detract from his great contribution to anthropology or from his excellent ethnographic works.

[102] To refer, for instance, as Eliade does, to Evans-Pritchard's book on Azande witchcraft as a "manual of black magic" raises the problem of whether Eliade has grasped the main point of the book and whether he is aware of its lasting impact on anthropology. Cf. Eliade, 1967a, p. 641.

[103] Eliade, 1966.

porary anthropologists tend to look on this debate as a product of its time, and today the leading authorities on the native Australians are not concerned with the high god theory in Australia. [104] Eliade admits that both sides in the debate were prejudiced, [105] but then he relies heavily on those authors whose bias seems to favor his own view on the subject matter.

Thirdly, Eliade's writings are a perfect example of grouping together of sources without the application of any criteria whatsoever. Scriptural texts, archaeological data, literary content, ethnographic reports and anthropological studies are all used as sources. There is no realization that the religious data which these different sources supply vary as regards accuracy, certainty, interpretation and content. For instance, much of the archeological data on pre-historic religions is highly speculative and can hardly be put on a par with the ethnographic reports of the last few decades. [106] To cite Homer as a religious source on the same level as Cicero or Herodotus, or all these classical writers on the same level as the Indian scriptures or Egyptian hieroglyphics is bound to lead to confusion. Eliade does not rely on the scholars of the respective fields he delves into for religious data in order to interpret the sources. For reasons never mentioned, he absolves himself from this patent academic duty. He writes in his introduction to *From Primitives to Zen:*

> But I should like to point out that this book must be judged as a whole, and not from the particular viewpoint of the anthropologist, or the classical scholar, or the orientalist. [107]

But is not the anthropological literature quoted in the book open to the critique and evaluation of the anthropologist himself? Are not the recognized experts in the Islamic tradition entitled to judge whether Eliade's selections from the Koran are representative of Muslim beliefs? And do not Egyptologists have the right to comment on the way Eliade quotes Egyptian sources and on the interpretation he gives to them? The growth of specialization demands that, whenever a scholar in one field uses material from another field, he should rely on the

---

[104] Cf. Elkin, 1954 and Berndt and Berndt, 1964.

[105] Eliade, 1966, pp. 116-117.

[106] Thus, for instance, Malefijt, 1968, dedicated a whole chapter to the archaeology of religion, but she does not use any of the material of this chapter for the rest of the book. Archaeological and ethnographic sources are rightly kept apart.

[107] Eliade, 1967a, p. vii.

experts in his new field of study. Eliade does not follow this academic procedure.

In dealing with some specific criticism of Eliade's use of anthropological sources it is convenient to distinguish between his earlier writings, written mainly in the 1940s and 1950s and his later writings produced in the last decade. All the major works of Eliade belong to the earlier period; his recent works consist mainly of articles, about half of which deal with the religions of non-literate societies.

The earlier writings, with the exception of his book on shamanism, are understandably based on anthropological sources now considered dated. Even if one takes into account, however, that much of Eliade's works were produced in a transition period for anthropology, his use of anthropological sources is still inferior. Frazer and Lévy-Bruhl are used extensively, particularly in *Patterns in Comparative Religion,* as ethnographic sources. It has been an accepted fact in anthropology for some time now that the data, amassed with great diligence by these writers, are open to doubt. [108] No anthropologist would use these sources as evidence to back up a theoretical position. Further, Eliade omitted important anthropological works which were available at the time when he wrote his earlier books and articles. *Rites and Symbols of Initiation* is a case in point. Except for his source material on the native Australians, his anthropological evidence for the many other tribes he cites from all over the world are generally poor and scanty. His African sources are extremely weak, especially when one recalls the ample literature on African tribes. [109] Moreover, his sources are much too selective. Negative data, as has been shown in the case of initiation rites and belief in high gods, are often not considered.

Eliade's more recent writings show increased familiarity with contemporary anthropological literature. There is, however, no evolution in Eliade's thought comparable to what has taken place in anthropology. His views on initiation rites, on the belief in high god, on non-literate man, and on religion and religious man are still the same ones propounded in his earlier works.

Notwithstanding Eliade's increased awareness of anthropological material, he still neglects many important anthropological sources. Though symbolism and ritual are two of the main themes in Eliade's works he does not quote the abundant anthropological literature on

---

[108] Cf. Evans-Pritchard, 1965b, p. 4ff.
[109] Cf., for example, some of the sources quoted by Young, 1965, pp. 182ff.

both topics. Some of the best monographs on religion, though quoted, have left no impact on his thoughts or on the content of his essays. [110]

In several instances his use of sources is unreliable. His first article on Australian religions is a case in point. The articles by Stanner, a major source of this essay, do not support Eliade's views on the Australian high god, on initiation, on myth and the sacred/profane dichotomy. [111] Elkin does not give initiation ritual the one function of enacting the birth and rebirth symbolism. [112] Upon reading the accusation that Catherine and Ronald Berndt have passed over "the religious beliefs of the Australian aborigines almost unnoticed," and then reflecting on the literary fact that one-fifth of their main work on these tribes is dedicated to religious beliefs and practices, and that both authors have individually written several articles on religious topics, it is necessary to conclude that Eliade's reading of sources leaves much to be desired. [113] In the same essay Eliade refers to an obscure nineteenth-century writer, A. Cameron, who has written a long description of the belief in the high god in some Australian tribes recorded in 1885. [114] Cameron's article referred to, however, contains only ten lines on the subject matter under discussion, and has no reference at all to belief in an "All-Father." It shows how little investigation the author has done on beliefs in the high god.[115] The reliability of Eliade's use of sources is thus open to question.

Anthropological sources which could have given some support to Eliade's views are not quoted, or are referred to without the realization that they could have been used effectively to strengthen some of his key concepts on religion and religious man. Victor Turner's articles on initiation, for instance, though they do not support Eliade's methodology nor his one-dimensional interpretation of the symbolism in-

---

[110] Some of the best monographs are Evans-Pritchard, 1956a; Lienhardt, G., 1960; Geertz, 1960; and Middleton, 1960.

[111] Stanner, 1959, p. 127; 1960a, pp. 264-265; 1961a, pp. 236ff., 258. Cf. Eliade, 1967b, p. 132.

[112] Elkin, 1954, p. 189. Cf. Eliade, 1967b, p. 124ff.

[113] Eliade, 1966, p. 124. Eliade may be referring to beliefs in the high god but he does not specify this. Berndt and Berndt have not written much on Australian belief in the high god, nor have they concentrated their main effort on writing a history of the controversy which took place fifty or so years ago. Their book leaves out any lengthy treatment on the subject because: (1) in their own ethnographic work they did not find the belief of high god to be a very prominent one; (2) when present, the nature of this belief is still debatable. Cf. Worms, 1963.

[114] Eliade, 1966, p. 115.

[115] Cameron, 1885, p. 359.

volved, amply corroborate the death/rebirth motif present in these rites. [116] The same can be said with regard to some of the works of Monica Wilson. [117] Some of Lévi-Strauss' tenets on myth, especially his view of myth as "coincidentia oppositorum," could have been used by Eliade to develop and support his own views of mythology. [118] Turner and Wilson are, however, apparently unknown to Eliade, and Lévi-Strauss is mentioned only to be criticised for his materialistic approach. [119]

Even from this brief and incomplete examination of Eliade's use of anthropological sources, it can be concluded that the student of religions who relies on Eliade for anthropological literature of non-literate societies will be misled and confused.

THE CONCEPT OF "PRIMITIVE" IN ELIADE

In agreement with the basic anthropological outlook, Eliade has grasped the significance of non-literate societies for the study of man. Most of the reasons he advances for the study of the religions of these cultures are acceptable to anthropologists. The most questionable tenet is his assumption that non-literate man of today represents a replica of the past. For a non-specialist it is safer to hold the more common anthropological view that the religions of non-literate peoples do not reflect a primordial state. [120]

Eliade's view of non-literate man, however, is not in harmony with that of contemporary anthropologists. Eliade formulated his concept of "primitive" in the 1930's and 1940's when Lévy-Bruhl's theory of primitive mentality was widely held. Briefly, Lévy-Bruhl maintained that the mind of non-literate man was pre-logical, that is, it operated on a logical system which differed from that of Western man; non-literate man's view of life was mystical, in the sense that he gave a religious, and unscientific interpretation to all aspects of life. [121] For

---

[116] Turner, V., 1964a, pp. 4ff. Leach, 1963b, p. 133, also sees the pattern of death and rebirth as an obvious symbol in the rites of passage.

[117] Wilson, 1957, pp. 205ff.

[118] Lévi-Strauss, 1964, pp. 17-18; 1958a, *passim*.

[119] Eliade, 1969a, p. 132.

[120] Cf. Watts, 1963, p. 18. The native Australians have often been held to represent archaic or primeval man. Elkin and Berndt and Berndt, however, do not accept this view; see Elkin, 1954, pp. 24-25, and Berndt and Berndt, 1964, pp. 8-11.

[121] See Lévy-Bruhl, 1910 and 1922. For the leading interpretation of Lévy-Bruhl in anthropological literature, see Evans-Pritchard, 1934 and 1965b.

Eliade non-literate man is in a "universe steeped in sacredness," and though he is "not totally incapable of logical thought," there seems to be something different in his logical make-up. [122] Eliade probably means that non-literate man approaches the universe with a set of logical assumptions and rules which are completely different from those of Western man. [123] This is the very heart of Lévy-Bruhl's theory. One of its fundamental errors, which Eliade shares, is the failure to distinguish between the intentions of the mind and its operations. It can be readily granted that in those non-literate cultures where, for instance, iron is in common use, the origin of the metal is given a religious rather than a scientific explanation. It is also certain that wherever iron was smelted the change in the metal was not explained in terms of molecules. It can further be admitted that the use of iron was often restricted to religious purposes. But iron had to be smelted in order to be transformed into the desired shape. This could never have been done without observation and/or trial and error experimentation. But observation and experimentation are the main ingredients of a scientific and logical mind. Thus, to give but one example, the building of the pyramids in ancient Egypt was certainly for a religious motive; but this does not rule out the fact that accurate geometrical calculations had to be made and planned organization of labor had to be achieved. [124] Again, these calculations and plans are evidence of a mind operating on the scientific level of observation and experimentation. The view which Eliade portrays in one of his earlier works, namely *The Forge and the Crucible*, a view reiterated in a more recent article, [125] is in many respects in harmony with Lévy-Bruhl's theory which denies the scientific attitude in non-literate cultures.

Eliade is aware that ethnologists and anthropologists have never looked favorably on Lévy-Bruhl's theory and that Lévy-Bruhl himself abandoned it towards the end of his life. [126] At times Eliade explicitly rejects some of Lévy-Bruhl's tenets; at other times he accepts them. There are instances when he quotes Lévy-Bruhl favorably and praises

---

[122] Eliade, 1962a, p. 144.
[123] Cf. Chapter III, pp. 67-69. See also Chapter II, pp. 46-49.
[124] Cf., for instance, Fakhry, 1961, pp. 9-19.
[125] Eliade, 1968a.
[126] Eliade, 1961a, p. 231, 1965a, pp. 189-190, 1969a, p. 16. Whether Lévy-Bruhl did completely abandon his view is probably still doubtfull; cf. Evans-Pritchard, 1965b, pp. 79 and 87.

his books. [127] Eliade never explains Lévy-Bruhl's theory which has often been misunderstood.

The statement that in non-literate societies we do not find the scientific attitude cannot be empirically demonstrated an is thus unacceptable in anthropology. Artifacts, domestication of animals and exploration can all be accredited to non-literate peoples, even though none has developed the advanced technology of the West. These former achievements had to be reached, at least in part, by scientific endeavor, even though the intention of the people involved may have been mainly, or solely, religious. As Lévi-Strauss has elaborately expressed it:

> To transform a weed into a cultivated plant, a wild beast into a domestic animal, to produce, in either of these, nutritious or technologically useful properties which were originally completely absent or could be only guessed at; to make stout, water tight pottery out of clay which is friable and unstable, liable to pulverize or crack, (which, however, is possible only if from a large number of organic and inorganic materials, the one most suitable for refining is selected, and also the appropriate fuel, the temperature and duration of firing and the effective degree of oxidation); to work out techniques often long and complex, which permit cultivation without soil or alternately without water; to change toxic roots or seeds into foodstuffs, or again to use their poison for hunting, war, or ritual—there is no doubt that all these achievements required a genuinely scientific attitude, sustained and watchful interest and a desire for knowledge for its own sake. For only a small proportion of observation and experiments ... could have yielded practical and immediately useful results. There is no need to dwell on the working of bronze and iron and of precious metals or even the simple working of copper ore by hammering which preceded metallurgy by several thousand years and even at that stage they all demand a very high level of technical proficiency.[128]

Thus, to maintain, as Eliade does, that the genius of non-literate peoples lies solely or mainly on the religious plane is to ignore the factual evidence so abundantly supplied by ethnographic sources. [129]

It must also be insisted that so-called non-literate man has the same mental structure as contemporary Western man. Even those peoples often mentioned for their "primitiveness" have to be accredited with intelligence and acumen. Writing on the native Australians, Berndt and Berndt remark:

> There is nothing as far as we know to hold them back as far as intelligence, or the capacity for intellectual development. [130]

---

[127] Eliade rejects the validity of Lévy-Bruhl's law of mystic participation, Eliade, 1958b, p. 269, 1965b, p. 189; but then he seems to accept it, Eliade, 1958b, pp. 367 and 445. Lévy-Bruhl is quoted favorably, Eliade, 1958b, pp. 389 and 444; but then again he is apparently rejected, Eliade, 1965b, p. 9 and 1969a, p. 16.

[128] Lévi-Strauss, 1962, pp. 14-15.

[129] For example, see the works of Forde, 1950a and Service, 1963.

[130] Berndt and Berndt, 1964, p. 11.

When it comes to religious thought, the evidence is overwhelming that these people possess the same basic mind structure as all people belonging to the biological species "homo sapiens."

Many of Eliade's general statements on non-literate societies stem from his assumption that they differ in mental structure from Western culture. Most of his confident assertions find no support in anthropological literature of today. Contrary to Eliade's repeated claims the interest of non-literate peoples is not limited to origins. [131] What is often foremost in the worldview of non-literate cultures is not cosmological considerations, but rather witchcraft and sorcery, spirits and their relations to men, and ancestral cults and beliefs. [132] And their fears are not, as Eliade would have us believe, of a cosmological nature. Eliade assures us that:

> Primitive man lived in constant terror of finding that the forces around him which he found so useful were worn out. For thousands of years men were tortured by the fear that the sun would disappear forever at the winter solstice, that the moon would not rise again, that plants would die forever... [133]

It would be difficult to supply any ethnographic evidence at all to support this ambiguous statement. Ethnographic reports do not give the slightest indication that people in non-literate societies live a life of constant worry and preoccupation about the heavenly bodies and the natural environment. To quote but one example, Lawrence and Meggitt, summarizing the work of several anthropologists on the Melanesians, note that:

> No Melanesia religion pays great attention to the total natural environment. Most treat it implicitly as something that can be taken for granted. It is no cause for anxiety except on the relatively rare occasions when it is threatened by disaster such as volcanic eruptions. [134]

Eliade is correct in his observations that irreligiosity is not common in non-literate cultures; but he gives the impression that in these societies religious considerations are always in the fore. This cannot be

---

[131] See for instance Maybury-Lewis, 1967, pp. 284-286; Oswalt, 1967, pp. 210ff.; Lawrence and Meggitt, 1965, p. 12; Edel, 1957, p. 161; Stefaniszyn, 1964, pp. 124ff.

[132] Cf. the literature cited in Chapter III, under footnotes 86 and 128. See Smith, J. Z., 1972, p. 146, who makes a similar critique of most historians of religions.

[133] Eliade, 1958b, p. 346. This is the picture which Lévy-Bruhl gives of non-literate man.

[134] Lawrence and Meggitt, 1965, p. 12.

corroborated by ethnographic evidence which shows that the concern of these peoples is also directed towards the ordinary daily activities of life. It is easy to conclude from Eliade's works that in non-literate societies men and women spend most of their time practicing religious rites and discussing religious matters, and that the lives of these people can be exhaustively described as "religion." Nothing could be further from ethnographic evidence.

A major flaw in Eliade's treatment of the differences between religion in non-literate cultures and in Western societies is his constant application of Western concepts to non-literate peoples. The distinctions between sacred and profane, natural and supernatural, religion and society, are Western concepts. It is only with great caution that one can apply them to non-literate cultures. [135] Because of this disregard of caution many of his statements on non-literate peoples lose their intelligible content. For instance, to state that for non-literate man all major profane activities are sacred is quite meaningless. [136] Unless one is certain that the distinction sacred/profane is an important category of thought among the people under study, one could just as well say that for them all major sacred actions are profane or social. Similarly, to assert that, unlike modern man, non-literate man considers the sacred as the "real" [137] does not convey anything meaningful unless one has first ascertained that the concepts "sacred" and "real" are present in the society under investigation. When Eliade develops the concept of "reality," he seems to rely upon some basic concepts from Indian philosophy and to apply them to non-literate cultures. But he fails to realize that philosophical concepts elaborated in the long Indian tradition may not necessarily be foremost in the minds of the majority of believers. The scriptures were a monopoly of the relatively few people who could read and write, and one has, therefore, to determine very carefully the universality of the scriptural philosophical concepts among the common people. Applying such concepts indiscriminately to non-literate cultures is unwarranted.

MYTH

Eliade gives great prominence to the place of myth in the religious life of non-literate societies. He neglects, however, several problems

---

[135] These distinctions are discussed in Chapter V where the main anthropological references are supplied.
[136] See Chapter II, pp. 48-49.
[137] Cf. Eliade, 1963a, passim.

dealing with the study of mythology. [138] An important question in the study of myth is to determine the sense in which people believe in their own myths. No explicit answer comes from Eliade, and it has to be admitted that anthropological material dealing with this matter is scarce. The problem cannot be solved by recourse to the myth/folklore distinction for, as was pointed out previously, [139] this distinction is not common in non-literate societies. Some mythical stories describe events which cannot possibly correspond to the experience, religious of otherwise, of the people who relate them as part of their cultural heritage. It is, therefore, necessary to determine very precisely whether these stories are believed in their entirety. Do people make distinctions within the myth itself, taking some elements literally, others not? What message does the story convey to the people who possess the myth? There is some, though admittedly not much, anthropological evidence to support the view that mythological accounts are not always taken seriously in their entirety. [140] If one wants, as Eliade does, to enter into the meaning of myth and embark on a comparative study of mythology on a large scale, these major questions cannot be ignored or left unanswered. There is no evidence that Eliade has taken up these problems, much less offered a solution.

Another issue which arises out of Eliade's treatment of religion and religious man is the question of the importance of myth. It has to be granted that many societies possess elaborate mythologies. But anthropologists have come across non-literate cultures which have in fact very little mythology. When present, myths may not be very important. To state that every human activity of some moment has a mythological explanation is to override the ethnographic evidence. [141] The same applies to myths of creation. Though common, they are found wanting in several societies. [142] At times, the creation myths are not elaborate and their importance is not always paramount. Further, myths are not necessarily looked upon as ideal prototypes. [143] It is certainly much

---

[138] These problems were outlined in Chapter III, pp. 72-73.

[139] Cf. Chapter III, p. 72.

[140] Stanner, 1960a, p. 265, observes that "the narration of the myth is sometimes accompanied by laughter among the listeners, and I have sometimes thought it has a sardonic tone."

[141] Edel, 1957, p. 161; Nadel, 1954b, p. 9; Oswalt, 1967, p. 210; Maybury-Lewis, 1967, p. 286; Stephaniszyn, pp. 124ff. For a typical example of a society where myths present legendary origins of ritual and its transmission see Frisbie, 1967, pp. 12ff.

[142] Cf. Salisbury, 1965, p. 55; Bulmer, 1965, p. 137; Lawrence, 1965, p. 214.

[143] See, for instance, the references in Chapter III, footnotes 38-41.

easier to collect voluminous books on mythology than it is to find out what part they play in the religious life of a particular culture. [144] Eliade does not take into consideration these discrepancies which are significant, and he seems to assume that myths always have a prominent place in a people's religious life. But this is often not the case. Where witchcraft looms large in the mental attitude of a people, their concerns are directed more to counteract the witch's action and its effects than to relate or recall to mind the myth of the origin of witchcraft. [145] It is legitimate to ask how often were these myths recalled before missionaries, travellers and ethnographers started asking questions about them.

Eliade restricts the importance of mythology to the past. In other words, the myth recounts what happened in the beginning and thus takes man back to his origins. This view of myth is, however, one-dimensional. Myth, the anthropologist would insist, is also often embedded in the present, in the contemporary cultural situation and need not always refer us back to the distant past. Millenarian myths often testify to this element in mythology. [146] Here myths may point out a desired future which has no justification, no prototype in the past. Those millenarian myths which forecast the advent of European goods in the near future do not, and indeed, cannot, take us back to a kind of primordial age where such goods were in abundance. The desired and promised acquisition of European goods is a new element in the development of mythology, an element, which cannot be explained by simply stating that all myths deal with origins. Even when societies have myths of a bygone paradise and when the advent of the European goods is accredited to the activity of the ancestors, the important element in the lives of the people seems to be the future acquisition of the goods, while the paradise of the past does not appear to occupy an important role.

The neglect of some of the main problems in mythology and the insistence that myths are stories of origins lead Eliade to a one-sided meaning of myth. While it is true, as Eliade holds, that man's religious values, ethical norms and human ideals are very often embodied in a

---

[144] Cf. Watts, 1963; Long, 1963; and Henderson and Oakes, 1963. While these books provide well-presented and ordered collections of myths, they do not sufficiently deal with the question of how important these myths are in the religious life of the people.

[145] Cf. references in Chapter III, footnotes 127 and 128.

[146] For references see Chapter III, footnote 152.

people's mythology, one must not lose sight of the fact that myths contain many elements which can hardly be considered idealistic. The impossible stories often recounted in the myth do not necessarily point to an ideal toward which the society is striving; and the social situation sometimes portrayed in myths does not imply that a lawless, asexual or promiscuous condition is the desired end. [147]

Eliade makes a number of observations on myth which could have led him away from the one-dimensional meaning, but, unfortunately, he does not follow through his own insights. We are told that myth has a logic of its own, but Eliade makes no attempt to expound on what this means and nowhere in his writings can we find a single example of a detailed study of the logical system of a myth. [148] There is no evidence in Eliade that he has read with profit the structural studies of mythology that have appeared in the last decade. The anthropological studies of the logic of myth, in spite of their short-comings, have brought out some meanings in mythology which have added to the multi-dimensional picture of mythology in general. From an anthropological standpoint, it is just too naive to reduce the meaningful content of myth to one element. Eliade is aware that myth is an attempt to unite contradictory elements in human experience. Myth is a "coincidentia oppositorum." [149] Once again, had he pursued this line of thought he would have toned down his insistence that myth deals largely with the past.

Just as the meaning of myth is restricted by Eliade to one level, so also is the function he assigns to it. For Eliade the function of myth is a religious one. Spelled out in detail myth provides an escape from time, from the human condition and from profane existence. Anthropologists do not reject this interpretation outright but, judging from the studies they have produced on myth, they consider this interpretation much too narrow. The functions of myth could take place on a number of levels; social, political, moral and religious. There is no reason why one should hold that the religious function is either the only one or the most important one. To limit the function of myth to that of providing an escape from profane existence creates insurmountable problems. First of all, the concept of time in non-literate

---

[147] Cf. Eliade, 1958b, p. 424 and 1960a, p. 174, where symbolic elements are ascribed to such myths. See also Turner, V., 1969a, pp. 183ff.

[148] It is difficult to ascertain what Eliade means by saying that myth has a logical structure. Cf., for example, Eliade, 1958b, p. 428.

[149] Cf. Eliade, 1958b, pp. 419-423.

cultures is not identical with the Western concept of time. In non-literate societies time is not conceived of as something one can escape from. Further, the assumption that myth is an escape from time is a difficult one to put to the test. Not only must the observer have a good grasp of the concept of time in a particular society, but he must also be able to show that myth does provide an escape from time for the native peoples. Moreover, the assumption that myth is an escape from time has the disadvantage of avoiding or bypassing the interpretative qualities of myth. Myth must be seen also, if not primarily, as a religious and social commentary on a people's beliefs. Myth expresses the total belief system of a society; it provides a stereotyped form for making known these beliefs and for transmitting them from one generation to the next. [150] The meanings and functions of myth are so numerous and varied that one cannot incapsulate them into one cryptic statement. For this reason "no serious scholar will now propose any general definition or comprehensive theory of myth—at least not without making serious numerous reservations." [151]

The element of the "past" is considered so important by Eliade that his fundamental definition of myth is sacred history. Nowhere does Eliade outline in any detail the relationship between myth and history. If the Western concept of history is not found in non-literate societies, then the statement "myth is a sacred history" is devoid of meaning. One is, therefore, led to conclude that the approach to mythology should not start by looking on myth as an account of sacred events which happened in the time of the beginnings. The attempt to educe the meaning and function of myth should rather start with an understanding of the relation of myth to its cultural background. This seems to be a more profitable line of approach because it takes into consideration the basic problems of mythology and because it brings into focus the fact that the meanings and functions of myth are many and varied. It is only after having explored the multi-dimensional meaning and function of myth on a cultural and social level that one can go ahead and make broad tentative generalizations on mythology.

TIME

Eliade's view of non-literate man's attitude to time is, from an anthropological standpoint, among the most difficult to support by

---

[150] Berndt, R., 1965, pp. 85-87; Berndt and Berndt, 1964, p. 223; Malefijt, 1968, p. 195; Watts, 1963, p. 3.
[151] Watts, 1963, p. 1.

ethnographic evidence. Some anthropologists have found his distinction between cyclic and linear time useful. [152] But it is quite another matter to go on and affirm that this emphasis on cyclic time connotes man's terror of linear or historical time. One cannot conclude that, because cyclic time predominates, linear time is conceived of as a condition to be avoided and escaped from; otherwise, in those societies which have developed consciousness of historical time there should be a corresponding fear of cyclic time. The "terror of history" concept is definitely overplayed in Eliade's *Cosmos and History*. It would be difficult to find ethnographic evidence [153] to support the main thesis of this book which Eliade states as follows:

> The essential theme of my investigation bears on the image of man himself by the man of archaic societies and on the place he assumes in the Cosmos. The chief difference between the man of archaic and traditional cultures and the man of modern societies with their strong imprint of Judaeo-Christianity lies in the fact that the former feels himself indissolubly connected with the Cosmos and the cosmic rhythms, whereas the latter insists that he is connected only with history. [154]

But if historical consciousness is in large part due to literature, [155] then the concept of history cannot be limited to the Judaeo-Christian tradition. The assertion that modern man, presumably under Christian influence, insists that he is "connected only with history" is hardly a self-evident proposition. Does not the yearly Christian calendar consist of a cyclical return of celebrations? Is not the central belief in the death and resurrection of Christ recurringly enacted in ritual? These are important cyclic elements in Christianity which cannot be ignored.

Eliade seems to make two major assumptions. Firstly, he presumes that cyclic and linear concepts of time cannot, or do not, exist side by side in the same tradition; secondly, the Judaeo-Christian tradition follows the linear conception, while other religions, especially "archaic" ones, opt for the cyclic dimensions of time. Both assumptions are overstated. Linear and cyclic views of time are opposite, but not necessarily contradictory and incompatible. Myth may provide not an escape from linear time, but a union of linear and cyclic time conceptions, a "coincidentia oppositorum," as Eliade himself would call it. With regard to the second assumption, it has to be insisted that the historic dimension

---

[152] Cf. Obeyesekere, 1969, p. 209.

[153] This is borne out by the fact that this book contains very few ethnographic and anthropological references.

[154] Eliade, 1959a, p. vii.

[155] Cf. Chapter III, pp. 76-78.

of time is found in other religious traditions, China being an excellent example.

Similarly, the distinction between sacred and profane time is given too much prominence. In non-literate societies, as in all societies, the ordinary human activities, such as work, leisure, and so on, regulate the divisions of the day. People do not seem perturbed to use time measurements which are based on both religious and social factors; they apparently see no contradiction in so doing. Ethnographic reports do not indicate that the dichotomy between sacred and profane occupies a major role in the formulation of the concept of time in non-literate cultures. To state, therefore, as Eliade does, that escape from profane time is foremost in the mind of religious man is doubtful. We know that people look on salvation in human terms; salvation seems to connote a desired escape not from time, but from the problems and difficulties of life, such as disease. Millenarian concepts of paradise also depict the state of bliss not as an escape from the earthly situation, but as an improvement of it. Cargo cults, for instance, predict the coming of the millennium not as a time when European goods will not be needed and wanted, but rather as a situation in which these goods are present in abundance.

RITUAL

Eliade ascribes to ritual the same function he gives to myth. He sees it mainly as an expressive and concretized way in which man escapes the human condition. [156] Rites, however, do not necessarily have the same function all the time. Eliade's view of ritual is based on the study of initiation rites, which, because they are not a daily occurrence, have a certain degree of solemnity about them. But in non-literate societies initiation rituals are not the only rites performed. There is ritual linked with economic and social activity. Magical, divinatory and sacrificial rites are all very widespread and often more common than rites of initiation. [157] Yet Eliade ignores them all. It is difficult to see how a scholar can form a concept of ritual when he does not take into consideration all the important rites of a society.

When dealing with the function of ritual Eliade fails to distinguish between the explicit reasons given by the people who practice the rites

---

[156] Cf. Chapter II, pp. 53-54.
[157] Cf., for example, Malinowski, 1922; Rappaport, 1967; Firth, 1963b; Malefijt, 1968, pp. 208ff. For magical rites see references under footnote 128 of Chapter III.

and the explanatory functions assigned by the researcher. [158] The many reasons ascribed to the rites by the native people themselves cannot be left out if the scholar is to enter the mentality of the people under study and if, as some historians of religions would insist, what is said about the religious behavior of other societies must be intelligible not just to the Western scholar but also to those who profess the belief and enact the rituals. [159] Even if one restricted the analysis to initiation rites it is clear that the death/resurrection motif is more often than not the investigator's interpretation. However, non-literate people frequently state that their rituals of male initiation are intended to endow the novice with the heroic qualities of their ancestors. [160] The rites may be explained as symbolizing manhood. [161] They may be seen as a means to foster good health, to strengthen and give prosperity to the initiate, to solidify the clan and even to weaken its enemies. [162] Female initiation ritual may suggest that the rite is intended to insure procreation, a thought very much in the minds of the people themselves. [163] The most common reason given for performing these rites is education, that is, the rite is believed to equip the girl with the knowledge necessary to assume an adult role in society. [164] The female initiation ritual may be said to strengthen the girls and to make them physically attractive. [165] Rarely do we come across non-literate societies where the death/resurrection theme is explicitly acknowledged. This should not come as a surprise. The concept of resurrection, as understood in the Christian tradition, has not been recorded in non-literate cultures. For Christians, resurrection implies a permanent existence beyond the grave. Though belief in some form of after-life is, as far as we know, universal, belief in personal and everlasting survival after death has not been recorded among non-literate peoples. [166] Thus to explain initiation rites as symbolizing death and resurrection would not make much sense to the people who practice them.

---

[158] Cf. Malefijt, 1968, *passim.*
[159] Smith, W. C., 1959, p. 42.
[160] Maybury-Lewis, 1967, p. 25.
[161] Glasse, 1965, p. 43.
[162] Bulmer, 1965, p. 151.
[163] Frisbie, 1967, p. 347.
[164] Frisbie, 1967, p. 349; Lawrence, 1965, p. 213.
[165] Lawrence, 1965, p. 213; Berndt, R., 1965, p. 92.
[166] Firth, 1955b, p. 331. For detailed observations on one particular society confer Reichard, 1950 vol. I, pp. 40-42; Kluckhohn and Leighton, 1962, p. 126; Frisbie, 1967, pp. 377-378. All these writers agree that the idea of personal immortality is not present among the people under study.

It has to be granted, however, that death/rebirth symbolism is often implicit in the rites themselves. [167] It can, therefore be said that one function of these rites is to give the initiates a new life, both on a religious and a social plane. Eliade would have this dimension into clear focus had he seen initiation rites, as anthroplogists have done since Van Gennep, as rites of passage. [168] These include birth, marriage and death rituals where life and death are often symbolically enacted. Taken as a whole these rites mark a point of entrance to an existence larger than, but including, the social sphere. [169] But the death/rebirth theme is only one of the many symbols involved; when present its importance varies. [170] In rituals of initiation, especially if one considers puberty rites, sexual symbolism may have a leading place. [171] Social and cultural values may be equally portrayed in initiation. The meaning and function of initiation cannot be limited to the one religious dimension which Eliade assigns to it.

Turning to the study of non-initiatory rites, the death/rebirth motif become less obvious. Many rites are directed towards a very definite purpose: the acquisition of desired ends in magical rites, the favor of the gods in sacrificial rites, knowledge and guidance in divinatory rituals, and food and means of livelihood in so-called increase rites. As far as the ethnographic evidence is concerned, the native people do not interpret these rites in terms of the death/rebirth theme. It is, besides, difficult to see how many of these rites could possibly be given this symbolical interpretation by an outside observer. Therefore, while the death/rebirth symbolism may be present in initiation rituals and in rites of passage in general, it cannot be said that in the total religious life of non-literate societies it has the dominant place. Eliade's over-emphasis on this symbolic aspect of initiation may lead to a misunder-standing of religious man in non-literate societies.

SYMBOLISM

The insistence in Eliade's writings on the need to study symbolism

---

[167] Frisbie, 1967, p. 350; Wilson, 1957, p. 205; Turner, 1964b, pp. 4ff. We prefer the terminology death/rebirth to death/resurrection for reasons mentioned in the text. Eliade himself seems to prefer the former terms as well.

[168] Van Gennep, 1909.

[169] Cf. Libby, 1959, p. 689.

[170] Stanner, for instance, points out that initiation rites must be understood in the light of sacrificial rites and that the death/rebirth theme is a minor symbol; Stanner, 1961a, p. 258.

[171] Cf. Maybury-Lewis, 1967, pp. 241 ff. Where circumcision is practised, sexual symbolism may often be given prominence.

is in harmony with more recent developments in anthropological studies of religion. From the outset, however, Eliade fails to make the crucial distinction between sign and symbol. Failure to do so may lead, as it has done in Eliade, to mis-interpretation. To give one example, stones marking a grave may be just a sign and not a symbol; in Eliade's lengthy treatment of stone symbolism it is assumed that stones are always symbols. [172]

Another difficulty with Eliade's study of symbolism is the fact that he does not distinguish between the ethnographic, the exegetical and explanatory levels of symbolism. [173] This can be very misleading. *Patterns in Comparative Religion,* one of the more ambitious of Eliade's works, provides many examples. Writing on the symbolism of stone he states that "the hardness, ruggedness and permanence of matter was itself a hierophany in the religious consciousness of the primitive." [174] Stone is then chosen or singled out as a symbol of matter, in that it is the typical symbol of the above mentioned qualities. On the ethnographic level, one will have to determine how often stone is used in religious rites and how often it figures in the religious thought of a people. Some of the more important religious symbols, the chiuringa of the Australians and the ritual adzes of the Polynesians, are made, not of stone, but of carved wood. On the exegetical level, one must investigate whether the people themselves assign the said qualities of hardness and so on to stone. It is conceivable that in those cultures where the use of iron is common, stone is never given such qualities. Further, one can ask whether such qualities did have mainly a religious connotation to the natives themselves. Eliade himself supplies evidence that this is not always the case. [175] Finally, one may move to the explanatory level and question whether stone is a religious symbol manifesting the divine to man because of its properties of hardness, ruggedness and permanency. This proposition will then have to be tested in a large number of instances to establish how universally applicable it is. Eliade skips the first two levels of investigation and states the single explanatory proposition as an obvious self-evident interpretation. The reader unfamiliar with ethnographic literature is bound to conclude that stone was the universal symbol of hardness, and

---

[172] The symbolism of stones is one of Eliade's major topics in *Patterns in Comparative Religion*; cf. Eliade, 1958b, pp. 216 ff.

[173] Cf. Chapter III, pp. 85-86.

[174] Eliade, 1958b, p. 216.

[175] Eliade, 1958b, p. 217.

so on, and that possibly this symbolism is explicitly recognized by the natives themselves. This could not be corroborated by ethnographic evidence.

In spite of Eliade's defective approach to symbolism, it has to be granted that he has pin-pointed a key element in the study of religion. Religious beliefs and practices cannot be grasped without an understanding of symbols. These are the keys which unlock the meaning of rites and beliefs. The symbols express a basic constituent of religion, namely, that what is being conveyed is abstract and often difficult to express and understand. Rightly, then, symbols are the religious language par excellance. Religious knowledge is passed on in symbolic form, and symbolism may be called the religious mode of cognition. But why should the use of symbols be restricted to religious matters? Surely not all abstract knowledge is religious. Many cultural and social values are passed on from one generation to another through symbols. [176] Limiting symbolism to religious matters is not beneficial to the study of religion, for such limitation closes other avenues which may aid the student in his task of understanding symbolism. Symbolism ought to be looked upon as a specifically human characteristic which is used especially in religious discourse.

If symbolism is a mode of cognition, it would appear that cognitive anthropology would have much to offer to the study of religion. [177] The study of symbolism demands a thorough knowledge of the language of the culture whose symbols are explored. The meaning which individual words connote to a particular social group has to be carefully investigated. Symbolism demands preciseness, which is one of the beneficial products of the new ethnography. However, Eliade is not aware that the new approach in anthropology can help the historian of religions who embarks on the study of symbolic systems.

Eliade, once again in harmony with contemporary anthropology, affirms that symbols have a logical structure and an emotional content. However, he has not made a single detailed study of a symbolic system. The logic of symbolism is stated, never explored. There is no evidence that Eliade has delved into anthropological material dealing with the logical structure of symbolism. Similarly we are assured that symbols have many dimensions. But when it comes to the study of particular symbols, Eliade does not bring out this multi-dimensional aspect of

---

[176] Cf. Chapter III, pp. 83.
[177] Cf. Chapter III, pp. 93-96.

symbolism. A typical example is his study of initiation where the only symbol he seems to see in these rites is that of death and rebirth. The same can be said about Eliade's reference to the emotional content of symbols; in his writings, the emotional element is stated, not specified.

When it comes to an understanding of particular symbols Eliade is intent on discovering the meaning of symbols. One of the main aims of symbolical studies is to find out what symbols mean to those who use them. The primary meaning of symbols is what they represent to their users. If this is the case, then the first step in the process of under- standing symbols is to see them in their cultural and historical con- text. Religious symbols could have cultural significance, while ap- parently social symbols may have their meaning embedded in religious beliefs. [178] To the anthropologist, Eliade does not pay enough attention to the cultural and social scene. The anthropologist would argue that to bypass or minimize the importance of the cultural and historical situation will not help the scholar in his quest to describe the symbols objectively and to give them an unbiased interpretation. It is only the cultural and social context which can restrain the scholar from giving meanings to symbols which are too arbitrary and subjective.

Religious Man

From Eliade's observations on myth and ritual it is not difficult to conclude that he tends to look on religion as a human response to the sacred through which man escapes from the human condition. Religion is therefore a constant reminder that another and better world exists outside the realm of historical time. Religious man seeks to escape from this world, which compared to the world of mythical prototypes, to the sacred origins, is but an illusion. Eliade had already formulated this view in his *Yoga: Immortality and Freedom*, his first major work and still one of the standard interpretations on the Indian scriptural sayings of yoga and its practice. [179] The conclusions Eliade reached in this book have left an impact on most of his later writings. Granted that his

---

[178] The dove as a symbol of peace is an example of a social symbol, popular in Western culture in the late 1960's, which has deep religious roots. Cf. McCullough, 1962 and McKenzie, 1965. On the other hand, the symbolism of hair, in spite of its religious elements, has social and sexual meanings. Cf. Leach, 1958, Hallpike, 1969, and Derrett, 1973.

[179] One gets the impression that Eliade based his book solely on a study of Indian scriptures. Eliade, however, had the opportunity to observe at first hand the practice of yoga in India. Cf. Ricketts, 1973, p. 16.

interpretation of yoga is correct, it still has to be determined how widespread this view is outside the Indian scriptures and the relatively few individuals who are committed practitioners of yoga. The anthropologist is worried by the fact that apparently Eliade neglected what might be called folk religion. Their concern is understandable if one recalls that till recently anthropologists had to concentrate their efforts on folk religion because the societies they studied were non-literate. The need to study scriptures when these are available may be primary, but the study of folk religion, especially when literacy is restricted to a small section of the population, is also a must if the scholar wants to arrive at a comprehensive study of a particular religion. Historians of religions themselves have acknowledged this need to study folk religion. [180] The differences between the ideal presented in the scriptures and the daily practical realization of that ideal may be significant in the scholar's attempt to understand religious man.

One can grant that deliverance from the human condition is often an important theme in the great religions. Christians, for example, have often looked upon their earthly life as a pilgrimage, a "vale of tears." But the exactly opposite attitude is present as well. Human suffering, particularly in Christianity, can be conceived as a desired end. In other words the religious attitude may not encourage a believer to escape from the human condition of suffering; on the contrary, the religious dimension may make suffering acceptable and meaningful. [181] Escape from the human condition is counterbalanced by the endeavor to get a grip on the situation and interpret it in the light of one's beliefs. Religion has another side to it, namely, it is also an attempt to cope with and accept the present human condition.

The one-sidedness of Eliade's view is even more glaringly apparent when one turns to non-literate societies. Magical rites, divinatory rites, hunting rites, fertility cults and curing rituals are not directed at providing the religious man with the time and space wherein he can gain a brief escape from the humdrum of daily existence. Rather, these rites direct man to control the human condition, to be able to predict it and to ensure that the food supply does not run short. Coping or dealing with human life and its problems is the primary goal of these

---

[180] See Earhart, 1967, pp. 196-197 and 201-204; Ashhy, 1967, p. 156; Adams, 1965, p. 115.

[181] Bukovsky and Riga, 1967, esp. pp. 776-777. Geertz, 1966, p. 19, states that "as a religious problem, the problem of suffering is, paradoxically, not how to avoid suffering but how to suffer..."

rituals. This aspect of religion as a technique to cope with the human condition is, if one were to judge from the frequency of the ritual performances, often paramount in the attitude of religious man. The role of religious specialists in the religious life of the society is often not to direct and teach men and women how to run away from the earthly condition. Many of these specialists have also been practical leaders who guided people in their striving to control human destiny and to better their condition here on earth. [182] Shamans are an obvious case in point, for one of their main duties as shamans is curing. [183] The use of medicinal herbs and drugs, sometimes effective even from the point of view of Western science, and the recourse to spirits for healing purposes are attempts to master disease by controlling the forces believed to bring it about. It would be difficult to quote ethnographic sources which showed religious specialists who are not, sometimes at least, involved in some kind of activity directly or indirectly beneficial to the material welfare of man and his environment. It is interesting to note that monasticism, common in the great religions, finds no parallel in non-literate societies where the ideal religious man is not conceived as the person who abandons the worldly state in order to achieve some form of paradisial happiness.

A view of religion which does not strive for a balance between these two elements, namely, an escape from the human condition and control of it, is bound to end with a one-sided and partial view of religious man. To neglect the element of control is unrealistic and liable to lead to incorrect and untenable conclusions. For attempts to control and improve the human situation have been of primary concern to all societies. No society would survive if it portrayed the human condition merely as something one should escape from in order to reach a state of bliss in another unseen world. Eliade's view of "primitive" man is very unlikely because the human species would hardly have survived with that vision. By neglecting those anthropological studies on non-literate cultures which manifest how religious beliefs and practices are often aimed at the control of life and of the human condition, Eliade limits the image of religious man. The religious man whose main or sole religious concern is to be freed from earthly life does not correspond to ethnographic reality.

The attempt by Eliade and phenomenologists in general to reach an

---

[182] Cf. Malefijt, 1968, pp. 228ff.
[183] Evidence for this is supplied by Eliade himself; cf. Eliade, 1964a, pp. 215ff.

understanding of religious man by studying religious experience is methodologically a good approach, for religious experience must include the attitude of the believer towards his own beliefs and practices. One could, therefore, seek to discover whether the desire to escape the human condition lies at the very heart of man's religious experience. Anthropologists, however, have neglected the study of religious experience because, in non-literate societies at least, people do not talk of their religious experiences but of their beliefs, myths and rites. The category of religious experiences is a relatively recent introduction even in the Western world and it requires further specification and precision before it can be used profitably. At the present state of our knowledge of non-literate societies it cannot be said that the craving for a non-earthly existence forms a central part of the people's religious experience.

As was pointed out in an earlier chapter, historians of religions, including Eliade, take a descending view of religion, while anthropologists opt for an ascending one. [184] The anthropological approach has the advantage that its procedure is fairly clear, its aims precise and its limits obvious. By restricting himself to empirical evidence and considering religion as a striving initiated by man himself, the anthropologist can embark on the study of religion without taking into account the problem of the truth or falsehood in religious beliefs. The anthropological approach leaves the study open to the new data which may be discovered by empirical research. This can be done only if man is seen as playing a creative part in his own religion, if he is seen as an active agent in the formulation of his own religious beliefs and practices. In a sense "man makes God in his own image." [185] The basic limitation of this approach is that it seems to bypass the well-recorded fact that most people look on their religious beliefs and rites as being given to them by God, or the gods or some spirits or ancestors. Religious man himself, so it would seem, takes a descending view of religion; he looks upon his religiousness as a given, even if he does make some attempt to acquire it or prepare himself for its reception.

This is exactly where the descending approach can supply insights into the study of religious man, for it does take seriously into account one of the main characteristics of the mentality of religious man himself. But whereas the ascending approach can operate on its own,

---

[184] Cf. Chapter I, pp. 40-41.
[185] Watts, 1963, p. 31.

prescending from the descending view, this latter cannot make any headway unless it takes into consideration the ascending view of the social scientist. The reasons for this are several.

First, the descending approach, which starts from the statement that the sacred manifests itself to man, cannot account by itself for the differences in religious beliefs and practices. These varieties could be more easily explained if man were given an active part in the formation of his religious views. Secondly, the common human claim to revelation shows that religion is also a quest on man's part. It is man himself who asserts that God or the spirits have made known truths to him. Religion is not a one-way communication between God and man; it is rather a dialogue. The human element cannot, therefore, be left out of the picture. Thirdly, man's knowledge of the sacred is largely derived in an empirical context. The experience of the sacred has empirical consequences without which it cannot be observed or studied. What the student of religions studies is ultimately not the sacred itself, but rather its effects on man. Fourthly, a purely descending view can be nothing else but an a priori approach. Historians of religions who adopt it can just as well be called theologians. Historians of religions, however, are adamant in their claim that they are engaged in doing something different from theological reflection.

The ascending approach can thus be seen not as an alternative to the descending one, but as a supplement to it. The former need not be judged as contradictory to and incompatible with the latter path. Both approaches present necessary and complementary ways to an integral study of religious man. The ascending approach will act as a check on the historian of religions; it will keep him from making hasty generalizations, from wanting to overstate his case as Eliade does; it will also lead him to question his own assumptions. The fundamental error of Eliade's approach is that he selects the descending approach and refuses to consider the ascending one. He starts from a set of well-adhered to metaphysical and theological presuppositions on man and his religion, and his main efforts when quoting anthropological literature are to fit ethnographic facts into the scheme. This explains why Eliade's views have remained unchanged in spite of the revolution in anthropology. Many of his conclusions are now highly questionable. Ethnographic evidence challenges most, if not all, of his sweeping generalizations. It is still open to discussion whether enough detailed ethnographic studies on non-literate religions exist to set out on a colossal endeavor along the lines of *Patterns in Comparative Religion*.

On the other hand the anthropologist can also profit by taking into consideration the descending view. In order to understand religious man from his own point of view one cannot possibly neglect religious man's own view of religion. This does not imply that religious man's views must be judged as true. Rather his views must be taken into account if the scholar is to arrive at an understanding of religion and religious experience. It is also possible that if anthropologists take serious consideration of the descending approach they will produce works which are less obviously reductionistic.

In conclusion, the picture which Eliade draws of religious man may appeal not to the anthropologist but to the Christian theologian, and to the student of literature. The Christian theologian will find Eliade's treatment in harmony with his basic religious assumptions, in particular if he looks on Christianity as a unique manifestation of the sacred which transcends all other self-revelations of God; the literateur can detect in Eliade the master of artistic creation and presentation of theme in a flowing and appealing style. The anthropologist, however, is aware that he has not encountered in his field experience the religious man of Eliade's vision and is more likely to place Eliade's contribution in the field of theology of religions or literature.

CHAPTER FIVE

ISSUES AND CONTRIBUTIONS

It has been stressed that much of what Eliade has to say on the religions of non-literate societies cannot be maintained in the light of
contemporary anthropological literature. Because of Eliade's uncritical
use of anthropological material he ends up with a onesided, and hence
distorted, view of religious man. Notwithstanding this critique, it can
still be held that Eliade has made some positive contribution to the
study of religion and religious man. Firstly, Eliade's works touch upon,
directly or indirectly, most of the basic problems inherent in any study
of religious beliefs and practices. These issues, which are at times
central in Eliade's approach, have been recognized and discussed in
anthropological literature. Secondly, some of Eliade's views on religion
and religious man find support in anthropological literature, even
though this literature does not uphold his main tenets.

THE STUDY OF RELIGION

One of the most pressing problems which any student of religion
has to face is a methodological one. Should one proceed inductively,
or deductively? Eliade opts for the latter approach. The general
anthropological tendency today is heavily in favor of the former.
Emphasis on the study of individual cultures and religions remains
prior in anthropological thought as well as in the training of an anthropologist. One common opinion among many anthropologists is that
formulation of generalizations can only be reliably reached after many
individual studies have been carried out. There are numerous advantages in this procedure. Since it is inductive, it is less aprioristic and
hence has a better chance of achieving objectivity. It also takes more
seriously into account the problems involved in understanding alien
belief systems. It is only by studying particular religions at some depth
that one can concentrate on the religious language which is the key
to the grasping of religious concepts. [1] Again, studying non-verbal or
ritual behavior is imperative if one is to make headway in understanding religious values and experiences. Since ritual varies, one must
start from a detailed study of particular religions. Further, a religion

---

[1] Firth, 1959, pp. 231-232; Evans-Pritchard, 1953b, p. 110.

forms a system of closely linked concepts. An understanding of a religion as a system of interconnected ideas is a necessary prerequisite for making comparisons and broad generalizations. Many religious values and concepts in non-literate societies can be better understood if seen in the light of cultural and social institutions. [2] This suggests that the study of particular religions should be the first step. Another advantage of the inductive method is that one avoids the danger of making unwarranted and careless identifications of beliefs from different religions. It will also help the student avoid reading his own views into the religion he is studying. The approach has been stressed by British anthropologists, in particular, by Evans-Pritchard who writes:

> To obtain objectivity in the study of primitive religions what is required is to build up general conclusions from particular ones. One must not ask "What is religion?" but what are the main features of, let us say, the religion of one Melanesian people; then one must seek to compare the religion of that people with the religions of several other Melanesian peoples who are nearest to the first in their cultures and social institutions; and then after a laborious comparative study of all Melanesian peoples, one may be able to say something general about Melanesian religions as a whole. One can only take this long road. There is no short cut. [3]

Such an approach has obvious drawbacks. It is certainly a very slow and tedious process which may never be completed. In-depth studies of non-literate religions are hampered both by the lack of historical records and of scriptural texts, as well as by the many changes these religions are presently undergoing. [4] It is not an easy task to decide when there are enough studies at one's disposal to start making generalizations. And even if these studies are at hand, one is faced with the all but insurmountable task of trying to collate material which is very uneven. The older works on the religions of non-literate peoples are mostly based on out-of-date theories and hence almost worthless. And contemporary anthropological studies on religion view the subject matter from different aspects, often making comparisons difficult if not altogether impossible. Clifford Geertz's comment on the newer studies of religion is well taken:

> In contrast to other approaches — evolutionary, psychological, sociological --
> the field of what we may loosely call "semantic studies" of religion is extre-

---

[2] Firth, 1959, p. 232; cf. Turner, V., 1967, p. 181; Brown, I. C., 1963, pp. 130-131.

[3] Evans-Pritchard, 1959b, pp. 8-9.

[4] This is admitted by Evans-Pritchard himself; cf. Evans-Pritchard, 1956a, p. 319.

mely jumbled. There is as yet no well-established central trend of analysis, no central figures around whom to order debate, and no readily apparent system of interconnections relating competing trends to one another. [5]

The difficulties encountered in relating the psychological, sociological and semantic studies on religion are numerous and not easily soluble.

Some anthropologists have therefore attempted to ask broader questions about religion, even though the number of monographs on non-literate religions is not large. [6] But the view of Evans-Pritchard seems to predominate. Even those anthropologists who have tried to formulate universal statements on religion have themselves carried out intensive field-studies on particular religions. [7] No contemporary anthropologist, and for that matter no contemporary historian of religions, has attempted to produce a work on religion on the scale of Frazer or Eliade. Evans-Pritchard's approach, though not flawless, seems to be much less hazardous. The need to produce more detailed studies on non-literate religions is obvious, even if some scholars try out, in the meantime, a few broader generalizations. In the light of our present knowledge of the many religions of non-literate peoples, Eliade's method is rather classical and archaic and his aims are too presumptous and premature. Eliade's works have raised the question of whether sweeping generalizations can be made. The answer is in the negative; such generalizations are neither helpful nor fruitful. [8]

Another important methodological problem regards the attitude of the student of religions. While writers agree that sympathy, understanding and impartiality should be attitudes cultivated by any scholar who embarks on the study of religions, it is still debatable whether the student's personal commitment to one religion is more conducive to the understanding of religious beliefs and practices. While it is relatively easy to avoid the public condemnations of an atheist and the naive proselytizing of a preacher, [9] the student is bound to be influenced to some extent by his own personal commitment, or lack of it. [10] While it is true that the student may be concerned with "the relevance of

---

[5] Geertz, 1968, p. 403.

[6] See the articles by Geertz, 1966 and Spiro, 1966a. Cf. also Lévi-Strauss, 1958a.

[7] Thus Geertz has made a study of the religion of Java and Spiro has published a monograph on Burmese religion. Lévi-Strauss has made a detailed analysis of some South American tribes. Cf. Geertz, 1960, Spiro, 1967 and Lévi-Strauss, 1964.

[8] Gluckman and Eggan, 1966, pp. xxxviii.

[9] Geertz, 1966, p. 39.

[10] Cf. Firth, 1959, p. 239.

such (religious) affirmations rather than with their ultimate validity," [11] his position on the latter may strongly influence his study of
the former. This is an old problem which has occupied the interests
of philosophers of religion since Renan. While perceiving the advan-
tageous viewpoint of the believing student, Renan maintained that an
investigator who was once a religious believer and had since abandoned
his creed would be in a better position to study religious beliefs and
practices. [12]

Historians of religions seem to agree that the believer brings in a
new insight to religious studies and that he is better equipped to interpret a faith. The unbeliever cannot really show appreciation or full
understanding. [13] The agnostic, one historian of religions has claimed,
is like "a blind man judging a rainbow." [14] Probably, one of the reasons
why historians of religions, including Eliade, have not been much influenced by anthropological studies of religion is because many anthropologists have had no personal religious commitment. The charge
of reductionism contains the implicit assertion that the non-believer
has no other way out but to reduce religious dimensions to something which he can understand.

Anthropologists have expressed divergent views on the matter. [15]
Wilhelm Schmidt, refuting Renan, wrote:

> But it is just in the investigation of the history of religion that a believing
> student of the subject has an advantage which his colleague who thinks
> otherwise can hardly equal. If religion is essentially of the inner life, it fol-
> lows that it can be grasped only from within. But beyond any doubt, this can
> better be done by one in whose own inward consciousness an experience of
> religion plays a part. There is but too much danger that the other will talk
> of religion as a blind man might of colors, or one totally devoid of ear, of a
> beautiful musical composition. [16]

More recently, Robin Horton has recognized that one wishing to
analyze an alien religion has an advantage if he begins by being himself a believer in some religion. [17] Other anthropologists seem to have

---

[11] Firth, 1959, p. 239.

[12] Renan, 1857, pp. 6-7.

[13] Cf. Zaehner, 1962, pp. 12-13; Smart, 1969, p. 4; James. 1956, p. 231;
Smith, W., 1962, p. 44; Wach, 1958, pp. 9-12; Parrinder, 1962, pp. 124-127;
Streng, 1969, pp. 7-9. More recently, Smart, 1973a, p. 34, has stated that there
is no strong reason to hold that particular commitment is necessary for the
study of religion.

[14] De Vries, 1967, p. 221.

[15] Writing about 15 years ago Raymond Firth surprisingly admits he had not
heard of the opposing view outlined here. Cf. Firth, 1959, p. 239.

[16] Schmidt, 1931, p. 6.

[17] Horton, 1964, p. 662.

taken this stand in their writings on religion. [18] And Evans-Pritchard, in particular, has explicitly endorsed the position of Schmidt. [19]

The opposite view, however, has as many, if not more, adherents. Robert Lowie, in a posthumously published essay, insists that the anthropologist must study religious values objectively. He then adds:

> Probably my own lack of religious training was an asset rather than a drawback, because I could not condemn any form of worship mainly because it differed from mine. I could only view it as a human manifestation worthy of scientific investigation.... In short I will study as many religions as I can, but I will judge none of them. I doubt if any other attitude is scientifically defensible. [20]

Not all anthropologists have followed Lowie's path of withholding judgment on the truth or falsehood of religious beliefs. [21] Many seem to think that an agnostic's attitude gives an objectivity which lies beyond the reach of a believer. A blanket denial of all religions is taken to be more impartial than an adherence to a particular faith.

Some have expressed the view that whether a student of religions is himself a believer or not does not really matter. Many religious and magical beliefs of non-literate societies are just as strange to a theist as to an atheist. Both would judge these beliefs as false and superstitious. [22] Such a view, however, does not seem to have much to recommend it. Christians have often judged the religious beliefs and practices of non-literate peoples as utterly false and superstitious, but they can, and often do, see in them a quest for God on man's part. Belief in God as creator, in the existence of a non-empirical reality and in life after death are commonly shared opinions among many peoples. Besides, anthropological works on religion seem to indicate that the interests one follows and the results of one's studies often depend on whether the writer is himself a religious believer. This appears to be the case in the study of religious experience; most of the anthropologists who have used the concept are themselves believers.

Many anthropologists claim that the quest for religious truth or falsehood does not enter into their investigations. Bharati writes that "the anthropologist, as an anthropologist, can neither make such state-

---

[18] The works of Lienhardt, G. and Turner, V are examples of this attitude.

[19] See Evans-Pritchard, 1965b, p. 121. It is interesting to note that this is one of the very few instances where Evans-Pritchard agrees with Schmidt.

[20] Lowie, 1963, p. 533. Cf. Fried, 1968, pp. 651-652, who commenting on Horton, 1964, finds his attitude rather strange.

[21] Firth, 1951, p. 247; Leach, 1968c.

[22] Mair, 1965, pp. 186-187.

ments (i.e. about the truth or falsehood of religion) nor do research with the intention of finding 'truth' in religion. This reviewer, for example, happens to be an ordained Hindu monk and regards himself as a committed Hindu, but he keeps his committment out of his anthropological research on Hindu society." [23] Bharati, who finds objection to the view that only a religiously committed person is fully suitable to study religion, seems to be propounding an approach very similar to the phenomenological *epoche,* or suspension of judgment. The anthropologist who is not a believer cannot approach the subject from the same angle since he has no religious committment. Downs, for instance, observes that the only reasonable way a person can study contradictory beliefs is "to accept the fact that human beings can and do believe things that cannot be proven or disproven by 'logical,' 'scientific,' or 'objective' argument. Accepting this, one can then develop a respect for man's ability to believe, and for any belief system as an expression of human nature." [24] Downs clearly exhibits a sympathetic approach, but he seems to rule out the concept of the sacred as 'illogical' and 'unscientific.' The consequence of this may be that the researcher will be led to seek a full explanation in terms of sociological and/or psychological criteria which are more logical to him.

Evans-Pritchard has offered a partial solution to the problem by specifying exactly the anthropologist's task in the study of religion and by leaving room for another approach. His view may be more attractive to phenomenologists and to historians of religions. He writes:

> As far as the study of religion as a factor of social life is concerned, it may make little difference whether the anthropologist is a theist or an atheist, since in either case he can only take into account what he can observe. But if either attempts to go further than this, each must pursue a different path. The non-believer seeks for some theory — biological, psychological or sociological — which will explain the illusion. The believer seeks rather to understand the manner in which a people conceive of a reality and their relations to it. For both, religion is part of social life, but for the believer it has also another dimension. [25]

That the anthropological study of religion has dealt primarily with its social and psychological functions and with the relations religious beliefs and practices have with the rest of culture requires no proof. [26]

---

[23] Bharati, 1972, p. 231. Smart, 1973a, p. 33, expresses a similar view when he writes that "the Religionist is concerned with those who express faith, but not with giving personal testimony."

[24] Downs, 1973, p. 297.

[25] Evans-Pritchard, 1965b, 121.

[26] See, for example, some of the standard textbooks, like Haviland, 1974, pp. 495 ff.; and Ember and Ember, 1973, pp. 377 ff.

Any scholar who is not blatantly one-sided in his approach can fulfill this task. Thus both the believer and the unbeliever can make useful, insightful studies of the place religion occupies in the life of a people, an understanding of which is preliminary to grasp religion itself. The phenomenologist tends to go beyond this study. His assumption is that there is, or might be, something more to religion that the sociological, cultural and psychological dimensions which social scientists have observed. While personal belief, or lack of it, need not make much difference to the scholar who restricts his study of religions to the areas mentioned above, it might produce a noteworthy difference in one who embarks on specifying the nature of religion and its ultimate significance.

Anthropological method presents another problem with regard to the study of religion. Participant-observation seems to imply that the researcher accepts to some degree the way of life, including the customs and sentiments, of the people under study. Now it is relatively easy to share in the political sentiments or the economic interests of a non-literate people because one can readily understand the nature of the reality upon which those sentiments and interests are based. It is not easy at all to share in religious beliefs and to participate fully in religious ritual if one has already taken an agnostic or atheistic stand in one's own life; that is, if one does not accept the reality from which such beliefs might flow or are believed to emanate. [27] One anthropological solution to this problem has been well articulated by James Downs. Writing about his field experience among the Navajo, he states that when he first arrived to start his research he did not believe in the Wolfman who, according to Navajo tradition, was a Navajo who had obtained the power to change into a wolf and, in that guise, to do harm to other people. Because of this belief the Navajo were reluctant to wander alone in the dark. Downs did not share this belief and for a while he had no qualms about going out in the dark on his own whenever he needed to do so. Within a short period, however, he found himself acquiring the same fearful attitude of the Navajo and ended up by not going out alone at night and by being afraid if he had to do so. This he explains by saying that "the social system in which one lives defines reality far more than any set of abstract ideas or any amount of objective knowledge." [28] This emphasizes the Durkheimian notion that social reality or structure is the prime factor in the shaping of

[27] Lienhardt, G., 1956, p. 312.
[28] Downs, 1973, p. 295.

religious beliefs and practices. It also suggests, as another anthropologist has put it, that "all religious ideas and institutions are explicable
solely in human, social terms." [29] These statements are ultimately about
the nature of religion; they are necessarily judgmental. The believer
will obviously reject them; so will the student of religions who applies
the phenomenological suspension of judgment. For the believer, religious beliefs are important not just because they are related to sociological and psychological factors, or because they have made an enormous impact on human culture, or because they are an excellent example
of human ingenuity. Rather, their importance lies in the fact that they
are thought to be based on a completely separate order of existence.
By giving religious beliefs and practices a dimension of their own,
the believer is in a realm of thought and experience which only those
who have faith can begin to understand and to share. One can hardly
maintain that sharing such beliefs in an academic manner can be even
remotely identified with the believer's own attitude. In like manner,
to adopt the "as if" attitude, which implies that the researcher puts on
the "appearance of acceptance at face value the phenomena of the
religion they study," [30] does not seem to be satisfactory.

One cannot, of course, approach anthropological literature of religion
with the dichotomy of books produced by believers and those by non-
believers. One has to recognize that both attitudes can contribute to
the study of religion and that both have their limitations. The task of
the scholar is to take into account all available literature and at the same
time to be aware of its contributions and limitations. There may finally
come a point, as Evans-Pritchard holds, when the believer and unbeliever must part company in their scholarly endeavors. [31]

THE DEFINITION OF RELIGION

The answer one gives to the preceding question is closely linked with
the definitional problem of religion. The definitions of religions by
scholars have been legion. Anthropologists have added to the already
long list. [32]

Perhaps the most common definition given by anthropologists is that

---

[29] Firth, 1968b, p. 31.

[30] Firth, 1959, p. 240.

[31] Evans-Pritchard, 1965b, p. 121; Bharati, 1972, p. 232. Cf. Yinger,
1970, p. 2.

[32] Leuba, 1912, pp. 339-361, lists many of the earlier definitions of religion.
Yinger, 1970, pp. 4 ff. discusses some of the more recent ones. Cf. also Horton,
1960a and Goody, 1961.

religion is the belief in spiritual or supernatural beings—a definition which stems from Edward Tylor. Many contemporary textbooks deal with religious matters under the title of the "supernatural." [33] But those anthropologists who have tackled the problem of defining religion have generally kept clear of such a definition, just as they have avoided the Durkheimian sacred/profane dichotomy. [34] Supernatural events are considered as such only in relation to what is accepted as natural occurrences. What may be considered as normal in one society may be attributed to the gods or the spirits in another. Thus even though many anthropologists still tend to classify magic under the supernatural, those non-literate peoples for whom belief in magic occupies a prominent role consider it as quite a natural event. As Nadel wrote:

> ... any definition of the supernatural must introduce the contrast with the domain of empirical and scientific knowledge; more precisely, when judging any action or notion to be concerned with the supernatural we assert by implication that it is concerned with existences and influences ("beings," "powers," "forces") the assumption of which conflicts with the principles of empirical inquiry and verification. And since those principles and their potentialities have been fully explored only in our own modern science, and can certainly not be assumed to govern the intellectual efforts of primitive peoples, the separation of the "natural" from the "supernatural" can have precise meaning only in our own system of thought. [35]

The division of events and human experiences into two contrasting spheres of the natural and the supernatural cannot, therefore, be assumed to be universal. People in non-literate societies have their own contrasting categories which make sense in their whole system of thought; but these categories may only be loosely related to our own natural/supernatural distinction. [36] To approach these societies with clear-cut Western categories may thwart the main aim of the study, namely, the understanding of another religion.

Two of the most common definitions found in anthropology take

---

[33] Cf. For instance, Titiev, 1963, pp. 501 ff.; Jacobs and Stern, 1952, pp. 199 ff; Haviland, 1974, pp. 497 ff. Some textbooks have ceased to write about religion under the rubric of "the supernatural"; cf. Keesing, 1958; Bohannan, 1963; Mair, 1965.

[34] Evans-Pritchard, 1965b, pp. 109-110; Beattie, 1964, p. 203; Count, 1960, p. 599; Glick, 1967, p. 33; Turner, V., 1964d, p. 302.

[35] Nadel, 1954b, pp. 3-4.

[36] One should note that even in the Western world what is classified under the supernatural and under the natural has changed over the last few centuries; cf. De Lubac, 1934. This makes the application of the natural/supernatural distinction to non-literate societies more difficult. Cf. Ember and Ember, 1973, p. 417; Taylor, R. B., 1973, p. 389.

either a psychological or a cultural approach to religion. Howells, for instance, writes:

> Religion is the normal psychological adjustment by which human societies build a barrier of fantasy against fear. And since, like any psychological adjustment, it is born in stress, it is therefore the source of emotion. [37]

Melford Spiro provides a typical definition which brings to the fore the cultural and institutional dimension of religion. He asserts:

> Religion is an institution consisting of culturally patterned interactions with culturally postulated superhuman beings. [38]

Some anthropological descriptions of religion tend to stress the artistic angle and see religion as a symbolic expression of human problems in dramatic form. [39] Others look on such a definition as too emotional and relate religion to science seeing them both as techniques aimed at explaining and predicting events. [40] Still others unite many factors in an attempt to give a comprehensive description of religious beliefs and practices. [41]

Definitions of this nature tend to depend mainly on the outward manifestations of religion. They ask what does a religion do; and the student tries to figure out some of the functional results of religious beliefs and practices. While such definitions may provide us with a wealth of information on the psychological dimension of religion and on the relations between religion and socio-cultural elements, they do not answer the basic question of what religion is. Fortunately, some anthropologists are aware of the defective character of these definitions and have tried different and perhaps more fruitful paths.

Godfrey Lienhardt, for example, has blended the anthropological notion that religion is a form of adjustment with the philosophical aspect which sees religion as a quest for truth. He writes:

> Religion is a way of knowing about and dealing with certain situations of human life. Religious knowledge and practice are ways in which men apprehend some truths and adjust themselves to their conditions in the light of that apprehension. [42]

---

[37] Howells, 1948, p. 21.

[38] Spiro, 1966a, p. 96.

[39] Beattie, 1964, pp. 202 ff.; 1966, pp. 65 ff.; Firth, 1951, pp. 215 ff.; 1959, p. 238.

[40] Horton, 1962a; cf. Geertz, 1960, p. 31, who points out that, like harmony, religion is ultimately a science.

[41] Cf. for example Lessa and Vogt, 1972, p. 1.

[42] Lienhardt, G., 1956, p. 327.

He is one of the few anthropologists who has recognized the element
of religious experience and given it prominence in describing the religion of a particular African tribe. [43] Evans-Pritchard has taken a
somewhat similar view. He explains that there are always two sides to
religion; one is concerned mainly with the social order, the other with
the relation of man to God. The personal expression of religion tells
us more of what religion is than its social and cultural manifestations.
There is, therefore, an element of religious experience, man's experience of God, which no social or cultural dimension can exhaust. This
experience transcends all cultural and social forms, even though it is
expressed in these same forms. [44] In what is still one of the best monographs on the religions of non-literate societies, he asserts:

> We can, therefore, say no more than that Spirit is an intuitive apprehension,
> something experienced in response to certain situations, but known directly
> only to the imagination and not to the senses. Nuer religious conceptions are
> properly speaking not concepts but imaginative constructions. [45]

Gallus, in a unique anthropological essay, incorporates the idea of
the sacred in a 'biofunctional' theory of religion. He sees religion
basically as a stage in the development of what he calls 'adaptive truth,'
which satisfies the demand for security and survival and is thus bio-
logically adaptive. Instead of bypassing the concept and experience of
the sacred, he includes it in his overall picture of religion. He states:

> The experience of the 'sacred' is an individual emotion that is the consequence
> of a *tension* (which does not exist in a scientific analysis) between the
> conscious ego and extrahuman reality (=*Veritas*=God, as expressed by St.
> Augustine). Extrahuman reality appears as an immense source of unknown
> power (or powers) which infinitely surpasses human capacity to know about
> it. This immense source of unknown power, when properly approached, be-
> comes responsive and links up with the hopes, fears, and endeavors of individ-
> ual life. [46]

While Gallus's description and analysis of religion borrows heavily
from the classical anthropological approach which gives religion a
positive sociological and/or psychological function in human life and
culture, he introduces a number of elements which are usually left out
by his colleagues in anthropology. The idea of a transcendent reality
with which the believer has a relationship is central. Otto's idea of
"mysterium tremendum" is also incorporated. Religious experience,

---

43 Lienhardt, G., 1960.
44 Evans-Pritchard, 1953a, p. 19; 1953b, pp. 125-126.
45 Evans-Pritchard, 1956a, p. 321.
46 Gallus, 1972, p. 554.

though described as an individual emotion, seems to be an emotion *sui generis* because it is not described simply in sociological or psychological terms. Beliefs and rituals are, in his analysis, secondary to the basic adaptive experience of the individual.

Those definitions which stress the fact that religion is a means for personal change are also concerned with religious experience. Wallace, for example, defines religion as "a set of rituals, rationalized by myth, which mobilizes supernatural power for the purpose of achieving or preventing transformations of state in man and nature." [47] The element of transformation in the definition of religion is also found in the work of some religionists. [48]

There is thus some support in anthropological literature for Eliade's emphasis on religious experience which implies that for a definition of religion one had better look at the inward response of the believer himself, and not at the outward manifestations. This experience is often described by historians of religions as an awareness of the invisible world, a consciousness which transcends sensory data and which achieves a new kind of knowledge and feeling. [49] Religious beliefs and experiences are based on the assumption that there is a realm of existence which goes beyond the knowledge provided by human sensory data. The meaning one gives to human life and to the universe as a whole is placed beyond the material world itself. Further, religion is not merely the affirmation of a transcendental world or reality. The believer goes as far as to establish relationships with the gods and spirits he believes in; relationships which are often very precisely determined. Because these relationships are expressed in anthropomorphic terms, that is, they are patterned on existing human social relations, religion cannot be understood without taking into account these spiritual relationships and their social models. Myths and rituals have also to be studied in the context of these relationships which form an important aspect of man's religious life. Such an approach can hardly lead to more than a description of religion. It has, however, two major advantages. First, it places the object of religion outside the material universe, thereby making it clear that not all human values, aspirations and relationships can be called religious. [50] Secondly,

---

[47] Wallace, 1966, p. 107. Cf. Norbeck, 1974, pp. 32 ff., where he talks about modes of transcendence.

[48] Streng et al., 1973, pp. 6-12.

[49] Smart, 1969, pp. 14-15.

[50] Cf. Hutchison, 1969, pp. 575-576 and 583.

by putting religious experience and life at the center of the concept of religion, one brings into focus the fact that religion involves the whole man and not merely his communal and/or psychological needs. Religion is, therefore, multi-dimensional and difficult to define.

When one studies the countless attempts by scholars in all disciplines to define religion more accurately, one is inclined to conclude that the quest for an exhaustive definition acceptable to all is a misdirected effort. Those who have defended the search of such a definition have ended up by providing the academic world with one which is almost meaningless to the believer himself and practically useless to the student of religions. [51] Anthropological definitions of religion often depend on the problem under investigation. A psychological study will give psychological factors the principal role, while a social study will make communal aspects prominent. A more recent case in point is Burridge's moral definition of religion stressing redemption, a definition very appropriate to the problem he is studying, namely, millenarian movements in a changing world of human values. [52]

Religion is a complex phenomenon and thus subject to many definitions; its many dimensions cannot possibly be exhausted by one simple criterion. To look for *the* one definition of religion would be an unprofitable task. As Milton Yinger wrote:

> Definitions, then, are tools; they are to some degree arbitrary; they lay stress on similarities *within* a delimited area and on the differences *outside* it, thus giving emphasis to one aspect of reality. They are abstract, which is to say they are oversimplifications. In dealing with a subject so complex and concerned with such a broad range of data as religion, a topic approached for many different purposes we must relinquish the idea that there is one definition that is "correct" and satisfactory for all. [53]

This explains why appealing definitions which emphasize "ultimate transformation." [54] or "ultimate value," [55] or "ultimate concern," [56] are not beyond critique and serious reservations. Pye, for instance,

---

[51] Ferre's definition of religion, for instance, does not assign a specific object to religious beliefs and experiences, thereby making his definition equally applicable to politics and economics. See Ferre. 1970, p. 11. The definitions of Smart, 1973b, p. 157 and of Geertz, 1966, p. 4, are more useful but still too theoretical and complex for the average believer.

[52] Burridge, 1969, pp. 6-7. His stress on redemption or salvation gives his definition a theological bent. Cf. Monk et al., 1973, pp. 8-10.

[53] Yinger, 1970, p. 4. Cf. Firth, 1959, p. 229.

[54] Streng et al., 1973.

[55] Monk et al., 1973.

[56] Tillich, 1963.

accurately notes that the element of ultimacy, which has been incorporated by some anthropologists in their definition of religion, [57] is not without difficulties. "In particular," he writes, "one wonders whether it (i.e. the element of ultimacy) is not just a little too far-reaching, too pure, or too profound. Not all persons involved in religion are conscious of the one overriding 'ultimate' concern. They may be more or less 'ultimate' in various circumstances." [58]

The main fault one finds with Eliade's view of religion is that he gives it a one-dimensional function and meaning with the result that his definition of religion is just too narrow. [59] Anthropological studies tend to show that the function of religion is not univocal and that its meaningful content cannot be exhausted by one cryptic statement.

RELIGION AND MAGIC

One way anthropologists have tried to define religion is to contrast it with magic. While anthropologists since Frazer have grappled with the problem of the relationship between religion and magic, we find in Eliade no attempt to study the issue explicitly, or to analyze the two concepts and specify their respective meanings. Yet one can make some deductions from Eliade's works where the reference to magic is often abundant. Eliade understands magic as the manipulation of the sacred. Its power is automatic and instrumental as Frazer had maintained. Magical power resides in the object itself. Frazer had contrasted this aspect with the element of supplication which is characteristic of religion; Eliade, however, while implying that magic and religion are not the same, does not use this Frazerian dichotomy. [60] Unlike Frazer, Eliade does not hold that magic was an evolutionary stage prior to religion. On the contrary Eliade maintains that magic became prevalent in developed societies, a process which he takes for granted. [61] He holds that the two phenomena are intimately linked; even the gods have magical power. Magic does not exist on its own, apart from religion. Whether religion can be free from magical elements Eliade does not say, but he never questions the fact that the religions of non-literate

---

[57] Lessa and Vogt, 1972.

[58] Pye, 1972, p. 11.

[59] One student of comparative religion has called Eliade's view "not unbiased." Cf. Pye, 1972, pp. 9-10 and p. 229, footnote 4.

[60] See Eliade, 1958b, pp. 108, 216. Eliade also accepts Frazer's definition of Sympathetic Magic; cf. Eliade, 1958b, pp. 9-10.

[61] Eliade, 1958b, p. 23.

societies imply magic as well. [62] Eliade uses the phrase "magico-religious" throughout his works and goes as far as to describe shamanism as a magico-religious experience. [63] One of the major links he sees between magic and religion is that both are projections into mythological time. The power of magic derives from this mythical return to origins. [64]

Most of what Eliade says on magic is in harmony with what several anthropological text-books say on the matter. [65] That anthropology has not made much progress since Frazer and Malinowski on the relation between magic and religion is fairly obvious. There is agreement in anthropological literature that magic and religion are distinct in theory but not in practice; that they both co-exist in ritual practice; and that both are as a rule important in the study of non-literate societies. One author has looked upon them as a kind of continuum with very little tension between them and with the balance shifting from one side to the other and differing from one society to another. [66] Whether this position helps towards understanding religion in non-literate societies is a moot question. One thing seems certain: the problem of the relationship between magic and religion is crucial for the study of non-literate cultures if for no other reason because most available literature on these cultures uses the two categories of thought.

The heart of the problem, however, is not the precise distinction between the two concepts. One must rather discuss whether the concepts themselves are applicable in the world of non-literate peoples. Magic and religion are ideas formulated in the Western Christian tradition which sees them as opposed to one another. Such an application to non-literate cultures will not hold. [67] Though there are similar conceptions or ways of looking at reality in both Western and non-literate societies which may be designated by the word "magic," there are enough differences to cause concern to any scholar in search of precision. Not many anthropologists have attempted to draw up these differences, much less to study them in any detail. [68]

---

[62] Eliade, 1958b, pp. 23, 80-81; 1964a, p. 76.

[63] Cf. for instance, Eliade, 1958b, pp. 13, 17, 392, and 439; 1959a, p. 98; 1964a, pp. 3 ff., 21, 107; 1965a, p. 72; 1969c, p. 121.

[64] Eliade, 1958b, pp. 392 ff.

[65] Herskovits, 1948, pp. 347 ff.; Beals and Hoijer, 1965, pp. 568 ff.; Hoebel, 1972, pp. 571 ff.

[66] Titiev, 1960. Cf. Aberle, 1966.

[67] See Gallus, 1972, pp. 555-556, who includes magic in his biofunctional theory of religion.

[68] Two exceptions are Malefijt, 1968, pp. 286 ff., and Mair, 1969a, pp. 222 ff.

A few anthropologists have attempted a somewhat different approach to the whole question. John Beattie has directed his attentions to the symbolic element in so-called magical rites. "The whole procedure or rite," he notes, "has an essentially expressive aspect whether or not it is thought to be effective instrumentally as well." [69] Rites enact what they are supposed to achieve. Hence by carrying out a rain-making ceremony, the participants are stating symbolically the importance they attach to rain and their earnest desire that it come when needed. The instrumentality of the rite is, of course, considered important in the minds of those performing or attending the ritual, but often the rites "are believed to be instrumental just because they are expressive." [70] To understand magical rites one must direct one's studies to what the rites are saying. Values, attitudes and desires are frequently manifested in these rites and in many instances these values are concerned not with the mythological era, but rather with the day to day needs of the people. Many magical rites have very little mythology and even when elaborate mythology does exist, what seems to be foremost in the minds of the participants are the tangible mundane results which coincide with their individual or societal needs. [71] This approach to magic avoids, to some degree, the magic/religion dichotomy by focusing on the symbolic element of all ritual behavior.

Another focus is taken by Murray Wax in a relatively recent essay. [72] He observes that the point of view of those societies where "magic" is a dominant feature of their culture presents the world around them not as a mechanism but as a society. Plants, animals and inanimate objects are not seen as things governed by physical laws of nature, but more as interrelated socially with each other and with men. This inter-relationship is the important element. What the participant seeks is not mechanical control but beneficial relationships. This is a very different view from that of Frazer, Malinowski, and some contemporary anthropologists who view magic as a sort of false science which gradually gives way to technological progress. [73] Wax's view is not a return to the animism of Tylor. Rather the "magical view" is seen as affirming that the world does influence human beings and human behavior. That environmental conditions affect human personality and consequently

---

[69] Beattie, 1964, p. 202.

[70] Beattie, 1964, p. 204.

[71] Nadel, 1956, pp. 189 ff.

[72] Wax, 1968.

[73] This view has also been used to explain water-divining practices in the United States of America. Cf. Hyman and Vogt, 1967.

human relations is an accepted view in Western culture. The difference
in non-literate societies lies in the fact that the relationships and the
objects which play a leading role in them are more precisely determined.
Human beings can influence, and at times control, these relations both
because of their charismatic personality and because of their superior
knowledge. This explains why some "magic" can only be performed by
specially designated people who have given proof of, or are assumed
to have, charism and knowledge. Consequently one can get a better
understanding of the fact that in non-literate societies magic can be
either good or harmful; this contrasts sharply with the Western view
which gives magic an evil connotation, linked especially with the
activity of the devil. The link, therefore, between magic and religion,
lies not only in their symbolic nature, but also in the shared concept
of relationship. Just as human beings can affect one another through
the physical environment because of the mutual relationship that exists
between man and the universe, so they can also affect the world of
gods and spirits; these latter in turn can direct and control man and
his world because, due to their superior standing, their relations with
man and the universe are more intimate and direct. There are analogies
of this in the Christian conception of the moral and spiritual world.
Good and bad influences of one person on another, or for that matter
of one situation over men, is an accepted fact. The activity of God on
men and the response of men is described in terms of relationships.
Good and bad spirits, or angels, are also a source of influence on human
activity—an influence often described in terms of personal relationship. [74]

What is important in the "magical" world, therefore, is not the control over, or manipulation of, the sacred or of the material world
through a well-defined ritual action. It is the relationship which counts.
The end result is possible only because relationships exist. It is interesting to note that many of these desired ends deal with prosperity,
good fortune and success in one's life and freedom from evil influences;
such desiderata are usually achieved by establishing mutual and harmonious relations with one's neighbors and with one's environment.
The power of magic does not depend on the putative return to a mythological era, but rather on the concrete experience of human relationships. "Magical experience" is not an awareness of one's return to

---

[74] Thus, for instance, Christian Spirituality is described in terms of relationships. Cf. Larkin, 1967.

mythological beginnings but a vivid realization of man's most inwardly felt relationships.

Magico-religious phenomena are, therefore, characterized both by their symbolic and expressive qualities and by their common basis in human relations which are expanded to include the material world and the world of non-human spirits. The study of religion cannot be carried out with any thoroughness unless one takes seriously into account the basic social relations of a given society and explores carefully the symbols used.

RELIGION AND CULTURE

The anthropological viewpoint has been influenced by Durkheim's theory that religion is nothing else but a symbol of society. Society was raised to the level of godhood. There is much evidence today in anthropological literature to show that religion is never a perfect idealization of social and cultural reality and that it cannot be regarded as an epiphenomenon of society. The relation of religion with the rest of culture seems to be closer in ethnic religions than in the universal religions like Christianity, Islam and Buddhism. Even in non-literate societies, which are ethnic religions, the observance of changing patterns has made it clear that religious and social change do not always go hand in hand. But neither is religion an independent entity, existing side by side with society; the relation between religion and society is not a tenuous one, but it is rather so deep that the study of man's religions has to be accompanied by an equally intensive study of social institutions. Writing on Indian society Embree remarks that "while it is probably true that it is difficult to consider religious ideas apart from their social structure in any society, in Indian culture it is manifestly impossible." [75] The same can be said about non-literate cultures. One cannot begin to understand some of their fundamental religious beliefs and values unless one has a good grasp of their social and cultural situation. Religion is an integral part of those cultures where the distinction between religion and society is not made. [76]

In a penetrating analysis of the Nuer concept of Spirit, Evans-Pritchard suggests that the many kinds of spirits believed in "are figures or representations of refractions of God, or Spirit, in relation to par-

---

[75] Embree, 1966, p. 32.
[76] One can note that this distinction is also absent in some of the great religions.

ticular activities, events, persons or groups." [77] The knowledge of social structure is necessary if we are to understand the various attributes ascribed to God and to spirits, and if we are to grasp the way in which a particular people envisages its relation to God. Similarly, in a study already referred to, [78] Meyer Fortes remarks that the religious institutions of the people he studied cannot be understood without reference to their social organization. Other anthropologists have taken similar positions. [79]

That human relationships are often the principal analogues used to express a people's conception of its God or gods and the relations these gods have with men does not appear to require much proof. Anthropomorphism is an attribute of all religions, though the type of anthropomorphic emphasis in one religion may vary in kind and in intensity from another. [80] Some anthropomorphic characteristics may be universal, others may be locally restricted to a particular society. To understand religious beliefs and practices it seems only logical to start from human relations and from other social or cultural elements. Even if one looks on religion, as Eliade does, as a manifestation of the sacred, one still has to begin from the socio-cultural situation for the sacred is manifested not in a vacuum but in man's total environment. The same can be said if one focuses one's study on religious experience; for this experience takes place in a specific socio-religious context which influences it and gives it shape and dimension.

Eliade's views on the relation between religion and society or culture are never clearly elaborated. It has been pointed out in an earlier chapter that his statements on this issue seem contradictory. [81] In general he tends to reduce the relationship between religion and culture to coincidental occurrences. For he writes that

> ...religious forms are non-temporal; they are not necessarily bound to time. We have no proof that religious structures are created by certain types of civilization or by certain historic moments. All one can say is that the predominance of this or that religious structure is occasioned or favored by a certain kind of civilization or a certain historic moment. [82]

However, in explaining some of the differences between Indo-European and Turko-Tibetan shamanism he openly admits that they were

[77] Evans-Pritchard, 1953b, p. 111.
[78] Fortes, 1959.
[79] Middleton, 1960; cf. Geertz, 1960.
[80] Cf. Malefijt, 1968, pp. 149-150.
[81] Cf. chapter IV, pp. 114-115.
[82] Eliade, 1960a, p. 178.

the results of the historical situation. The agrarian oriental civilization and the urban Mediterranean one are respectively specified as the two cultural sources. [83] Elsewhere he remarks that there "are differences in religious experiences explained by differences in economy, culture and social organization—in short, by history." [84] And again he assures us that "since the religious life of humanity is realized in history, its expressions are inevitably conditioned by the variety of historical moments and cultural styles." [85]

Even if one interprets Eliade as endorsing the causal influence of culture on religious forms and beliefs, it would be difficult to quote more than a handful of examples from his works where he analyzes such an influence. As a rule he does not take seriously into account human social relations, or the cultural background, or the historical context. But does not man often express his relations with God and with spirits in the same way as he describes human relations? And are not the relations between the various gods and spirits constructed on the human model? How can one understand, for instance, Australian religions, if one is not given the slightest indication of their environmental and cultural background? [86] How can one see the believers' point of view if one does not try and enter into the total life of the people under study? The anthropomorphic elements in the religions of non-literate peoples can only be judged as exotic unless the social and cultural traits behind them are first discovered.

While Eliade and contemporary anthropologists do not seem to agree on the nature of the relationship between religion and culture and on the influence of the latter on the former, they all admit that religions have left their indelible mark on cultures. Shamanism, Eliade asserts, has made possible or stimulated cultural creations, lyric poetry being a typical example. [87] The influence of religion on culture receives priority in Eliade's works; as a rule, however, this influence is not specified or outlined.

As has already been noted, anthropologists admit that religion has played an important role in the history of mankind and in the life of all peoples. [88] Cultural institutions may be a direct product of religious ideas and attitudes. The classical example is Weber's study of how the

---

[83] Eliade, 1964a, p. 379.
[84] Eliade, 1961a, p. 17.
[85] Eliade, 1961a, pp. 62-63.
[86] His articles on Australian Religions are a case in point.
[87] Eliade, 1964a, pp. 508-511.
[88] Cf. also Norbeck, 1974, pp. 23 ff.

Protestant ethic was the main factor in the rise of capitalism in the West. [89] Though it is more difficult, at times even impossible, to produce similar works on non-literate societies because of the lack of reliable historical records, it is almost a truism to state that in these cultures religious values and beliefs often dictate political, economic, legal and family matters.

It is a common theme in anthropological literature that religion often upholds the norms of a society, thereby contributing to the maintenance of the social order. Rules and customs on which the peaceful working of a social system depends are reinforced by religious sanctions. Especially where no elaborate system of governmental control exists, religious ideas may be the main cause of maintaining peaceful relations. [90] In such societies there can be no appeal to a regular court nor a convincing threat by a police force, and it is often the religious dimension which is left to exert pressure and keep the balance. One way in which religious beliefs can more specifically influence the maintenance of order is by upholding and endorsing the offices of those whose task it is to rule over a social group. Political power is given religious validation, and it is precisely because of this religious element that political power is respected. Religion may validate political control in many ways, investing the chief or ruler with religious functions is one of the more common means. The same result can be obtained by creating a class of priests or other religious specialists who sanctify the office of the ruler, assist the king in the task of ruling his subjects, and at the same time check and control his actions. [91]

Religious beliefs can also regulate economic activities. Magico-religious beliefs may be of great value to a people because they regulate, order and systematize human labor. [92] Great economic activities and enterprises are frequently carried out within a religious framework which may have been the cause of their coming into being and of their continuing in existence. In like manner religion can have a lasting impact on the family and on marriage patterns within a society. Inheritance laws, to give one example, may be ruled by religious values. [93] This lasting impact of religion on society is one of the main reasons

---

[89] Weber, 1905.

[90] Evans-Pritchard, 1940b, p. 291; Hoebel, 1954, pp. 157-159; Cf. Mair, 1962, *passim*.

[91] Cf. Gluckman, 1940; Wilson, 1959.

[92] See Ames, 1964; Firth, 1963a. Malinowski, 1922, provides one of the best examples in anthropological literature.

[93] Cf. Forde, 1950b.

why the study of religion has been a major preoccupation in the social sciences. As Clifford Geertz remarked:

> Religion is sociologically interesting not because it describes the social order, but because, like environment, political power, jural obligation, personal affection and a sense of beauty, it shapes it. [94]

The important fact to bear in mind is that the impact of religion on culture differs from society to society and that anthropologists have not succeeded in working out clear patterns of influence which are universally applicable. The tendency in anthropological literature is to assume that the impact of religion on human culture has been generally good and useful, though studies on the dysfunctional aspects of religion are not wanting. [95] The beneficial results are especially seen as contributing to man's nobler aspirations. Robert Lowie, for instance, after affirming that religion has a definite place in human life, adds:

> There are many people who might like to see the extermination of all religion, but perhaps they might take a closer look at what happens when religious attitudes are destroyed: the accompanying ethical standards also disappear, and one is left with a society not only without religion but also without restraining virtues. It is extremely doubtful that a nation can keep its ethics after it loses its religion. [96]

And Margaret Mead writes that religions are the means "by which the dignity of man in his quest for spiritual values has been reinforced and enhanced." [97]

It is in this area of inter-relating religion and culture, believed by some to be the main task of anthropologists, that some of the most fruitful work on the religions of non-literate societies has been done. Though Durkheim's sociology still lies at the root of these endeavors, few anthropologists today accept his theory in its complete form. However, as one assessment of the contemporary scene has it:

> the more moderate proposition that religious ritual and belief both reflect and act to support the moral framework underlying social arrangements (and are in turn animated by it) has given rise to what has become perhaps the most popular form of analysis in the anthropological study of religion. [98]

---

[94] Geertz, 1966, pp. 35-36. Cf. Evans-Pritchard, 1959b, p. 6.

[95] For examples, see Simoons, 1961, p. 3. Some anthropologists have maintained that apparently dysfunctional religious beliefs and practices were in fact economically beneficial rather than harmful. Cf. Spiro, 1966a; Harris, 1966.

[96] Lowie, 1963, p. 539.

[97] Mead, 1964, p. 100. Cf. Norbeck, 1974, pp. 65-66.

[98] Geertz, 1968, p. 402.

Anthropologists, therefore, tend to see religion as one dimension of culture which both influences and is influenced by other cultural elements. Studies which aim at bringing out the interrelations often put into focus the important aspect of religion in man's life. One can hardly begin a study of the religious life of man without considering the manifold interactions of religious beliefs and other socio-cultural dimensions. Religious man is caught up in these actions and interactions, some of which he experiences consciously, others he bypasses without much attention. To understand his attitudes and experiences one must see them in the light of these cultural interrelations, the study of which reveals religious man as an instrument of social change, seeking, at times consciously, to mold his own way of life. Such a view of religious man would consider his desire to escape from this wordly condition as non-existent, or at best as secondary in importance.

While studies of the relations between religion and society are indispensible for understanding man and his religions, they still have two major shortcomings. First, though some aspects of religious beliefs and practices are closely related to the social structure, others are relatively loosely linked and operate as semi-independent variables. Thus the studies of the relationships between religion and society may leave out some important religious aspects; they also tend to neglect the fact that religions form systems of ideas. Further, emphasis on cultural relationships can lead the scholar to forget that religions have a philosophical content expressed frequently enough in symbolic form. Secondly, sociological studies avoid psychological reflections which are inescapable when dealing with religious man. The concept of religious experience tends to be left out altogether; also neglected is the consideration that religious beliefs and practices are often based on the paradoxical situations of life which are charged with emotion and which affect not just the social group but also the individuals. Human relations, which lie behind many religious and magical practices, are definitely sociologically determined, but they are also psychologically felt. Anthropologists have made serious attempts to cope with both deficiencies, though they have not always been successful.

RELIGION AND PHILOSOPHY

One of Eliade's main contributions to the study of religious man is his keen awareness, detectable throughout his works, that religion constitutes a philosophical system. The nature of man is central to all religions. [99] So also are considerations about the nature of the world and man's place in it. Eliade insists that behind religion lies an ontology which explains how the world came into being; [100] underlying many myths, symbols and rites is a metaphysics. [101] "Symbol, myth and rite express a complex system of coherent affirmations about the ultimate realities of things." [102] Myth is a kind of early philosophy for "the earliest philosophical speculations derive from mythology." [103] Eliade asserts that the behavior of non-literate peoples can be understood in the framework of their philosophical systems. [104] This implies that religious beliefs and practices are often based on deeply rooted philosophical speculations which need not be explicitly formulated by the religious believers themselves. The philosophy is usually portrayed in symbolic form and therefore the understanding of symbols is essential if one is to grasp the meaning of religious beliefs and practices. [105] Eliade goes as far as to specify the type of philosophy present in non-literate societies; he writes:

> Hence it could be said that this primitive ontology has a platonic structure; and in that case, Plato could be regarded as the outstanding philosopher of "primitive mentality," that is, as the thinker who succeeded in giving philosophic currency and validity to the modes of life and behavior of archaic humanity. [106]

Just as in Platonic philosophy, the archetype plays a leading role in the philosophical system of non-literate peoples who tend to reduce "events to categories and individuals to archetypes." [107] Eliade's emphasis that for non-literate man the repetition of the archetype is at the heart of his religious practices, has to be seen in the light of Platonic philosophy. [108]

---

[99] Cf. Hutchison, 1969, p. 20.

[100] Eliade, 1963a, p. 108.

[101] Eliade, 1959a, p. 3; 1958b, *passim.*

[102] Eliade, 1959a, p. 3; cf. 1960a, pp. 17-18.

[103] Eliade, 1963a, p. 112; cf. 1961a, p. 95.

[104] Eliade, 1959a, p. 92.

[105] Eliade, 1960a, p. 10.

[106] Eliade, 1959a, p. 34; cf. *ibid.*, pp. 124 ff.; 1960a, p. 92. Platonic philosophy is also attributed to the native peoples of Australia; cf. Eliade, 1967b, pp. 219-220 and 1967d, p. 166.

[107] Eliade, 1959a, p. 44.

[108] Cf. Eliade, 1959a, p. ix, where he states that he uses the word "archetype" in the Augustinian sense. See also Ricketts, 1969. Altizer holds that Eliade solved the problem of writing in an abstract conceptual language about archaic man's symbols and ideas by adopting the categories of neo-platonism; Altizer, 1963, p. 42.

While it would be difficult to quote references to support the con-
tention that the philosophy of non-literate societies is Platonic, there
is ample evidence in contemporary anthropology that religion is also a
philosophical system of ideas. Religious views often give meaning to
life. [109] Evans-Pritchard, for one, insists that "a number of systematic
studies of primitive philosophies have to be made," [110] studies which
go hand in hand with the study of religions. The philosophies of non-
literate peoples are as varied as their religions; just as the theory of
ideas is a dominant theme in Platonic philosophy, so also the philosophies of non-literate cultures give dominant roles to different themes.
No common philosophical theme can be said to be universally dominant
in non-literate societies.

> Among all African peoples we find in one form or another theistic beliefs,
> manistic cults, witchcraft notions, interdictions with supernatural sanctions,
> magical practices, etc., but the philosophy of each has its own special
> character in virtue of the way in which among that people these ideas are
> related to one another. It will be found that one or other belief, or set
> of beliefs, dominates the others and gives form, pattern and colour to the
> whole. Thus, among some peoples, notably a large proportion of the Bantu,
> the dominant motif is provided by the cult of ancestors; among others, some
> of the Sudanic peoples, for example, it is found in the notion of witchcraft,
> with which are bound magical and oracular techniques; among others, such
> as the Nuer, Spirit is the center of the picture and manistic and witchcraft
> ideas are peripheral; and among other peoples yet other notions pre-
> dominate. [111]

The quest for the philosophical categories of thought of various peoples
has been carried out by a number of scholars, notably anthropologists.
Though the results of these studies are not immune from criticism,
they all seem to point to the fact that philosophy and religion have to
be taken together. [112] Religious concepts, myths and rituals may be
employed to express philosophical ideas about the nature of man and
of the universe and about the relations between man and his total
environment. [113] Another link between philosophical and religious
ideas is seen in that both attempt to cope with the problem of evil, moral
or otherwise.[114] Also in magical practices, as has already been pointed

---

[109] Berndt and Berndt, 1964, pp. 77-78; Firth, 1951, p. 241.

[110] Evans-Pritchard, 1956a, p. 315.

[111] Evans-Pritchard, 1956a, p. 315.

[112] Confer, for instance, the works on African philosophy by Temples, 1959,
Jahn, 1961 and Taylor, J.V., 1963. These books are evaluated by Mbiti, 1970,
pp. 10-12.

[113] Fortes and Dieterlen, 1965, to give one example, supply many instances
of this.

[114] Cf. Geertz, 1966, pp. 19 ff.

out, [115] the question of evil looms large. The understanding of religious and magical beliefs and practices cannot be achieved without an analysis of the way a society conceives of evil and of the solutions offered to explain it and deal with it.

One way in which some American anthropologists have attempted to deal with the philosophical systems of non-literate peoples is under the category of "worldview." [116] This approach tries to describe the way a people characteristically look upon the universe. Worldview includes patterns of thought, affective and cognitive aspects of things, the dimension of time and space and attitudes towards the cosmos. While the few available in-depth studies of particular worldviews bring out the variety of philosophical systems in non-literate cultures, it can be accepted that some basic philosophical problems are commonly confronted in every society. Robert Redfield, to whom we owe the concept of worldview, [117] asserted that a people's worldview always included an arrangement of groupings of people according to qualitative differences connected with the groups. Some conception of human nature, distinguishing man from the rest of the world, is present. Further, earth itself is usually categorized and distinguished into different aspects, such as water, fire, and so on. Finally, the place of human experiences, such as death and birth, are the object of clearly formulated attitudes and opinions.

Some writers have tended to relate the worldview of a particular society to its economic, kinship and political institutions, while others have restricted their analysis to its religious dimensions. [118] That studies of worldview have enormous implications for the study of religious man and his religions can hardly be doubted. Redfield, for instance, concluded that for non-literate peoples man is *in* nature and hence we cannot speak of man *and* nature. [119] In this worldview, he argues, there can be no mysticism for this implies a prior separation of man and nature and an effort to overcome the separation. Similarly, non-literate man's worldview tends to conceive of man and the universe as bound together in one moral order where mutual relations are the

---

[115] See the references to studies on witchcraft in footnote 128, Chapter III.
[116] Confer Redfield, 1953, pp. 84 ff.; Mendelson, 1968, pp. 576 ff.; Jones, 1972. For individual studies on worldviews see Leslie, 1960; Guiteras-Holmes, 1961; Gruhn, 1971; and Tierney, 1973.
[117] Redfield, 1952, pp. 30-36; 1953, pp. 84-110.
[118] Confer Geertz, 1957; Tax, 1941 and Mendelson, 1958.
[119] Redfield, 1953, pp. 105-106.

norm. Dichotomies of sacred/profane, natural/supernatural, and so on, would therefore have no place in such a worldview orientation.

RELIGION AND PSYCHOLOGY

While religious beliefs and practices definitely contain a coherent philosophical system, it must be stressed that for understanding religious man it is not sufficient to bring out the structural dimensions of his beliefs. Religious man himself may never consider the philosophical implications and presuppositions of his religious actions. Thus if we are to understand religious man we cannot be content solely with the analysis of philosophical systems. Religion is not an intellectual pastime; [120] on the contrary, to the believer, it implies a commitment of some sort and is linked with the normal day to day living. The whole man is involved in religious beliefs and practices. No complete study of religious man can thus leave out the psychological dimension. This involvement of the whole man in religion is accurately expressed by John Mbiti who writes on African societies:

> ... because traditional religions permeate all departments of life, there is no formal distinction between the sacred and the secular, between the religious and the non-religious, between the spiritual and the material areas of life. Wherever the African is, there is his religion: he carries it to the fields where he is sowing seeds or harvesting a new crop; he takes it with him to the beer party or to attend a funeral ceremony; and if he is educated, he takes religion with him to the examination room at school or in the university; if he is a politician he takes it to the house of parliament. Although many African religions do not have a word for religion as such, it nevertheless accompanies the individual from long before his birth to long after his physical death. [121]

One way of taking into account this aspect of religion has been the use of the term "religious experience" which has become common among historians of religions. Eliade's use of this concept in dealing with non-literate peoples has to be regarded as one of his contributions. For the concept of religious experience implies that religion is a way of life and not merely a set of beliefs strongly adhered to. It also assumes that religion affects man on many levels: intellectually, socially and emotionally. Though the category of religious experience is not free from difficulties, as has been shown, [122] the need for such cate-

---

[120] This is one of the main problems of Lévi-Strauss's method; pursued by itself it could easily become a sort of mathematical game.

[121] Mbiti, 1970, p. 2.

[122] Confer Chapter IV, pp. 138-139.

gories to take into account the religious life of a people seems beyond question.

While anthropological studies on the relation between religion and society, and on the philosophical systems underlying religious beliefs, have been pursued for some time, it has to be regretted that attempts to study the religious experience of non-literate peoples have been largely neglected. Psychological studies have on the whole left little impact on the anthropology of religion. There have been basic differences especially between psychoanalysis and anthropology ever since Freud published his *Totem and Tabu*. [123] Despite the ambivalent anthropological reaction to this work, it is now an accepted fact in anthropology that Freud's book does not help us understand the man of non-literate societies, nor his religions. [124] The disputed areas covered by the two disciplines are several. Anthropologists contend that the study of religion cannot possibly achieve any degree of impartiality if one sets out with the Freudian presupposition that religion is a form of social neurosis. Again, the attempt of Freud and his followers to reduce everything to the sexual dimension is considered naive and unrealistic by most anthropologists. The comparison, taken as a self-justifying assumption by Freud and many psychoanalysts, between the neurotic adult or the child in our society and the average man in non-literate cultures borders on the ludicrous to many an anthropologist who has lived and to some extent adapted himself to the life of a non-literate people.

Not all psychoanalysts have carried on those tradional Freudian slants in their studies. Roheim, Bettleheim, Kardiner and Erikson, to mention but a few, have all shed a number of Freudian assumptions in their attempts to incorporate non-literate cultures in their studies. [125] Roheim and Kardiner reject Freud's basic principle that the religious institutions of non-literate peoples are the result of the unconsciously remembered religious drama of the killing and eating of their patriarchal father. While Roheim still looks on the Oedipus complex as central to religious institutions, Kardiner shifts his emphasis to the various observable traumas produced by childrearing practices, a study of which has been carried out by several American anthropologists. [126] Bettle-

---

[123] Freud, 1913.

[124] See Kroeber, 1920 and 1939. Evans-Pritchard, 1965b, pp. 41-43, sums up most of the anthropological critique of Freud's views on non-literate peoples.

[125] See Roheim, 1950; Bettelheim, 1954; Kardiner, 1945; and Erikson, 1963.

[126] Confer Whiting and Child, 1953; Mead and Wolfenstein, 1955. Note,

heim, taking up the initiation rites of non-literate cultures, sees them as socially instituted mechanisms which are aimed at helping the individual reach sexual identity. And Erikson, writing on two American Indian cultures, takes into account the cultural context as well as psychological maturation. He looks on their religious notions in terms of basic modes of relation to the world; these relations gradually develop in the course of one's childhood and adolescence. He points out that "small differences in child-training are of lasting and sometimes fatal significance in differentiating a people's image of the world, their sense of decency and their sense of identity." [127] In harmony with contemporary anthropological theory he asserts:

> The discovery of primitive child-training systems makes it clear that primitive societies are neither infantile stages of mankind, nor arrested deviations from the proud progressive norms which we represent: they are complete forms of mature human living, often of a homogeneity and simple integrity which we at times might well envy. [128]

Studies along these lines might lead to a better understanding of religious life and of the way it develops from childhood onwards. Another promising psychological approach is the study of the influence of individuals on the religious beliefs and practices of their own culture. The rise of religious movements easily lends itself to such investigations, though few anthropologists have pursued this line of inquiry. [129] Much work has still to be done. It is interesting to note that none of these writers has gone into the question of religious experience which seems so central in any psychologically-oriented study of religion. Sociocultural studies are well ahead in their intensive field-work and their analytical studies. The assessment of Clifford Geertz on the matter seems justified. He writes:

> In all such (i.e., psychoanalytical) studies, even when individual authors have dissented from many of Freud's specific views, the basic premise has been Freudian: that religious practices can be usefully interpreted as expressions of unconscious psychological forces—and this has become, amid much polemic, an established tradition of inquiry. In recent years, however, responsible work of this type has come to question the degree in which one is justified in subjecting historically created and socially institution-

---

however, that these studies do not deal with religion exclusively and that some do not take into account the religious dimension at all.

[127] Erikson, 1963, p. 124.

[128] Erikson, 1963, p. 112.

[129] Erikson, 1958 and 1969 are two of the best studies along these lines. Comparable studies by anthropologists on prophets and religious leaders in non-literate societies are not easy to find.

alized culture forms to a system of analysis founded on the treatment of the mental illness of individuals. For this reason, the future of this approach depends perhaps more upon developments within psychoanalysis, now in a somewhat uncertain state, than within anthropology. [130]

Perhaps one of the main reasons why psychoanalytical studies have lagged behind socio-cultural ones is inherent in the discipline itself. In the study of the relations between religion and society the socially-minded student is aided by the fact that both sides of the relations he is investigating are directly observable. Similarly, the scholar who concentrates on the philosophical aspect examines the relationships between the various concepts all of which are on the same level. And Lévi-Strauss's linguistically oriented approach enjoys the same advantage. The psychologist or psychoanalyst, however, tackles the innermost feelings of man. When he talks of relations he is hampered by the fact the believer's relationships are with gods and spirits which are by definition unobservable. The student can thus scrutinize only one side of what is essentially a mutual relationship.

Psychological theories which try and explain religion in terms of awe and anxiety-reduction, though once popular, have now been largely abandoned by anthropologists. [131] Yet one can hardly neglect the emotional element often present in religious rites. Religion is not merely something thought out, or received as cultural heritage; it is also something felt or experienced by the whole man. The problem is to find concepts in which all these elements can be taken into account, and techniques for carrying out the appropriate fieldwork.

One minor attempt to do this has been the use of the term "value" which seems to be fairly common in the social sciences. [132] "A value," wrote Kluckhohn, "is a conception, explicit or implicit, distinctive of an individual or characteristic of a group, of the desirable which influences the selection from available modes, means and ends." [133] Values can synthesize cognitive and affective elements in one's orientation to an objective world. They point to people's aspirations and goals. Religions everywhere supply many values for society as well as for individuals and the study of values can contribute to our knowledge

---

[130] Geertz, 1968, p. 401.

[131] Muller, 1880; Marett, 1909; Lowie, 1924. For a critique of those views see Evans-Pritchard, 1965b, pp. 20 ff.

[132] Ayoub, 1968. "Attitudes" seems to be a more common word in psychological studies. Confer Allport, 1935; 1937, passim; Byrne, 1966, passim.

[133] Kluckhohn, 1951, p. 395.

of what are the most prized religious ideals in a particular society. Religious man may also be recognized by certain specific values.

What Eliade is saying is that otherworldliness is the most valued orientation of religious man; living in a sacred place and within sacred time, attempting to return to the origins, is the prime value in man's religious life. That otherworldliness does play a role in the religious life of man is certainly true. But so far the studies of values do not point to this specific religious ideal as the dominant theme or value in religious beliefs and practices. Here one must often distinguish carefully between the values inculcated in sacred scriptures and those which occupy the attention of most believers. Ninian Smart has shrewdly observed that religion for the masses often has immediate practical significance oriented toward worldly benefits. [134] This implies that for many believers the prime values are still this-wordly.

RELIGION AS PARADOX

Attempts to study the philosophical and experiential dimensions of religion have pointed to the fact that religion is also a paradox. In other words the system of ideas is not a completely unified one, but contains contradictions which are also experienced by religious man in his everyday life. Eliade is therefore correct in highlighting the concept of "*coincidentia oppositorum*" and in seeing it as a necessary element in religion. Religious man does not claim to know all the answers to the questions which his beliefs give rise to. Some of the key concepts in religion unite apparently incompatible ideas. Thus God is presented as someone to fear and to love, as a revealed and as a hidden entity, and as a near and yet withdrawn personality. This should not occasion surprise for "it is in the nature of the subject that there should be ambiguity and paradox." [135] Failure to understand the paradoxical nature of religion may lead a student to over-emphasize one aspect of religious beliefs. Eliade himself is a victim of this error. His insistence on the "withdrawn" god in the religions of non-literate peoples is done at the expense of neglecting the common concept of God as a near, provident father. Writing on African religions, John Mbiti has said:

> The attribute of God's trancendence must be balanced with that of His immanence, since these two are paradoxically complementary. This means that He is so "far" (transcendental) that men cannot reach Him; yet, he is

---

[134] Smart, 1969, p. 162.
[135] Evans-Pritchard, 1956a, p. 318. Cf. Radcliffe-Brown, 1951, pp. 123-124.

"near" (immanent) that He comes close to men. Many foreign writers have gone astray here, in emphasizing God's remoteness to the exclusion of his nearness. [136]

Religious man could, therefore, easily be described as a paradoxical being. The paradoxes of religion are based in part at least on the paradoxes and contradictions of life. Some of these vary according to the particular life-style of a society.

The life-style of a society is often preliminary to the study of its religion. To understand, for instance, the role cattle play in the religious rites of some people, one must first of all grasp the significance of cattle in the over-all picture of their daily life. Whether a society leads a nomadic or settled life may leave a lasting impact on their religious life. In a study of the tribal peoples of Northern Siberia, W. W. Malandra points out that the understanding of this people's nomadic existence and dependence on the roving reindeer is essential if one intends to get a picture of their religious life. Physical movement, for these peoples, is a basic mode of religious living. He writes:

Among the reindeer peoples we find a kind of religious orientation which to a large extent is comprehensible only with reference to economic and material conditions of reindeer pastoralism and hunting. We should be sensitive to the fact that the physical, economic givenness of nomadic existence will be a sine qua non for the religious experience of peoples engaged in such a life. [137]

THE STUDY OF LIFE-STYLES

The study of the life-style of a society seems to be the best starting point for the student of religions, no matter whether he is sociologically, psychologically, philosophically or religiously inclined. Such studies, however, carry with them two major methodological problems or questions. The first deals with the aim of understanding. For one does not aim at understanding paradoxes. By their very nature the paradoxes and contradictions of life are not subject to that kind of mental scrutiny which leads to perfect understanding. If religion is also a paradox, the goal should be not just understanding, but more precisely a careful presentation of the paradoxes involved and of the various ways in which people attempt to explain them and live with them. Complete intelligibility is not a feasible aim in the study of religions. Without decrying the need to promote understanding, one has to be realistic enough to admit that the nature of the subject imposes certain limits to that kind

---

[136] Mbiti, 1970, p. 33.
[137] Malandra, 1967, p. 31.

of inquiry which gives a final answer to the nature of religion. The study of religious man has to be approached with this same consideration in mind. Understanding has, therefore, to be pursued within clearly defined limits.

The second problem deals with the training of the historian of religions. If he is to present an understandable picture of a particular religion, the student of religion must be fully aware of the life-style of the society. A life-style, however, is not something one can easily comprehend in the quiet setting of a library reading-room. Participation in that life-style would seem to be a prerequisite for the student of religions who embarks on the study of the religions of non-literate societies. And since no one person can possibly participate in but a few life-styles, one must learn to rely on scholars who have participated in the life-styles of other cultures. Many historians of religions, Eliade in particular, do not seem to have sufficiently grasped the significance of this methodological procedure. While Eliade is to be highly recommended for his attempt to incorporate the study of non-literate religions in the history of religions, it has to be admitted that neither he, nor his colleagues, have developed a methodology, nor a training program for historians of religions who intend to pursue such a study.

Several proposals seem appropriate here for the development of method in the history of religions. Students who are planning to study the religions of non-literate societies should start with that kind of intensive fieldwork followed in anthropology. This method has now stood the test of time and it has been clearly defined. Secondly, the historian of religions could look to the social sciences for conceptual tools; the advantage of this will be that they will be more true to their claim that their method is inductive. Further, inspired by the procedure of the social sciences, the historians of religions will be encouraged to refine their terminology. Finally, the approach taken by social anthropologists seems to be the most suitable one for the historians of religions. Social anthropology and history are certainly closely allied and the historical bent seems appropriate for the historian of religions. Social anthropologists have produced the best writings on the religions of non-literate societies and some have taken an interpretative approach, thus reducing to a minimum purely social or psychological explanations of religion. Eliade himself, as has been pointed out, finds some of their work commendable. [138]

---

[138] Eliade, 1967e, p. 502.

One does not question the standing of the history of religions as an academic discipline on its own. But one doubts whether its aim of including all religions of mankind can be reached without adopting some of the methods of social anthropology. The relation between social anthropology and the history of religions is not, however, one-sided. Some of the leading British social anthropologists have explicitly stated that what the historians of religions say must be taken into account by anthropologists themselves. [139]

The task of the student of religions would be first to understand the cultural heritage and the life-style of a particular society whose religion he intends to study. Here he must often rely on the works of anthropologists, unless he has done fieldwork himself. Then he has to unearth the specific systems which expand human relations to the metaphysical or ontological realm. Here the studies by anthropologists on worldview, value-systems and relations between religion and society will be of immense help. The historian of religions who has pursued fieldwork may make his own contributions in this area. The final step would be that of comparison and correlation leading to some broad generalizations. The specific task of the historian of religions would seem to lie here.

RELIGION AND RELIGIOUS MAN

The task of the historian of religions is by no means an easy one. Religion is multi-dimensional: the cultural, social, psychological and philosophical dimensions are all present in every religious system. One is faced with the problem not only of uniting these elements, but also of finding a perspective which takes them all into account and a terminology which expresses them suitably. Cantwell Smith's argument that the word "religion" is not a very appropriate word seems to be supported by the anthropological studies of non-literate societies. [140] To unite the various studies of religions under the Western rubric of religion and culture, or religion and magic or some other culture-bound dichotomy does violence to the life-styles of non-literate societies where there is no word or concept equivalent to our concept of "religion." Eliade is aware of this problem, and he prefers to use such phrases as "religious man," "religious life," and "religious experience." But the problem remains unsolved; "religion" and "religious" are etymologically the same word and they share the same disadvantages. "Faiths" and

---

[139] Firth, 1959, p. 228.
[140] Smith, W. C., 1964.

"belief systems" may be more appropriate words to use. They denote a worldview and a value system which would include not just theoretical formulations but also practical, symbolical enactments of the theory. They also contain or imply fewer culture-bound dichotomies and presuppositions. What characterizes these belief systems is the fact that they are based on the assumption of non-empirical realities which influence and affect the course of human events and the world in general.

Like religion, religious man cannot be defined; one can only attempt approximate descriptions. The religious man would be the person whose beliefs lead him to establish relations which go beyond those he has with his fellow men and with the world in general. These new metaphysical relations do not necessarily contradict empirical sense data. They often supplement it, or else they exist on a separate plane of their own. Besides, they frequently have repercussions on man's relationships with his follow men and with the universe at large. The practical form these relationships take depends more often than not on the cultural and social situation. In other words, the human dimension of man's religious experience has to be sought in his own particular life-style. The holy or the sacred, to use the terminology of the historians of religions, manifests itself in the context of a personal total life-experience which is intimately related to the social and physical environment.

Especially when dealing with non-literate societies religious life must be seen in the context of life in general. Different religions and different religious men are best understood in the light of the divergent life-styles of their respective cultures. For in these societies at least, religious beliefs and practices do not constitute a separate domain of one's life. Rather religion is integrated with life to such a degree that what exists is a total way of life. The life-styles of these societies do not include the experience of the Western dichotomy between the sacred and the secular. Religion is not, as it is in the Western world, a department on its own, both intellectually and in practice.

The concept of "homo religiosus," therefore, developed in the tradition of the West may not even be a useful analytical tool for the study of the belief systems of non-literate peoples. Here all men are "religious;" the contrast between the religious and non-religious man—crucial for the understanding of belief systems in the West—does not exist. Religious specialists in non-literate cultures are considered as specialists but not as the ideal religious men. These specialists are members of the community and though respected for their abilities they participate in the common life-style of the culture to which they belong. In these societies religious man in the sense understood in Western culture does not exist. What the student comes across are people belonging to different cultural milieus where divergent belief systems, values and rituals dominate the lives of all members of society.

BIBLIOGRAPHY

Aberle, David F.
   1962 "A Note on Relative Deprivation Theory as applied to Millenarian and other Cult Movements." In: *Millennial Dreams in Action*, Sylvia Thrupp, ed. The Hague, Mouton and Company. Pp. 209-214.
   1966 "Religio-Magical Phenomena and Power, Prediction and Control." *Southwestern Journal of Anthropology*, 22: 221-230.
Ackerknech, E. H.
   1942 "Problems of Primitive Medicine." *Bulletin of the History of Medicine*, 11: 503-521.
   1946 "Natural Diseases and Rational Treatment in Primitive Medicine." *Bulletin of the History of Medicine*, 19: 467-497.
   1954 "On the Comparative Method in Anthropology." In: *Method and Perspective in Anthropology*, R. F. Spence, ed. Minneapolis, University of Minnesota Press. Pp. 117-125.
Adams, Charles J., Ed.
   1965 *A Reader's Guide to the Great Religions*. New York, Free Press.
Agassi, J. and Jarvie, J. C.
   1973 "Magic and Rationality Again." *British Journal of Sociology*, 24: 236-245.
Allan, C. H.
   1951 "A Nativistic Cult in the British Solomon Islands." *South Pacific*, 5: 79-85.
Allen, Douglas
   1972 "Mircea Eliade's Phenomenological Analysis of Religious Experience." *History of Religions*, 52: 170-186.
Allen, M. R.
   1967 *Male Cults and Secret Initiations in Melanesia*. Victoria, Australia, Melbourne University Press.
Allport, G. W.
   1935 "Attitudes." In: *A Handbook of Social Psychology*, C. C. Murchison, ed. Worcester, Mass., Clark University Press. Pp. 798-844.
   1937 *Personality. A Psychological Interpretation*. New York, Holt and Co.
Altizer, Thomas J.
   1963 *Mircea Eliade and the Dialectic of the Sacred*. Philadelphia, Westminster Press.
American Anthropological Association
   1972 *Guide to Departments of Anthropology 1972-73*.
Ames, Michael M.
   1964 "Magical-Animism and Buddhism: A Structural Analysis of the Sinhalese Religious System." In: *Religion in South Asia*, E. B. Harper, ed. Seattle, University of Washington Press. Pp. 21-52.
Anderson, Robert T.
   1971 *Traditional Europe: A Study in Anthropology and History*. Belmont, California, Wadsworth Publishing Company.
Aranguren, Jose Luis
   1974 "Freedom, Symbols and Communication." *The Annals of the American Academy of Political and Social Science*, 412: 11-20.
Ashby, Philip H.
   1963 "The History of Religions." In: *Religion*, Paul Ramsey, ed. Englewood Cliffs, Prentice-Hall. Pp. 1-49.

1967 "The History of Religions and the Study of Hinduism." In: *The History of Religions*, J. M. Kitagawa, ed. Chicago, University of Chicago Press. Pp. 143-159.
Ayoub, Victor F.
1968 "The Study of Values." In: *Introduction to Cultural Anthropology*. J. A. Clifton, ed. New York, Houghton Mifflin Co. Pp. 244-273.

Bacon, Elizabeth
1953 Review of: *Shamanism — Archaic Techniques of Ecstasy* by Mircea Eliade. *American Anthropologist*, 55: 600-601.
Barden, Garrett
1973 "Reflections of Time." *The Humanist Context*, 5: 331-344.
Barnouw, Victor
1971 *An Introduction to Anthropology*. Homewood, Illinois, The Dorsey Press, 2 vols.
Barth, F.
1974 "Analytical Dimensions in the Comparison of Social Organization." *American Anthropologist*, 76: 207-220.
Barton, R. G.
1955 *Mythology of the Ifugaos*. Austin, University of Texas Press.
Bascom, William
1968 "Folkways." *International Encyclopaedia of the Social Sciences*, vol. 5: 496-500.
Beals, Ralph L. and Hoijer, Harry
1965 *An Introduction to Anthropology*. New York, Macmillan, 3rd ed.
Beattie, John H. M.
1956 "Social Anthropology." In: *The Outline of Modern Knowledge*, A. Pryce-Jones, ed. London, V. Gollancz. Pp. 252-278.
1959a "Rituals of Nyoro Kingship." *Africa*, 29: 134-144.
1959b "Understanding and Explanation in Social Anthropology." *British Journal of Sociology*, 10: 45-60.
1960 *Bunyoro: An African Kingdom*. New York, Holt, Rinehart and Winston.
1964 *Other Cultures*. New York, Free Press.
1965 *Understanding an African Kingdom: Bunyoro*. New York, Holt, Rinehart and Winston.
1966 "Ritual and Social Change." *Man* (N.S.), 1: 60-74.
1968 "Aspects of Nyoro Symbolism." *Africa*, 38: 413-442.
Beidelman, T. O.
1961 "Right and Left among the Kaguru: A Note on Symbolic Classification." *Africa*, 31: 359-392.
1964 "Three Tales of the Living and the Dead: The Ideology of Kaguru Ancestral Propitiation." *Journal of the Royal Anthropological Institute*, 94: 109-137.
1965 "Notes on Boys' Initiation among the Ngulu of East Africa." *Man*, 65: 143-147.
1966 "The Ox and Nuer Sacrifice: Some Freudian Hypotheses about Nuer Symbolism." *Man* (N.S.), 1: 453-467.
Bellah, Robert N.
1964 "Religious Evolution." *American Sociological Review*, 29: 358-394.
1965 (Ed.) *Religion and Progress in Modern Asia*. New York, Free Press.
Benedict, Ruth
1934 *Patterns of Culture*. Boston, Houghton Mifflin, 1959.

Benz, E.
1959 "On Understanding non-Christian Religions." In: *The History of Religions*, M. Eliade and J. M. Kitagawa, eds. Chicago, University of Chicago Press. Pp. 115-131.
1961 "Theological Meaning and the History of Religions." *Journal of Religion*, 41: 1-16.
Berlin, B., Breedlove, D. E. and Raven, P.
1966 "Folk Taxonomies and Biological Classifications." In: *Cognitive Anthropology*, S. A. Tyler, ed. New York, Holt, Rinehart and Winston, 1969. Pp. 60-66.
Berndt, Catherine
1960 "The Concept of Primitive." In: *The Concept of the Primitive*, Ashley Montagu, ed. New York, Free Press, 1968. Pp. 7-31.
1964 "The Role of Native Doctors in Aboriginal Australia." In: *Magic, Faith and Healing*, A. Kiev, ed. Glencoe, Illinois, Free Press. Pp. 264-281.
Berndt, Ronald M.
1965 "The Kamano, Usurufa, Jata and Gore of the Eastern Highlands." In: *Gods, Ghosts and Men in Melanesia*, P. Lawrence and J. M. Meggitt, eds. Melbourne, Oxford University Press. Pp. 78-104.
1966 "The Wuradilagu Song Cycle of Northeastern Arnhem Land: Content and Style." In: *The Anthropologist looks at Myth*, J. Greenway, ed. Austin, Texas University Press. Pp. 195-243.
Berndt, Catherine and Berndt, Ronald, M.
1964 *The World of the First Australians.* Chicago, University of Chicago Press.
1967 *The First Australians.* Sydney, Ure Smith, 2nd ed.
Berreman, G. D.
1966 "Anemic and emetic Analysis in Social Anthropology." *American Anthropologist*, 68: 346-354.
1968a "Ethnography: Method and Product." In: *Introduction to Cultural Anthropology*, J. A. Clifton, ed. New York, Houghton Mifflin. Pp. 337-373.
1968b "Is Anthropology Alive?" In: *Readings in Anthropology*, M. H. Fried, ed. New York, Thomas Crowell, 2nd ed. Vol. 2, pp. 845-857.
Bettis, Joseph D., ed.
1969 *Phenemenology of Religion.* New York, Harper and Row.
Bettelheim, Bruno
1954 *Symbolic Wounds: Puberty Rites and the Envious Male.* New York, Collier, rev. ed., 1962.
Bharati, A.
1972 "Anthropological Approaches to the Study of Religion: Ritual and Belief Systems." In: *Biennial Review of Anthropology*, 1971, B. J. Siegel, ed. California, Stanford University Press. Pp. 230-282.
Bidney, David
1963 "So-Called Primitive Medicine and Religion." In: *Man's Image in Medicine and Anthropology*, I. Gladston, ed. New York, International Universities Press. Pp. 141-156.
1967 *Theoretical Anthropology.* New York, Schocken Books, 2nd ed.
Bilaniuk, P. B. T.
1967 "Anima naturaliter Christiana." *New Catholic Encyclopaedia*, vol. 1: 545.
Bleeker, C. J.
1954 "The Relation of the History of Religions to Kindred Religious Sciences." *Numen*, 1: 141-155.
1959 "The Phenomenological Method." *Numen*, 6: 96-111.

1962 "The Significance of Initiation." In: *Millennial Dreams in Action*, S. Thrupp, ed. The Hague, Mouton.

1963 *The Sacred Bridge. Researches into the Nature and Structure of Religion.* Leiden, E. J. Brill.

1971 "Comparing the Religio-Historical and the Theological Method." *Numen*, 18: 9-29.

1972 "The Contribution of the Phenomenology of Religion to the Study of the History of Religions." In: *Problems and Methods of the History of Religions*, H. Bianchi, C. J. Bleeker and A. Bausani, eds. Leiden, E. J. Brill. Pp. 35-45.

Boas, Franz

1896 "The Limitations of the Comparative Method of Anthropology." In: *Race, Language and Culture*, by F. Boas. New York, Free Press, 1966. Pp. 270-280.

1940 *Race, Language and Culture.* New York, Macmillan.

Bock, Philip K.

1970 *Culture Shock.* New York, A. Knopf.

1974 *Modern Cultural Anthropology.* New York, A Knopf, 2nd ed.

Bohannan, Paul

1953 "Concepts of Time among the Tiv of Nigeria." In: *Myth and Cosmos*, J. Middleton, ed. New York, Natural History Press, 1967. Pp. 315-329.

1963 *Social Anthropology.* New York, Holt, Rinehart and Winston.

Bolle, K. W.

1957 "History of Religions with a Hermeneutic oriented toward a Christian Theology?" In: *The History of Religions*, J. M. Kitagawa, ed. Chicago, University of Chicago Press. Pp. 89-118.

1967 "Introduction." In: *The Study of Religion* by J. de Vries. New York, Harcourt, Brace and World Inc. Pp. vii-xxiii .

Bouquet, A. C.

1956 *Comparative Religion.* Baltimore, Pelican.

Bourdillon, Michael

1968 "Lévi-Strauss and Myth." *The Month*, 225: 149-163.

1972 "The Manipulation of Myth in a Tavara Chiefdom." *Africa*, 42: 112-121.

Brace, C. L.

1967 *The Stages of Human Evolution.* Englewood Cliffs, Prentice-Hall.

Bradbury, R. E.

1960 "Father and Son in Edo Mortuary Ritual." In: *African Systems of Thought*, M. Fortes and G. Dieterlen, eds. London, Oxford University Press, 1965. Pp. 96-115.

1963 "Fathers, Elders and Ghosts in Edo Religion." In: *Anthropological Approaches to the Study of Religion*, M. Banton, ed. London, Tavistock, 1966. Pp. 127-153.

Brandon, S. F. G.

1959 "The Origin of Religion." *The Hibbert Journal*, 57: 349-355.

1962 *Man and His Destiny in the Great Religions.* Toronto, University of Toronto Press.

1967 *The Judgment of the Dead.* London, Weidenfeld and Nicholson.

Braroe, N. W. and Hicks, G. L.

1967 "Observations on the Mystique of Anthropology." *Sociological Quarterly*, 8: 173-186.

Brauer, Jerald C.

1967 "Preface." In: *The History of Religions*, J. M. Kitagawa, ed. Chicago, University of Chicago Press. Pp. v-x.

Bright, William
1968 "Language and Culture." *International Encyclopaedia of the Social Sciences*, vol. 9: 18-22.
Brown, Ina C.
1963 *Understanding other Cultures*. Englewood Cliffs, Prentice-Hall.
Brown, Robert
1963 *Explanation in Social Science*. Chicago, Aldine.
Bruijn, J. V. de
1951 "The Mansren Cult of Biak." *South Pacific,* 5: 1-10.
Bukovsky, J. and Riga, P.
1967 "Suffering." *The New Catholic Encyclopaedia*, vol. 13: 775-777.
Bulmer, R. H. N.
1965 "The Kyaka of the Western Highland." In: *Gods, Ghosts and Men in Melanesia*, P. Lawrence and J. M. Meggitt, eds. Melbourne, Oxford University Press. Pp. 132-161.
Bunzel, Ruth
1932 *Introduction to Zuni Ceremonialism*. Washington, D.C., Bureau of American Mythology.
Burridge, K. O. L.
1957 "Social Implications of some Tangu Myths." In: *Myth and Cosmos*, J. Middleton, ed. New York, Natural History Press, 1967. Pp. 27-46.
1960 *Mambu. A Melanesian Millenium*. New York, Barnes and Noble.
1964 "Lévi-Strauss and Myth." In: *The Structural Study of Myth and Totemism*, E. Leach, ed. London, Tavistock. Pp. 91-115.
1969 *New Heaven, New Earth. A Study of Millennarian Activities*. Oxford, Blackwell.
Burtt, Edwin A.
1957 *Man Seeks the Divine*. New York, Harper and Row, 2nd ed.
Butt, Audrey
1960 "The Birth of a Religion." In: *Gods and Rituals,* J. Middleton, ed. New York, Natural History Press, 1967. Pp. 377-435.
Byrne, Donn
1966 *Introduction to Personality. A Research Approach*. Englewood Cliffs, Prentice-Hall.

Cameron, A. L. P.
1885 "Notes on Some Tribes of New South Wales." *Journal of the Royal Anthropological Institute*, 14: 344-370.
Cantor, Norman, and Schneider, Richard
1967 *How to Study History*. New York, Thomas Crowell.
Carlyle, Mary L.
1956 "A Survey of Glossolalia and Related Phenomena in non-Christian Religions." *American Anthropologist*, 58: 75-96.
Carr, Edward Hallet
1967 *What Is History?* New York, Knopf.
Chaney, Richard P.
1973 "Comparative Analysis and Retroductive Reasoning or Conclusions in Search of a Premise." *American Anthropologist*, 75: 1358-1375.
Childe, Gordon V.
1951 *Social Evolution*. New York, Schuman.
Clifton, J. A., ed.
1968 *Introduction to Cultural Anthropology*. New York, Houghton Mifflin.

Cohen, Yehudi A.
  1964 *The Transition from Childhood to Adolescence*. Chicago, Aldine.
  1968 (Ed.) *Man in Adaptation*. 2 vols. Chicago, Aldine.
Colby, B. N.
  1966 "Ethnographic Semantics: A Preliminary Survey." *Current Anthropology*, 7: 3-32.
Collier, John Jr.
  1967 *Visual Anthropology: Photography as a Research Method*. New York, Holt, Rinehart and Winston.
Colson, E.
  1954 "Ancestral Spirits among the Plateau Tonga." In: *Cultures and Societies of Africa*, S. and P. Ottenberg, eds. New York, Random House, 1960. Pp. 372-387.
Conklin, H.
  1955 "Hanunoo Color Categories." *Southwestern Journal of Anthropology*, 11: 339-344.
  1962 "Lexicographical Treatment of Folk Taxonomies." In: *Cognitive Anthropology*, S. A. Tyler, ed. New York, Holt, Rinehart and Winston, 1968. Pp. 41-59.
  1968 "Ethnography." *International Encyclopaedia of the Social Sciences*, vol. 5: 172-178.
Count, E.
  1960 "Myth as World View: a Biosocial Synthesis." In: *Culture in History*, J. Diamond, ed. New York, Columbia University Press, Pp. 580-630.
Crawford, J. R.
  1967 *Witchcraft and Sorcery in Rhodesia*. London, Oxford University Press.

Danielou, Jean
  1959 "Phenomenology of Religions and Philosophy of Religion." In: *The History of Religions*, M. Eliade and J. M. Kitagawa, eds. Chicago, University of Chicago Press. Pp. 67-85.
Darnell, Regna
  1974 *Readings in the History of Anthropology*. New York, Harper and Row.
De Lubac, H.
  1934 "Remarques sur l'Histoire du Mot Surnaturel." *Nouvelle Revue Théologique* 61: 225-249.
Derrett, J. M. Duncan
  1973 "Religious Hair." *Man*, 8: 100-103.
De Vries, Jan
  1967 *The Study of the Religion*. New York, Harcourt, Brace and World.
Dhavamony, M.
  1969 "The History of Religions and Theology." *Gregorianum*, 50: 805-836.
Diamond, Stanley
  1963 "The Search for the Primitive." In: *The Concept of the Primitive*, Ashley Montagu, ed. New York, Free Press, 1968. Pp. 96-147.
Dorson, Richard M.
  1973 "Mythology and Folklore." In: *Annual Review of Anthropology*, vol. 2, B. J. Siegel, ed. California, Annual Reviews Inc. Pp. 107-126.
Douglas, Mary
  1955 "Social and Religious Symbolism of the Lele of the Kasai." *Zaire*, 9: 385-402.
  1957 "Animals in Lele Religious Thought." In: *Myth and Cosmos*, J. Middleton, ed. New York, Natural History Press, 1967. Pp. 231-247.

1964 "The Meaning of Myth, with Special Reference to 'La Geste d'Asdiwal'."
In: *The Structural Study of Myth and Totemism*, E. Leach, ed. London,
Tavistock, 1967. Pp. 49-69.
1967 "Witch Beliefs in Central Africa." *Africa*, 37: 72-80.
1970 *Natural Symbols. Explorations in Cosmology*. New York, Pantheon
Books.

Downs, James F.
1973 *Human Nature; An Introduction to Cultural Anthropology*. New York,
Glencoe Press.

Dozier, Edward P.
1955 "The Concepts of 'Primitive' and 'Native' in Anthropology." In: *The
Concept of the Primitive*, Ashley Montagu, ed. New York, Free Press,
1968. Pp. 228-256.

Driver, Harold E.
1968 "Robert E. Lowie." *International Encyclopaedia of the Social Sciences*,
vol. 9: 480-483.

Dubois, Cora
1963 "Anthropology: Its Present Interests." In: *The Behavioral Sciences
Today*, B. Berelson, ed. New York, Basic Books. Pp. 26-37.

Dundes, Alan, ed.
1968 *Everyman His Way. Readings in Cultural Anthropology*, Englewood
Cliffs, Prentice-Hall.

Durbin, Marshall
1967 "Language." In: *Biennial Review of Anthropology*, B. J. Siegal and
A. R. Beals, eds. Stanford, California, Stanford University Press. Pp.
209-251.

Earhart, H. Byron
1967 "Toward a Unified Interpretation of Japanese Religion." In: *The History
of Religions*, J. M. Kitagawa, ed. Chicago, University of Chicago Press.
Pp. 195-225.

Edel, May
1957 *The Chiga of Western Uganda*. London, Oxford University Press.

Edel, May and Edel, Abraham
1968 *Anthropology and Ethics*. Cleveland, Case Western Reserve University
Press, 2nd ed.

Eggan, Fred
1953 "Social Anthropology and the Method of Controlled Comparison." In:
Readings in Cross-Cultural Methodology, F. W. Moore, ed. HRAF
Press, Pp. 107-127.
1962 "Some Reflections on the Comparative Method in Anthropology." In:
Context and Meaning in Cultural Anthropology, M. Spiro, ed. New York,
Free Press, 1965. Pp. 357-371.
1968 "One Hundred Years of Social Anthropology." In: *One Hundred Years
of Anthropology*, J. O. Brew, ed. Cambridge, Harvard University Press.
Pp. 119-149.

Eliade, Mircea
1938 *Metallurgy, Magic and Alchemy*. Paris, Librairie Orientale, Paul
Geuthner.
1946 "Le problème du Chamanisme." *Revue de l'Histoire des Religions*, 131:
5-52.
1949 "Shamanism." In: *Forgotten Religions*, V. Ferm, ed. New York, Philosophical Library. Pp. 297-308.

1952 "Mythe et Histoire dans la Littérature Orale." *Bulletin du Centre Romain de Recherches* 1: 26-31.

1954a "The Problem of the Origins of Yoga." In: *Forms and Techniques of Altruistic and Spiritual Growth*, P. A. Sorokin, ed. Boston, Beacon Press. Pp. 63-70.

1954b "Shamanism and Indian Yoga Techniques." In: *Forms and Techniques of Altruistic and Spiritual Growth*, P. A. Sorokin, ed. Boston, Beacon Press. Pp. 70-84.

1955a "Littérature Orale." *Encyclopédie de la Pléiade,* R. Queneau, éditeur. Paris, Gallimard. Vol. 1, pp. 3-26.

1955b "Symbolisme et Rituels Métallurgiques Babyloniens." In: *Studien zur Analytischen Psychologie C. G. Jung.* C. G. Jung Institute, Zurich, Roschen Verlag. Vol. 2, pp. 42-46.

1955c "Smiths, Shamans and Mystagogues." *East and West*, 6: 206-215.

1955d "Aspects Initiatiques de l'Alchimie Orient-Occident." *Archivio de Filosofia: Studi di Filosofia della Religione*, no. 2, pp. 215-225.

1957a "La Vertu Créatrice du Mythe." *Eranos-Jahrbuch*, 25: 59-85.

1957b "Time and Eternity in Indian Thought." In: *Man and Time*, J. Campbell, ed. New York, Pantheon. Pp. 173-200.

1958a *Yoga, Immortality and Freedom.* New York, Routledge and Kegan Paul.

1958b *Patterns in Comparative Religion.* New York, Sheed and Ward. (First published in 1949.)

1958c "The Prestige of the Cosmogonic Myth." *Diogenes*, 23: 1-13.

1959a *Cosmos and History. The Myth of the Eternal Return.* New York, Harper Torchbooks. (First published in 1954).

1959b "Methodological Remarks on the Study of Religious Symbolism." In: *The History of Religions*, M. Eliade and J. M. Kitagawa, eds. Chicago, University of Chicago Press. Pp. 86-107.

1960a *Myths, Dreams and Mysteries.* New York, Harper and Brothers.

1960b "History and the Cyclical View of Time." *Perspectives*, 5: 11-14.

1960c "Structure and Changes in the History of Religions." In: *City Invincible.* Chicago, University of Chicago Press. Pp. 351-366.

1960d "The Structure of Religious Symbolism." *Proceedings of the IX International Congress for the History of Religions.* Tokyo, Maruzen. Pp. 506-512.

1960e "Encounter at Ascona." In: *Spiritual Disciplines*, J. Campbell, ed. New York, Pantheon. Pp. xvii-xxi.

1961a *The Sacred and the Profane. The Nature of Religion.* New York, Harcourt, Brace and Co. (First published in 1957.)

1961b "Recent Works on Shamanism." *History of Religions*, 1: 152-186.

1961c "Note pour un Humanisme." *La Nouvelle Revue Française*, 9: 872-878.

1961d "Art and the Divine." *Encyclopaedia of World Art*, vol. 4, pp. 382-387.

1962a *The Forge and the Crucible.* New York, Harper and Brothers. (First published in 1956.)

1962b "Cargo-Cults and Cosmic Regeneration." In: *Millennial Dreams in Action*, S. Thrupp, ed. The Hague, Mouton. Pp. 139-143.

1963a *Myth and Reality.* New York, Harper and Row.

1963b "Yoga and Modern Philosophy." *Journal of General Education*, 15: 124-137.

1964a *Shamanism: Archaic Techniques of Ecstasy.* New York, Routledge and Kegan Paul. (First published in 1951.)

1964b "Introduction à l'Étude des Mythes." *Acta Philosophica et Theologica*, 2: 145-159.

186   BIBLIOGRAPHY

1964c "Myth and Reality." In: *Alienation. The Cultural Climate of Modern Man*, G. Sykes, ed. New York, Braziller. Vol. 2, pp. 748-753.
1965a *Rites and Symbols of Initiation*. New York, Harper Torchbooks. (First published in 1958.)
1965b *The Two and the One*. New York, Harper Torchbooks.
1965c "L'Initiation et le Monde Moderne." In: *Initiation*, C. J. Bleeker, ed. Leiden, E. J. Brill. Pp. 1-14.
1966   "Australian Religions. Part I: An Introduction." *History of Religions*, 6: 108-134.
1967a *From Primitives to Zen. A Thematic Source Book on the History of Religions*. New York, Harper and Row.
1967b "Australian Religions. Part II: An Introduction." *History of Religions*, 6: 208-35.
1967c "Australian Religions. Part III: Initiation Rites and Secret Cults." *History of Religions*, 7: 61-90.
1967d "Australian Religions. Part IV: The Medicine Men and Their Supernatural Models." *History of Religions*, 7: 159-83.
1967e "Understanding Primitive Religions." In: *Glaube, Geist, Geschichte. Festschrift für Ernst Benz*, G. Muller and W. Zeller, eds. Leiden, E. J. Brill. Pp. 498-505.
1968a "The Forge and the Crucible: A Postscript." *History of Religions*, 8: 74-88.
1968b "Australian Religions. Part V: Death, Eschatology and Some Conclusions." *History of Religions*, 7: 244-68.
1968c "Notes on the Symbolism of the Arrow." In: *Religions in Antiquity*, J. Neusner, ed. Leiden, E. J. Brill. Pp. 463-75.
1969a *The Quest*. Chicago, University of Chicago Press.
1969b *Pantajali and Yoga*. New York, Funk and Wagnalls.
1969c *Images and Symbols. Studies in Religious Symbolism*. New York, Sheed and Ward. (First published in 1952.)
1969d "South American High Gods. Part I." *History of Religions*, 8: 338-54.
1970   *Two Tales of the Occult*. New York, McGraw-Hill.
1971a "South American High Gods. Part II." *History of Religions*, 10: 234-266.
1971b "Spirit, Light and Seed." *History of Religions*, 11: 1-30.
1972   *Zalmoxis, The Vanishing God*. Chicago, University of Chicago Press.
1973   "The Dragon and the Shaman. Notes on a South American Mythology." In: *Man and his Salvation*, Eric J. Sharpe and John R. Hinnells, eds. Great Britain, Manchester University Press. Pp. 99-105.
Elkin, A. P.
1954   *The Australian Aborigines*. New York, Doubleday, 1964.
Ember, Carol R. and Ember, Melvin
1973   *Anthropology*. New York, Appleton-Century-Crofts.
Embree, Ainslie, ed.
1966   *The Hindu Tradition*. New York, Modern Library.
Erasmus, Charles J.
1952   "Changing Folk Belief and the Relativity of Empirical Knowledge." *Southwestern Journal of Anthropology*, 8: 411-428.
Erikson, Erik H.
1958   *Young Man Luther*. New York, Norton.
1963   *Childhood and Society*. New York, Norton, 2nd. ed.
1969   *Ghandi's Truth*. New York, Norton.
Evans-Pritchard, E. E.
1929   "The Morphology and Function of Magic: A Comparative Study of

Trobriand and Zande Ritual and Spells." In: *Magic, Witchcraft and Curing*, J. Middleton, ed. New York, Natural History Press, 1967. Pp. 1-22.

1934 "Lévy-Bruhl's Theory of Primitive Mentality." *Bulletin of the Faculty of Arts*, vol. 2. Cairo, Egyptian University.

1937 *Witchcraft, Oracles and Magic among the Azande*. Oxford, Clarendon Press.

1939 "Nuer Time-Reckoning." *Africa*, 12: 189-216.

1940a *The Political System of the Anuak of the Anglo-Egyptian Sudan*. London, Percy Lund, Humphries and Co.

1940b "The Nuer of the South Sudan." In: *African Political Systems*, M. Fortes and E. E. Evans-Pritchard, eds. Glencoe, Free Press. Pp. 272-296.

1949 *The Sanusi of Cyrenaica*. London, Oxford University Press.

1950 "Social Anthropology: Past and Present." In: *Social Anthropology and Other Essays* by E. E. Evans-Pritchard. Glencoe, Free Press, 1962. Pp. 135-154.

1951 "Social Anthropology." In: *Social Anthropology and Other Essays*. Glencoe, Free Press, 1962. Pp. 1-134.

1953a "Nuer Spear Symbolism." *Anthropological Quarterly*, 26: 1-19.

1953b "The Nuer Concept of Spirit and Its Relation to the Social Order." In: *Myth and Cosmos*, J. Middleton, ed. New York, Natural History Press, 1967. Pp. 109-126.

1954 "A Problem of Nuer Religious Thought." In: *Myth and Cosmos*, J. Middleton, ed. New York, Natural History Press, 1967. Pp. 127-148.

1956a *Nuer Religion*. London, Oxford University Press.

1956b "Sangi, Characteristic Feature of Zande Language and Thought." In: *Social Anthropology and Other Essays* by E. E. Evans-Pritchard. New York, Free Press, 1962. Pp. 330-354.

1959a "Religion and the Anthropologist." In: *Social Anthropology and Other Essays* by E. E. Evans-Pritchard. New York, Free Press, 1962. Pp. 155-191.

1959b "Religions." In: *The Institutions of Primitive Society*. New York, Free Press, 1962. Pp. 1-11.

1961 "Anthropology and History." In: *Social Anthropology and Other Essays* by E. E. Evans-Pritchard. New York, Free Press, 1962. Pp. 172-191.

1963 "The Comparative Method in Social Anthropology." In. *The Position of Women in Primitive Societies and Other Essays in Social Anthropology*. New York, Free Press, 1965. Pp. 13-36.

1965a *The Position of Women in Primitive Societies and Other Essays in Social Anthropology*. New York, Free Press.

1965b *Theories of Primitive Religion*. London, Oxford University Press.

1967 *The Zande Trickster*. London, Oxford University Press.

Fabrega, H.
1972 "Medical Anthropology." In: *Biennial Review of Anthropology*, 1971, B. J. Siegel, ed. California, Stanford University Press. Pp. 167-229.

Fakhry, Ahmed
1961 *The Pyramids*. Chicago, University of Chicago Press.

Faron, L. C.
1961 "On Ancestor Propitiation among the Mapuche of Central Chile." *American Anthropologist*, 63: 824-829.

Fenton, John Y.
1970 "Reductionism in the Study of Religion." *Soundings*, 53: 61-76.

Ferré, Frederick
  1970 "The Definition of Religion." *Journal of the American Academy of Religion*, 38: 3-16.
Field, M. J.
  1937 *Religion and Medicine of the Ga People.* London, Oxford University Press.
Firth, Raymond
  1950 "An Anthropological View of Mysticism." In: *Essays on Social Organization and Values,* by R. Firth. London, Athlone Press, 1964. Pp. 294-306.
  1951 *Elements of Social Organization.* London, Watts and Co.
  1953 "The Study of Values by Social Anthropologists." In: *Essays on Social Organization and Values,* by R. Firth. London, The Athlone Press, 1964. Pp. 206-224.
  1955a "The Theory on 'Cargo-Cult'." *Man,* 55: 130-132.
  1955b "The Fate of the Soul." In: *Tikopia Ritual and Belief,* by R. Firth. Boston, Beacon Press, 1967. Pp. 330-353.
  1958 *Social Anthropology as Science and Art.* Dunedin, University of Otago.
  1959 "Problem and Assumption in an Anthropological Study of Religion." In: *Essays on Social Organization and Values* by R. Firth. London, The Athlone Press, 1964. Pp. 225-256.
  1960 "The Plasticity of Myth." In: *Tikopia Ritual and Belief,* by R. Firth. Boston, Beacon Press, 1967. Pp. 284-292.
  1961 "Oral Tradition in Relation to Social Status." In: *Studies on Mythology,* R. A. Georges, ed. Homewood, Dorsey Press, 1968. Pp. 168-183.
  1963a *We, The Tikopia.* Boston, Beacon Press. Abridged ed.
  1963b "Offering and Sacrifice: Problems of Organization." *Journal of the Royal Anthropological Institute,* 93: 12-24.
  1968a "Social Anthropology." *International Encyclopaedia of the Social Sciences,* vol. 1: 320-324.
  1968b "Gods and God: An Anthropologist's Standpoint." In: *The Humanist Outlook,* A. J. Ayer, ed. London, Pemberton. Pp. 31-44.
  1973 *Symbols: Public and Private.* Ithaca, New York, Cornell University Press.
Fischer, John L.
  1966a "A Ponapean Oedipal Tale: Structural and Socio-Psychological Analysis." In: *The Anthropologist Looks at Myth,* J. Greenway, ed. Austin, University of Texas Press. Pp. 109-129.
  1966b "Syntax and Social Structure." In: *Sociolinguistics,* W. Bright, ed. New York, Mouton and Co. Pp. 168-187.
Forde, Daryll
  1949 "First Fruit Rituals." In: *Yako Studies* by Daryll Forde. London, Oxford University Press, 1964. Pp. 109-129.
  1950a *Habitat, Economy and Society.* London, Methuen.
  1950b "Double Descent among the Yako." In: *African Systems of Kinship and Marriage,* A. R. Radcliffe-Brown and D. Forde, eds. London, Oxford University Press. Pp. 285-332.
Fortes, M.
  1959 *Oedipus and Job in West African Religion.* Cambridge, Cambridge University Press.
  1960 "Some Reflections on Ancestor Worship." In: *African Systems of Thought,* M. Fortes and G. Dieterlen, eds. London, Oxford University Press, 1965. Pp. 122-144.
  1961 "Pietas in Ancestor Worship." *Journal of the Royal Anthropological Institute,* 91: 166-191.

1962 "Ritual Office in Tribal Society." In: *Essays on the Ritual of Social Relations*, M. Gluckman, ed. Manchester, Manchester University Press. Pp. 53-88.

1966 "Religious Premises and Logical Technique in Divinatory Ritual." In: *Philosophical Transactions of the Royal Society of London*. Pp. 409-422.

Fortes, M. and Dieterlen, G., eds.

1965 *African Systems of Thought*. London, Oxford University Press.

Fortune, R. F.

1932 *Sorcerers of Dobu*. New York, Dutton and Co., 1963.

Fox, Robin

1967 *Kinship and Marriage*. Baltimore, Pelican.

Frake, Charles O.

1961 "The Diagnosis of Disease among the Subanun of Mindanao." *American Anthropologist*, 63: 111-132.

1962 "The Enthnographic Study of Cognitive Systems." In: *Cognitive Anthropology*, S. A. Tyler, ed. Holt, Rinehart and Winston, 1968. Pp. 28-41.

1964 "Notes on Queries in Ethnography." *American Anthropologist*, 66: 132-145.

1965 "A Structural Description of Subanun 'Religious Behavior'." In: *Reader in Comparative Religion*, W. A. Lessa and E. Z. Vogt, eds. New York, Harper and Row. Pp. 582-593.

Frazer, James

1890 *The Golden Bough*, Th. Gaster, ed. New Yorker, Mentor, 1959.

Freud, Sigmund

1913 *Totem and Taboo*. New York, Vintage Books, 1946.

Fried, Morton H.

1968 *Readings in Anthropology*. Vol. 2, *Cultural Anthropology*. New York, T. Y. Crowell Co.

Frisbie, Charlotte J.

1967 *Kinaalda'. A Study of the Navaho Girl's Puberty Ceremony*. Middleton, Connecticut, Weslyan University Press.

Frye, Northrop

1959 "World Enough Without Time." *The Hudson Review*, 12: 423-431.

Furer-Haimendorf, C. von

1962 "Morality and the Social Order among the Apa Tanis." In: *Gods and Rituals*, J. Middleton, ed. New York, Natural History Press, 1967. Pp. 1-19.

1967 *Morals and Merits*. Chicago, University of Chicago Press.

Gallus, A.

1972 "A Biofunctional Theory of Religion." *Current Anthropologist*, 13: 543-558.

Geertz, Clifford

1957 "Ethos, World-View and the Analysis of Sacred Symbols." *Antioch Review*, 17: 421-437.

1960 *The Religion of Java*. Glencoe, Free Press.

1964 "The Transition to Humanity." In: *Horizons of Anthropology*, S. Tax, ed. Chicago, Aldine. Pp. 37-48.

1965 "The Impact of the Concept of Culture on the Concept of Man." In: *Man in Adaptation*, Y. Cohen, ed. Chicago, Aldine, 1968. Vol. 2, pp. 17-29.

1966 "Religion as a Cultural System." In: *Anthropological Approaches to the Study of Religion*, M. Banton, ed. London, Tavistock. Pp. 1-46.

1968 "Religion. Anthropological Study." *International Encyclopaedia of the Social Sciences*, vol. 11: 398-406.

Geiser, Peter
1973 "The Myth of the Dam." *American Anthropologist,* 75: 184-194.
Gennep, Arnold van
1908 *The Rites of Passage.* London, Routledge and Kegan Paul, 1960.
Georges, Robert A.
1968 "Prologue." In: *Studies on Mythology,* R. A. Georges, ed. Homewood, Illinois, Dorsey Press. Pp. 1-14.
Glasse, R. M.
1965 "The Huli of the Southern Highlands." In: *Gods, Ghosts and Men in Melanesia,* P. Lawrence and J. M. Meggitt, eds. Melbourne, Melbourne University Press. Pp. 27-49.
Gleason, H. A., Jr.
1962 "Linguistics in the Service of the Church." *Practical Anthropology,* 9: 205-219.
Glick, Leonard B.
1967 "Medicine as an Ethnographic Category: The Gini of New Guinea Highlands." *Ethnology,* 6: 31-56.
Glover, Jesse R.
1972 "The Role of the Witch in Gurung Society." *The Eastern Anthropologist,* 25: 221-226.
Gluckman, Max
1940 "The Kingdom of the Zulu of South Africa." In: *African Political Systems,* E. E. Evans-Pritchard and M. Fortes, eds. London, Oxford University Press. Pp. 22-55.
1952 *Rituals of Rebellion in South-East Africa.* Manchester, Manchester University Press.
1962 "Les Rites de Passage." In: *Essays on the Ritual of Social Relations.* Manchester, Manchester University Press. Pp. 1-52.
Gluckman, Max and Eggan, Fred
1965 "Introduction." In: *The Relevance of Models for Social Anthropology,* M. Banton, ed. London, Tavistock. Pp. ix-xl.
1966 "Introduction." In: *Anthropological Approaches to the Study of Religion,* M. Banton, ed. London, Tavistock. Pp. xi-xlii.
Goffman, E.
1959 *The Presentation of Self in Everyday Life.* New York, Doubleday.
Goldenweiser, Alexander
1925 "Cultural Anthropology." In: *The History and Prospects of the Social Sciences,* H. E. Barnes, ed. New York, Knopf. Pp. 210-254.
Goldschmidt, Walter
1968 "The Anthropological Study of Modern Society." *International Encyclopaedia of the Social Sciences,* vol. 1: 330-339.
Goode, William J.
1951 *Religion among the Primitives.* Glencoe, Free Press.
Goodenough, Ward H.
1964 "Cultural Anthropology and Linguistics." In: *Language in Culture and Society,* Dell Hymes, ed. New York, Harper and Row. Pp. 36-39.
Goody, Jack
1961 "Religion and Ritual: The Definitional Problem." *British Journal of Sociology,* 12: 142-164.
1968 "Time: Social Organization." *International Encyclopaedia of the Social Sciences,* vol. 16: 30-42.
Goody, Jack and Watt, Ian
1962 "The Consequences of Literacy." *Comparative Studies in Society and History,* 5: 314-345.

Gorman, Carl N.
  1973 "Navajo Vision of Earth and Man." *Indian Historian,* 6: 19-22.
Gottschalk, Louis, ed.
  1963 *Generalization in the Writings of History.* A Report of the Committee on Historical Analysis of the Social Sciences Research Council. Chicago, University of Chicago Press.
Greenberg, Joseph H.
  1964 "Linguistics and Ethnology." In: *Language in Culture and Society,* Dell Hymes, ed. New York, Harper and Row. Pp. 27-31.
  1968 "Anthropology: The Field." *International Encyclopaedia of the Social Sciences,* vol. 1: 304-313.
Greenway, John, ed.
  1965 *The Primitive Reader.* Hatboro, Pa., Folklore Associates.
  1966 *The Anthropologists Looks at Myth.* Austin, University of Texas Press.
Gruhn, Ruth
  1971 "A Preliminary Analysis of the World-view of the Tsivitca Movement in Northern North America." *Canadian Review of Sociology and Anthropology,* 8: 185-189.
Gualtieri, A. R.
  1967 "What is Comparative Religion Comparing?" *Journal for the Scientific Study of Religion,* 6: 31-39.
Gudschinsky, Sarah C.
  1967 *How to Learn an Unwritten Language.* New York, Holt, Rinehard and Winston.
Guiteras-Holmes, C.
  1961 *Perils of the Soul: The World View of the Tzotzil Indian.* New York, Free Press.
Gunther, Erna
  1968 "Art in the Life of Primitive Peoples." In: *Introduction to Cultural Anthropology,* J. A. Clifton, ed. New York, Houghton Mifflin. Pp. 76-114.

Haddon, A. C.
  1910 *History of Anthropology.* London, Watts and Co.
Hallowell, A. I.
  1935 "Primitive Concepts of Disease." *American Anthropologist,* 37: 365-368.
  1960 "Ojibwa Ontology, Behavior and World View." In: *Culture in History,* J. Diamond, ed. New York, Columbia University Press. Pp. 19-52.
Hallpike, C. R.
  1969 "Social Hair." *Man* (N.S.), 4: 256-264.
Hammond, Peter B.
  1971 *An Introduction to Cultural and Social Anthropology.* New York, Macmillan.
Harper, E. B., ed.
  1964 *Religion in South Asia.* Seattle, Washington University Press.
Harris, Marvin
  1966 "The Cultural Ecology of India's Sacred Cow." *Current Anthropology,* 7: 51-66.
  1968 *The Rise of Anthropological Theory.* New York, Thomas Crowell.
Hart, Donn V. and Hart, Harriet, C.
  1966 "Maka-andog: A Reconstructed Myth from Eastern Samar, Philippines." In: *The Anthropologists Looks at Myth,* J. Greenway, ed. Austin, Texas University Press. Pp. 84-108.

Haviland, William A.
  1974 *Anthropology*. New York, Holt, Rinehart and Winston.
Hayley, Audrey
  1968 "Symbolic Equations: The Ox and the Cucumber." *Man* (N.S.), 3:
       262-271.
Haynes, Renee
  1965 Review of: *The Two and the One* by Mircea Eliade. *The Tablet*, July
       17th, 1965, pp. 803-804.
Hays, H. R.
  1958 *From Ape to Angel: An Informal History of Social Anthropology*. New
       York, Capricorn Books.
Henderson, Joseph L. and Oakes, Maud
  1963 *The Wisdom of the Serpent. The Myths of Death, Rebirth and Resur-
       rection*. New York, Braziller.
Herskovits, Melville J.
  1948 *Man and His Works. The Science of Cultural Anthropology*. New York,
       Knopf.
  1965 "A Genealogy of Ethnological Theory." In: *Context and Meaning in
       Cultural Anthropology*, M. Spiro, ed. New York, Free Press. Pp. 403-415.
Hobsbawm, E. J.
  1959 *Primitive Rebels*. New York, Norton and Co.
Hodgen, Margaret T.
  1964 *Early Anthropology in the Sixteenth and Seventeenth Centuries*. Phila-
       delphia, University of Pennnsylvania Press.
Hoebel, E. Adamson
  1954 *The Law of Primitive Man*. Cambridge, Harvard University Press.
  1972 *Anthropology: The Study of Man*. New York, McGraw-Hill, 4th. ed.
Hoijer, Harry
  1953 "The Relation of Language to Culture." In: *Anthropology Today*, A. L.
       Kroeber, ed. Chicago, University of Chicago Press. Pp. 554-573.
Holloway, Ralph L., Jr.
  1969 "Culture: A Human Domain." *Current Anthropology*, 10: 395-412.
Holmberg, Alan R.
  1968 "Among the Siriono Nomads of the Long Bow." In: *Readings in Anthro-
       pology*, M. Fried, ed. New York, Thomas Crowell. Vol. 2, pp. 136-141.
Homans, George C.
  1967 *The Nature of Social Science*. New York, Harcourt, Brace and World.
Horner, George R.
  1966 "A Bulu Folktale: Content and Analysis." In: *The Anthropologist Looks
       at Myth*, J. Greenway, ed. Austin, Texas University Press. Pp. 145-156.
Horton, Robin
  1960a "A Definition of Religion and Its Uses." *Journal of the Royal Anthro-
        pological Institute*, 90: 201-226.
  1960b *The Gods as Guests. An Aspect of Kalabari Religious Life*. Lagos, Nige-
        ria Magazine.
  1962a "The Kalabari World-View: An Outline and Interpretation." *Africa*,
        32: 197-219.
  1962b "The High God: A Commentary on Father O'Connell's Paper." *Man*,
        62: 137-140.
  1964 "Ritual Man in Africa." *Africa*, 34: 85-104.
  1967a "African Traditional Thought and Western Culture. Part I, From
        Tradition to Science." *Africa*, 37: 50-71.
  1967b "African Traditional Thought and Western Science. Part II, The 'Closed'
        and 'Open' Predicaments." *Africa*, 37: 155-187.

Hostetler, J. A.
1964 "The Amish Use of Symbols and Their Function in Bounding the Community." *Journal of the Royal Anthropological Institute*, 94: 11-21.
Hostetler, J. A. and Huntington, G. E.
1967 *The Hutterites in North America*. New York, Holt, Rinehart and Winston.
Howells, William
1948 *The Heathens*. New York, Doubleday, 1962.
Hsu, F. L. K.
1952 *Religion, Science and Human Crisis*. New York, Grove Press.
1969 *The Study of Literate Civilizations*. New York, Holt, Rinehart and Winston.
1972 (Ed.) *Psychological Anthropology*. Cambridge, Mass., Schenkman.
Hughes, Charles C.
1968 "Ethnomedicine." *International Encyclopaedia of the Social Sciences*, vol. 10: 87-93.
Hultkrantz, A.
1965 "Some Aspects of Religio-Ethnographic Fieldwork." In: *Fourth Conference of Nordic Anthropologists. Ethnos*, supplement to vol. 31.
Hunt, Robert, ed.
1967 *Personalities and Cultures*. New York, Natural History Press.
Husserl, Edmund
1931 *Ideas: General Introduction to Pure Phenomenology*. New York, Macmillan.
Hutchison, John A.
1969 *Paths of Faith*. New York, McGraw-Hill.
Hyman, Ray and Vogt, Evon Z.
1967 "Water Witching: Magical Ritual in Contemporary United States." *Psychology Today*, 1: 35-42.
Hymes, Dell
1964 "Directions in (Ethno-) Linguistic Theory." *American Anthropologist*, 66: 6-56.

International Directory of Anthropological Institutions
1967 *Current Anthropology*, 8: 648-651.

Jacobs, Melville
1964 *Pattern in Cultural Anthropology*. Homewood, Dorsey Press.
Jacobs, Melville, and Stern, B. J.
1952 *General Anthropology*. 2nd edition. New York, Barnes and Noble.
Jahn, J.
1961 *Muntu: an outline of the New African Culture*. Grove Press, 1962.
James, E. O.
1938 *Comparative Religion*. New York, Barnes and Noble, 1961.
1954 "The History, Science and Comparative Study of Religion." *Numen*, 1: 91-105.
1956 *History of Religions*. New York, Harper.
Jarvie, I. C.
1963 "Theories of Cargo-Cults: A Critical Analysis." *Oceania*, 32: 1-31, 109-136.
Jennings, Jesse D.
1963 "Anthropology and the World of Science." *Bulletin of the University of Utah*, vol. 54, no. 18, pp. 5-18.

194 BIBLIOGRAPHY

Jones, W. T.
1972 "World Views: Their Nature and their Function." *Current Anthropology*, 13: 79-109.

Kaminsky, Howard
1962 "The Problem of Explanation." In: *Millennial Dreams in Action*, S. Thrupp, ed. The Hague, Mouton. Pp. 215-217.
Kardiner, Abram
1945 *The Psychological Frontiers of Society*. New York, Columbia University Press, 1963.
Kardiner, A. and Preble, E.
1961 *They Studied Man*. New York, World Publishing Co.
Keesing, Felix M.
1958 *Cultural Anthropology*. New York, Holt, Rinehart and Winston.
Kennedy, John G.
1967 "Psychological and Sociological Explanations of Witchcraft." *Man* (N.S.) 2: 216-225.
Kerman, Keith T.
1972 "Language." In: *Biennial Review of Anthropology*, 1971, B. J. Siegel, ed. Pp. 326-372.
Khare, R. S.
1967 "Predictions of Death among the Kanya-Kula Brahmans: A Study of Predictive Narratives." *Contributions to Indian Sociology* (N.S.). Pp. 1-25.
Kim, Jay J.
1972 "Belief or Anamnesis: Is A Rapprochement between History of Religions and Theology possible?" *Journal of Religion*, 52: 150-169.
King, A. R.
1964 "Myth." *A Dictionary of the Social Sciences*, J. Gould and W. L. Kolb, eds. P. 450.
King, Winston L.
1968 *Introduction to Religion. A Phenomenological Approach*. New York, Harper and Row.
Kishimoto, Hideo
1961 "An Operational Definition of Religion." *Numen*, 8: 236-240.
1967 "Religiology." *Numen*, 14: 81-86.
Kitagawa, Joseph M.
1959 "The History of Religions in America." In: *The History of Religions*, M. Eliade and J. M. Kitagawa, eds. Chicago, University of Chicago Press. Pp. 1-30.
1967 "Primitive, Classical and Modern Religions: A Perspective on Understanding in the History of Religions." In: *The History of Religions*, J. W. Kitagawa, ed. Chicago, University of Chicago Press. Pp. 39-66.
1968 "The Making of a Historian of Religions." *Journal of the American Academy of Religion*, 35: 191-202.
Kluckhohn, Clyde
1942 "Myths and Rituals: A General Theory." *The Harvard Theological Review*, 35: 45-79.
1944 *Navaho Witchcraft*. Boston, Beacon Press, 1967.
1949 "The Philosophy of the Navaho Indians." In: *Readings in Anthropology*, M. Fried, ed. New York, Crowell, 1968. Vol. 2, pp. 675-699.
1951 "Values and Value-Orientation in the Theory of Action." In: *Toward*

a *General Theory of Action,* Talcott Parsons and E. Shils, eds. Cambridge, Harvard University Press. Pp. 388-433.

1961 *Anthropology and the Classics.* Providence, Rhode Island, Brown University Press.

1964 "Navaho Categories." In: *Primitive Views of The World,* S. Diamond, ed. New York, Columbia University Press. Pp. 93-125.

Kluckhohn, Clyde and Leighton, D.
1962 *The Navaho.* New York, Natural History Press.

Kottack, Conrad Phillip
1974 *Anthropology. The Exploration of Human Diversity.* New York, Random House.

Krige, J. D.
1947 "The Social Function of Witchcraft." *Theoria,* 1: 8-21.

Krige, J. D. and Krige, E. J.
1954 "The Lovedu of the Transvaal." In: *African Worlds,* D. Forde, ed. London, Oxford University Press. Pp. 55-82.

Kristensen, W. Brede
1957 *The Meaning of Religion. Lectures in the Phenomenology of Religion.* The Hague, M. Nijhoff, 1960.

Kroeber, A. L.
1920 "Totem and Taboo: An Ethnographic Psychoanalysis." *American Anthropologist,* 22: 48-55.

1939 "Totem and Taboo in Retrospect." *American Journal of Sociology,* 45: 446-451.

1963 *An Anthropologist looks at History,* Theodore Kroeber, ed. Berkeley, University of California Press.

Kroeber, A. L. and Kluckhohn, C.
1952 *Culture: A Critical Review of Concepts and Definitions.* New York, Random House.

Kuper, Hilda
1964 *The Swazi.* London, International African Institute.

Lamphere, Louis
1969 "Symbolic Elements in Navajo Ritual." *Southwestern Journal of Anthropology,* 25: 279-305.

Langer, S. K.
1957 *Philosophy in a New Key.* New York, Mentor.

Langness, L. L.
1965 *The Life History in Anthropological Science.* New York, Holt, Rinehart and Winston.

Lanternari, V.
1962 "Messianism: Its Historical Origin and Morphology." *History of Religions,* 2: 52-72.

1964 "Il Comparativismo Storico-dialettico nell'ethnologia religiosa." VIe Congrès International des Sciences Anthropologiques et Ethnologiques. Musée de l'Homme, Paris. Vol. 2, pp. 419-420.

Larkin, E. E.
1967 "Spirituality, Christian." *The New Catholic Encyclopaedia.* Vol. 13: 599-603.

Laughlin, William S.
1963 "Primitive Theory of Medicine: Empirical Knowledge." In: *Man's Image in Medicine and Anthropology,* I. Gladston, ed. New York, International Universities Press. Pp. 116-140.

Lawrence, P.
  1965 "The Ngaing of the Raid Coast." In: *Gods, Ghosts and Men in Mela-nesia*, P. Lawrence and J. M. Meggitt, eds. Melbourne, Oxford Univer-sity Press. Pp. 198-223.
Lawrence, P. and Meggitt, J. M., eds.
  1965 "Introduction." In: *Gods, Ghosts and Men in Melanesia*. Melbourne, Oxford University Press. Pp. 1-25.
Leach, Edmund
  1949 "Primitive Magic and Modern Medicine." *Health Education Journal*, 7: 162-170.
  1958 "Magical Hair." In: *Myth and Cosmos*, J. Middleton, ed. New York, Natural History Press, 1967. Pp. 77-108.
  1961 "Lévi-Strauss in the Garden of Eden: An Examination of Some Recent Developments in the Analysis of Myth." In: *Reader in Comparative Religion*, W. A. Lessa and E. Z. Vogt, eds. New York, Harper and Row, 2nd ed., 1965. Pp. 574-581.
  1962 "Genesis as Myth." In: *Myth and Cosmos*, J. Middleton, ed. New York, Natural History Press, 1967. Pp. 1-13.
  1963a *Rethinking Anthropology*. Cambridge, Cambridge University Press.
  1963b "Two Essays Concerning the Symbolic Representation of Time." In: *Rethinking Anthropology*. Cambridge, Cambridge University Press. Pp. 124-136.
  1964a "Myth as a Justification for Faction and Social Change." In: *Studies on Mythology*, R. A. Georges, ed. Homewood, Dorsey Press, 1968. Pp. 184-198.
  1964b "Ritual." In: *A Dictionary of the Social Sciences*, J. Gould and W. L. Kolb, eds. Pp. 607-608.
  1966a "The Legitimacy of Solomon: Some Structural Aspects of Old Testa-ment History." *European Journal of Sociology*, 7: 58-101.
  1966b "Ritualization in Man in Relation to Conceptual and Social Development." In: *Philosophical Transactions of the Royal Society of London*. Pp. 403-408.
  1968a "Ritual." *International Encyclopaedia of the Social Sciences*, vol. 13: 521-526.
  1968b "The Comparative Method in Anthropology." *International Encyclopaedia of the Social Sciences*, vol. 1: 339-345.
  1968c "We Scientists Have the Right to Play God." *The Saturday Evening Post*, November 16th, 1968, p. 16.
  1968d (Ed.) *Dialectic in Practical Religion*. Cambridge, Cambridge University Press.
  1970 *Claude Lévi-Strauss*. New York, The Viking Press.
Leeuw, G. van der
  1933 *Religion in Essence and Manifestation: A Study in Phenomenology*. Magnolia, Mass., Peter Smith, 1967.
Leiris, Michel
  1958 *Race and Culture*. New York, Unesco.
Leslie, C. M.
  1960 *Now We Are Civilized: A Study of the World View of the Zapotec Indians of Mitla, Oaxaca*. Detroit, Wayne University Press.
Lessa, William A.
  1959a Review of: *Patterns in Comparative Religion* by Mircea Eliade. *Ameri-can Anthropologist*, 61: 122-123.
  1959b Review of: *The Sacred and the Profane* by Mircea Eliade. *American Anthropologist*, 61: 1146-1147.

1961 *Tales for Ulithi Atoll. A Comparative Study of Oceanic Folklore.* Berkeley, University of California Press.

1966 "Discoverer-of-the-Sun: Mythology as a Reflection of Culture." In: *The Anthropologist Looks at Myth*, J. Greenway, ed. Austin, University of Texas Press. Pp. 3-51.

Lessa, William A. and Vogt, E. Z., eds.

1972 *Reader in Comparative Religion.* 3rd ed. New York, Harper and Row.

Leuba, James

1912 *A Psychological Study of Religion.* New York, Macmillan.

Levin, M. G. and Potapov, L. P., eds.

1964 *The Peoples of Siberia.* Chicago, University of Chicago Press.

Lévi-Strauss, Claude

1958a "The Structural Study of Myth." In: *Structural Anthropology*, by Lévi-Strauss. New York, Basic Books, 1963. Pp. 206-231.

1958b "The Story of Asdiwal." In: *The Structural Study of Myth and Totemism*, E. Leach, ed. London, Tavistock, 1967. Pp. 1-47.

1960 "Four Winnebago Myths: A Structural Sketch." In: *Myth and Cosmos*, J. Middleton, ed. New York, Natural History Press, 1967. Pp. 15-26.

1961 *Conversations with Claude Lévi-Strauss*, G. Charbonnier, ed. London, Jonathan Cape, 1969.

1962 *The Savage Mind.* Chicago, University of Chicago Press, 1966.

1963 *Structural Anthropology.* New York, Basic Books.

1964 *The Raw and the Cooked*, vol. 1. New York, Harper and Row, 1969.

1966 "Anthropology: Its Achievements and Future." *Current Anthropology*, 7: 124-127.

1967 "Today's Crisis in Anthropology." In: *Anthropology,* S. Rapport and H. Wright, eds. New York, New York University Press. Pp. 129-138.

Lévy-Bruhl, L.

1910 *How Natives Think.* New York, Washington Square Press, 1966.

1922 *Primitive Mentality.* Boston, Beacon Press, 1966.

Levy, Jerrold E.

1969 "Some Comments upon the Ritual of the Sanni Demons." *Comparative Studies in Society and History*, 11: 217-226.

Lewis, I. M., ed.

1968 *History and Social Anthropology.* London, Tavistock.

Lewis, Oscar

1956 "Comparisons in Cultural Anthropology." In: *Readings in Cross-Cultural Methodology*, F. W. Moore, ed. New Haven, HRAF Press, 1961. Pp. 55-88.

Libby, D.

1959 Review of: *Birth and Rebirth* by Mircea Eliade. *American Anthropologist*, 61: 688-689.

Lieban, Richard W.

1962 "The Dangerous Ingkantos: Illness and Social Control in a Philippine Community." *American Anthropologist*, 64: 306-312.

1967 *Cebuano Sorcery: Malign Magic in the Philippines.* Berkeley, University of California Press.

Lienhardt, Godfrey

1956 "Religion." In: *Man, Culture and Society*, H. L. Shapiro, ed. London, Oxford University Press. Pp. 310-329.

1958 Review of: *Patterns in Comparative Religion* by Mircea Eliade. *The Tablet,* May 3rd, 1958, p. 416.

1960 *Divinity and Experience. The Religion of the Dinka*. London, Oxford University Press.

1966 *Social Anthropology*. London, Oxford University Press.

Lienhardt, Peter

1960 Review of: *Myth, Dreams and Mysteries* by Mircea Eliade. *The Tablet*, November 26th, 1960, pp. 1091-1092.

Linton, Ralph

1943 "Nativistic Movements." *American Anthropologist*, 45: 230-240.

1944 "The Scope and Aims of Anthropology." In: *The Science of Man in the World Crisis*, R. Linton, ed. New York, Columbia University Press. Pp. 3-18.

Lisitzky, Gene

1956 *Four Ways of Being Human*. New York, The Viking Press.

Little, Kenneth L.

1958 *Race and Society*. New York, Unesco.

Long, Charles

1963 *Alpha: The Myths of Creation*. New York, Collier, 1969.

1967 "Archaism and Hermeneutics." In: *The History of Religions*, J. M. Kitagawa, ed. Chicago, University of Chicago Press. Pp. 67-88.

1969 "Science and Signification." In: *Myths and Symbols*, J. M. Kitagawa and Ch. Long, eds. Chicago, University of Chicago Press. Pp. 141-150.

Lotz, John

1964 "On Language and Culture." In: *Language in Culture and Society*, Dell Hymes, ed. New York, Harper and Row. Pp. 182-184.

Lowie, Robert

1924 *Primitive Religion*. New York, Grosset and Dunlap, 1952.

1937 *History of Ethnological Theory*. New York, Holt, Rinehart and Winston.

1963 "Religion in Human Life." *American Anthropologist,* 65: 533-542.

Luyster, Robert

1966 "The Study of Myth: Two Approaches." *Journal of Bible and Religion*, 34: 235-243.

Maguire, James J.

1960 "The New Look in Comparative Religion." *Perspectives*, 5: 8-10.

Mair, Lucy

1959 "Independent Religious Movements in Three Continents." In: *Gods and Rituals*, J. Middleton, ed. New York, Natural History Press, 1967. Pp. 307-335.

1962 *Primitive Government*. Baltimore, Penguin.

1964 "Witchcraft as a Problem in the Study of Religion." In: *Anthropology and Social Change*, by L. Mair. London, Athlone Press, 1969. Pp. 185-200.

1965 *Introduction to Social Anthropology*. London, Oxford University Press.

1969a *Witchcraft*. New York, World Universities Press.

1969b *Anthropology and Social Change*. London, Athlone Press.

Malandra, W. W.

1967 "The Concept of Movement in the History of Religions." *Numen*, 14: 23-69.

Malefijt, A. de Waal

1968 *Religion and Culture*. New York, Macmillan.

Malinowski, B.

1922 *Argonauts of the Western Pacific*. New York, Dutton and Co., 1961.

1925 *Magic, Science and Religion*. New York, Doubleday, 1954. Pp. 17-92.

1926 "Myth in Primitive Psychology." In: *Magic, Science and Religion* by B. Malinowski. New York, Doubleday, 1954. Pp. 93-148.

Mandelbaum, David G.
  1966 "Transcendental and Pragmatic Aspects of Religion." *American Anthropologist*, 68: 1174-1191.
  1968 "Cultural Anthropology." *International Encyclopaedia of the Social Sciences*, vol. 1: 313-319.
  1973 "The Study of Life-History: Gandhi." *Current Anthropology*, 14: 177-196.
Manners, R. A. and Kaplan, D., eds.
  1968 *Theory in Anthropology.* Chicago, Aldine.
Maranda, Pierre
  1972 "Structuralism in Cultural Anthropology." In: *Annual Review in Anthropology*, vol. 1, B. J. Siegel, ed. California, Annual Reviews, Inc. Pp. 329-348.
Marett, R. R.
  1909 *The Threshold of Religion.* London, Methuen and Company.
Marwick, M. G.
  1963 "The Sociology of Sorcery in a Central African Tribe." In: *Magic, Witchcraft and Curing*, J. Middleton, ed. New York, Natural History Press, 1967. Pp. 127-134.
  1965 *Sorcery in Its Social Setting.* Manchester, Manchester University Press.
  1967 "The Study of Witchcraft." In: *The Craft of Social Anthropology*, A. L. Epstein, ed. London, Tavistock. Pp. 231-244.
  1972 "Anthropologists' declining Productivity in the Sociology of Witchcraft." *American Anthropologist*, 74: 378-385.
Maybury-Lewis, David
  1967 *Akwe-Shavante Society.* Oxford, Clarendon Press.
Mbiti, John S.
  1970 *African Religions and Philosophy.* New York, Doubleday and Company.
McCullough, W. S.
  1962 "Dove." In: *The Interpreter's Dictionary of the Bible.* New York, Abington Press. Vol. 1: 866-867.
McDermott, R. A.
  1968 "Religion as an Academic Discipline." *Cross-Currents*, 18: 11-33.
McKenzie, John L.
  1965 "Dove." In: *Dictionary of the Bible*, by J. L. McKenzie. Milwaukee, Bruce. P. 203.
Mclean, Milton D., ed.
  1967 *Religious Studies in Public Universities.* Carbondale, Illinois, Central Publications.
Mead, Margaret
  1928 *Coming of Age in Samoa.* New York, W. Morrow and Co.
  1930 *Growing up in New Guinea.* New York, Mentor, 1953.
  1940 *The Mountain Arapesh. Vol. 2, Supernaturalism.* New York, American Museum of Natural History, 37: 319-451.
  1964 *Anthropology. A Human Science.* Princeton, VanNostrand.
  1969 *Culture and Commitment. A Study of the Generation Gap.* New York, Natural History Press.
Mead, M. and Wolfenstein, M., eds.
  1955 *Childhood in Contemporary Cultures.* Chicago, University of Chicago Press.
Meland, B. E.
  1961 "Theology and the Historian of Religions." *Journal of Religion*, 41: 263-276.

Mendelson, E. M.
  1958 "The King, the Traitor and the Cross: An Interpretation of Highland Maya Religious Conflict." *Diogenes,* 21: 1-10.
  1965 "Initiation and the Paradox of Power. A Sociological Approach." In: *Initiation,* C. J. Bleeker, ed. Leiden, E. J. Brill. Pp. 214-221.
  1968 "World View." *International Encyclopaedia of the Social Sciences,* 16: 576-579.
Metzger, Duane and Williams, Gerald
  1963 "Tenejapa Medicine: The Curer." *Southwestern Journal of Anthropology,* 19: 216-23.
Middleton, John
  1954 "Some Social Aspects of Lugbara Myth." In: *Myth and Cosmos,* J. Middleton, ed. New York, Natural History Press, 1967. Pp. 47-61.
  1955 "The Concept of 'Bewitching' in Lugbara." In: *Magic, Witchcraft and Curing,* J. Middleton, ed. New York, Natural History Press, 1967. Pp. 55-67.
  1960 *Lugbara Religion.* London, Oxford University Press.
  1967 "Introduction." In: *Magic, Witchcraft and Sorcery,* J. Middleton, ed. New York, Natural History Press.
Middleton, J. and Winter, E. H.
  1963 *Witchcraft and Sorcery in East Africa.* New York, Praeger.
Mike, Douglas
  1973 "Prophylactic Medicine and Kin Units among the Yao Ancestor Worshippers." *Mankind,* 9: 77-88.
Monk, Robert et al.
  1973 *Exploring Religious Meaning.* New Jersey, Prentice-Hall, Inc.
Montagu, Ashley
  1962a "The Fallacy of the 'Primitive'." In: *The Concept of the Primitive,* A. Montagu, ed. New York, Free Press, 1968. Pp. 1-16.
  1962b *The Humanization of Man.* New York, Grove Press.
  1968a "Preface." In: *The Concept of the "Primitive,"* A. Montagu, ed. New York, Free Press. Pp. vii-ix.
  1968b "The Concept of 'Primitive' and Related Anthropological Terms: A Study in Systematics of Confusion." In: *The Concept of the "Primitive,"* A. Montagu, ed. New York, Free Press. Pp. 148-168.
  1968c (Ed.) *Culture: Man's Adaptive Mechanism.* New York, Oxford University Press.
Morey, Robert V.
  1971 "Gauhibo Time-Reckoning." *Anthropological Quarterly,* 44: 22-36.
Morris, Desmond, ed.
  1967 *Primate Ethology.* Chicago, Aldine.
Morris, Desmond and Morris, Ramona
  1966 *Men and Apes.* New York, Bantam Books.
Muller, Max
  1880 *Lectures on the Origins and Growth of Religion.* London, Longmans, Green and Co.
Murdock, George P.
  1934 *Our Contemporary Primitives.* New York, Macmillan, 1965.
  1961 (Ed.) *Outline of Cultural Material.* New Haven, HRAF Press.
Murphy, R. F.
  1958 *Mundurucu' Religion.* Berkeley, University of California Press.
Murray, Margaret
  1963 *The Genesis of Religion.* London, Routledge and Paul.

Nadel, S.
1951　*The Foundations of Social Anthropology.* New York, Free Press.
1952　"Witchcraft in Four African Societies: An Essay in Comparison." *American Anthropologist,* 54: 18-29.
1954a "Morality and Language among the Nupe." *Man,* 54: 55-57.
1954b *Nupe Religion.* London, Oxford University Press.
1956　"Malinowski on Magic and Religion." In: *Man and Culture,* R. Firth, ed. London, Oxford University Press. Pp. 189-208.
Nash, Dennison
1973　"A Convergence of Psychological and Sociological Explanations of Witchcraft." *Current Anthropology,* 14: 545-546.
Needham, Rodney
1960　"The Left Hand of the Nugue: An Analytical Note on the Structure of Meru Symbolism." *Africa,* 30: 20-33.
1967　"Right and Left in Nyoro Symbolic Classification." *Africa,* 37: 425-452.
Nida, Eugene A.
1954　"Customs and Cultures. New York, Harper and Row.
1964　"Linguistics and Ethnology in Translation Problems." In: *Language in Culture and Society,* Dell Hymes, ed. New York, Harper and Row. Pp. 90-97.
Norbeck, Edward
1961　*Religion in Primitive Society.* New York, Harper and Row.
1964　"The Study of Religion." In: *Horizons of Anthropology,* Sol Tax, ed. Chicago, Aldine. Pp. 212-233.
1967　"Anthropological Views of Religion." In: *Religion in Philosophical and Cultural Perspective.* J. C. Feaver and W. Horosz, eds. Princeton, Van-Nostrand. Pp. 414-435.
1974　*Religion in Human Life.* New York, Holt, Rinehart and Winston.
Norbeck, E., Walker, D. and Cohn, M.
1962　"The Interpretation of Data: Puberty Rites." *American Anthropologist,* 64: 463-485.
Northrop, F. S. C. and Livingston, H. H.
1964　*Cross-Cultural Understanding: Epistemology in Anthropology.* New York, Harper and Row.
Noss, John B.
1963　*Man's Religions.* New York, Macmillan.

Obeyesekere, G.
1969　"The Ritual Drama of the Sanni Demons: Collective Representation of Disease in Ceylon." *Comparative Studies in Society and History,* 11: 174-216.
O'Connell, James
1962　"The Withdrawal of the High God in West African Religion: An Essay in Interpretation." *Man,* 62: 67-69.
Oswalt, Wendell H.
1967　*Alaskan Eskimos.* San Francisco, Chandler Publishing Co.
Otto, Rudolph
1950　*The Idea of the Holy.* 2nd. ed. London, Oxford University Press.

Paine, Robert
1972　"Contractual Ritual in Absence of Descent Groups: The Betrothal Ritual of the Reindeer Lapps of Kautokeino." *Anthropologica,* 14: 61-81.

Park, George K.
  1963 "Divination in Its Social Contexts." In: *Magic, Witchcraft and Curing*,
        J. Middleton, ed. New York, Natural History Press, 1967. Pp. 233-254.
Park, Willard Z.
  1965 Review of: *Shamanism, Archaic Techniques of Ecstacy* by Mircea
        Eliade. *American Anthropologist*, 67: 1305-1306.
Parrinder, Geoffrey
  1962 *Comparative Religion*. New York, Macmillan.
  1963 *Witchcraft: European and African*. New York, Barnes and Noble.
  1966 "The Origins of Religion." *Religious Studies*, 1: 257-261.
Parrish, Fred L.
  1941 *The Classification of Religions, Its Relation to the History of Religions*.
        Scottdale, Pa., Herald Press.
  1965 *History of Religion: Destiny-Determining Factor in the World's Cultures*.
        New York, Pageant Press.
Parsons, Anne
  1964 "Is the Oedipus Complex Universal?" In: *Personalities and Cultures*,
        R. Hunt, ed. New York, Natural History Press, 1967. Pp. 352-399.
Parvathamma, C.
  1972 "A Study of the Functional Aspect of Temple Ceremonial." *The Eastern
        Anthropologist*, 52: 123-133.
Pearson, Roger
  1974 *Introduction to Anthropology*. New York, Holt, Rinehart and Winston.
Peck, John G.
  1968 "Doctor Medicine and Bush Medicine in Kaukira, Honduras." In: *Essays
        on Medical Anthropology*, T. Weaver, ed. Athens, University of Georgia
        Press. Pp. 78-87.
Pelto, Pertti J.
  1966 *The Nature of Anthropology*. Columbus, Ohio, Charles Merrill.
Penner, Hans H.
  1969 "Myth and Ritual: A Wasteland or a Forest of Symbols." In: *On
        Method in the History of Religions*, J. S. Helfer, ed. Middletown,
        Weslyan University Press. Pp. 46-57.
Penner, Hans H. and Yoman, Edward A.
  1972 "Is the Science of Religion Possible?" *The Journal of Religion*, 51:
        107-133.
Penniman, T. K.
  1952 *A Hundred Years of Anthropology*. 2nd ed. London, Duckworth and Co.
Pettazzoni, Raffaello
  1954 *Essays on the History of Religions*. Leiden, E. J. Brill.
  1959 "Il Metodo Comparativo." *Numen*, 6: 1-14.
Piddington, Ralph
  1950 *An Introduction to Social Anthropology*. New York, Praeger.
Pinney, Roy
  1968 *Vanishing Tribes*. New York, Thomas Crowell.
Pletcher, Galen K.
  1973 "Mysticism, Contradiction and Ineffability." *American Philosophical
        Quarterly*, 10: 201-211.
Pocock, David
  1964 "The Anthropology of Time-Reckoning." In: *Myth and Cosmos*,
        J. Middleton, ed. New York, Natural History Press, 1967. Pp. 303-314.
Popper, K. R.
  1957 *The Poverty of Historicism*. London, Routledge and Kegan Paul.

Powdermaker, Hortense
1966 *Stranger and Friend. The Way of an Anthropologist.* New York, Norton.
Price-Williams, D. R.
1962 "A Case Study of Ideas Concerning Disease among the Tiv." *Africa,* 32: 123-131.
Pummer, Reinhard
1972 "Religionswissenschaft or Religiology?" *Numen,* 19: 91-127.
Pye, Michael
1972 *Comparative Religion.* New York, Harper and Row.

Radcliffe-Brown, A. R.
1922 "The Interpretation of Andamanese Customs and Beliefs: Myths and Legends." In: *Studies on Mythology,* R. A. Georges, ed. Homewood, Dorsey Press, 1968. Pp. 46-71.
1951 "The Comparative Method in Social Anthropology." In: *Method in Social Anthropology: Selected Essays* by A. R. Radcliffe-Brown, M. N. Srinivas, ed. Chicago, University of Chicago Press, 1958. Pp. 108-127.
1952 *Structure and Function in Primitive Society.* New York, Free Press.
1958 *Method in Social Anthropology: Selected Essays* by A. R. Radcliffe-Brown, M. N. Srinivas, ed. Chicago, University of Chicago Press.
Raglan, Lord
1959 Review of: *Patterns in Comparative Religion* by Mircea Eliade. *Man,* 59: 53-54.
Rahner, Karl
1969 "Christianity." In: *Sacramentum Mundi.* Vol. 1: 299-311.
Rappaport, Roy A.
1967 *Pigs for the Ancestors.* New Haven, Yale University Press.
Rapport, Samuel and Wright, Helen
1967 *Anthropology.* New York, New York University Press.
Rasmussen, David
1968 "Mircea Eliade: Structural Hermeneutics and Philosophy." *Philosophy Today,* 12: 138-146
Read, M.
1948 "Attitudes towards Health and Disease among Preliterate Peoples." *Health Education Journal,* 6: 166-172.
Redfield, Robert
1952 "The Primitive World View." *American Philosophical Society, Proceedings,* 96: 30-36.
1953 *The Primitive World and Its Transformations.* Ithaca, New York, Cornell University Press.
Reichard, G. A.
1950 *Navaho Religion.* New York, Pantheon Books.
Renan, E.
1857 *Études d'Histoire Religieuse.* Paris, Levy.
Reno, S. J.
1972 "Eliade's Progressional View of Hierophanies." *Religious Studies,* 8: 153-160.
Rhoades, D. H.
1962 "What Social Science Has Done to Religion." *Numen,* 9: 69-80.
Richards, A. I.
1956 *Chisungu.* New York, Grove Press.
Ricketts, Mac Linscott
1967 "Mircea Eliade and the Death of God." *Religion in Life,* 36: 40-52.

1969 "The Nature and Extent of Eliade's 'Jungianism'." *Union Seminary Quarterly Review*, 25: 211-234.

1973 "In Defense of Eliade. Toward Bridging the Communications Gap between Anthropology and the History of Religions." *Religion. Journal of Religion and Religions*, 3: 13-34.

Rigby, Peter
1966 "Dual Symbolic Classification among the Gogo of Central Tanzania." *Africa*, 36: 1-16.

Robinson, M. S. and Joiner, L. E.
1968 "An Experiment in the Structural Study of Myth." *Contributions to Indian Sociology* (N.S.) No. 2, pp. 1-37.

Roheim, Geza
1950 *Psychoanalysis and Anthropology: Culture, Personality and the Unconscious.* New York, International Universities Press.

Royal Anthropological Institute
1951 *Notes and Queries in Anthropology.* London, Routledge and Kegan Paul. 6th ed.

Rubel, Arthur J.
1960 "Concepts of Disease in Mexican-American Culture." *American Anthropologist*, 62: 795-814.

Saler, Benson
1964 "Nagual, Witch and Sorcerer in a Quiche Village." In: *Magic, Witchcraft and Curing*, J. Middleton, ed. New York, Natural History Press, 1967. Pp. 69-99.

1967 Review of: *Mephistopheles and the Androgyne* by Mircea Eliade. *American Anthropologist*, 69: 262-263.

Salisbury, R. F.
1965 "The Siane of the Eastern Highlands." In: *Gods, Ghosts, and Men in Melanesia*, P. Lawrence and J. M. Meggitt, eds. Pp. 50-77.

Sapir, E.
1937 "Symbolism." *Encyclopaedia of the Social Sciences*, vol. 14: 492-495.

Schapera, Issac
1953 "Some Comments on Comparative Method in Social Anthropology." In: *Cross-Cultural Approaches*, C. S. Ford, ed. New York, HRAF Press. Pp. 55-64.

1962 "Should Anthropologists be Historians?" *Journal of the Royal Anthropological Institute*, 92: 143-156.

Schleiermarcher, Friedrich
1893 *On Religion: Speeches to Its Cultured Dispisers.* New York, Harper and Row, 1958.

Schlette, H. R.
1966 *Towards a Theology of Religions.* New York, Herder and Herder.

Schmidt, Wilhelm
1931 *The Origin and Growth of Religion. Facts and Theories.* New York, The Dial Press.

1939 *The Culture Historical Method of Anthropoloy.* New York, Fortuny's.

Schusky, Ernest L.
1965 *Manual for Kinship Analysis.* New York, Holt, Rinehart and Winston.

Schwartz, B. M. and Ewald, R. E.
1968 *Culture and Society: An Introduction to Cultural Anthropology.* New York, Ronald Press.

Schwartz, Theodore
1973 "Cult and Context: The Paranoid Ethos in Melanesia." *Ethos*, 1: 153-174.

Scorza, David
  1972 "Classification of Au Myths." *Practical Anthropoloy,* 19: 214-219.
Seijas, Haydée
  1973 "An Approach to the Study of Medical Aspects of Culture." *Current Anthropology,* 14: 544-545.
Seligman, Breda Z.
  1952 Review of: *Shamanism—Archaic Techniques of Ecstacy* by Mircea Eliade. *Man,* 52: 74-75.
Service, E. R.
  1962 *Primitive Social Organization.* New York, Random House.
  1963 *Profiles in Ethnology.* New York, Harper and Row.
Shapiro, Harry L.
  1953 *Race Mixture.* New York, Unesco.
Sharpe, Eric J.
  1971 "Some Problems of Method in the Study of Religion." *Religion. Journal of Religion and Religions,* 1: 1-14.
Shelton, Austin J.
  1964 "On Recent Interpretation of Deus Otiosus: The Withdrawn God in West African Religion." *Man,* 64: 53-54.
  1965 "The Presence of the 'Withdrawn' God in North Ibo Religious Beliefs and Worship." *Man,* 65: 15-18.
Siegel, Bernard J., ed.
  1965–71 *Biennal Review of Anthropology.* California, Stanford University Press.
  1972 *Annual Review of Anthropology,* vol. 1. California, Annual Reviews Inc.
  1973 *Annual Review of Anthropology,* vol. 2. California, Annual Reviews Inc.
Simoons, Fredrick J.
  1961 *Eat Not This Flesh: Food Avoidances in the Old World.* Madison, University of Wisconsin Press.
Slotikin, J. S., ed.
  1965 *Readings in Early Anthropology.* Chicago, Aldine.
Smart, Ninian
  1968 "Recent Books on the Comparative Study of Religion." *The Expository Times,* 79: 196-200.
  1969 *The Religious Experience of Mankind.* New York, Scribner.
  1973a *The Phenomenon of Religion.* New York, Herder and Herder.
  1973b *The Science of Religion and the Sociology of Knowledge.* New Jersey, Princeton University Press.
Smith, Edwin
  1952 "African Symbolism." *Journal of the Royal Anthropological Institute,* 82: 13-37.
  1966 (Ed.)*African Concepts of God.* London, Edinburgh House Press, 3rd ed.
Smith, J. Z.
  1972 "Wobbling Pivvot." *Journal of Religion,* 52: 134-149.
Smith, Wilfred Cantwell
  1959 "Comparative Religion: Whither and Why?" In: *The History of Religions,* M. Eliade and J. M. Kitagawa, eds. Chicago, University of Chicago Press. Pp. 31-58.
  1962 *The Faith of Other Men.* New York, New American Library.
  1964 *The Meaning and End of Religion.* New York, Mentor.
Social Science Research Council
  1954 *The Social Sciences in Historical Study*; a Report of the Committee of Historiography. Bulletin 64. New York, Social Science Research Council.

Spencer, Herbert
1876 *Principles of Sociology.* London, Williams and Norgate.
Spencer, Robert F.
1966 "Ethical Expression in a Burmese Jataka." In: *The Anthropologist Looks at Myth,* J. Greenway, ed. Austin, University of Texas Press. Pp. 278-301.
Spiro, Melford
1964a "Introduction." In: *Symposium on New Approaches to the Study of Religion,* J. Helm, ed. Seattle, University of Washington Press. Pp. 1-3.
1964b "Religion and the Irrational." In: *Symposium on New Approaches to the Study of Religion,* J. Helm, ed. Seattle, University of Washington Press. Pp. 102-115.
1966a "Religion: Problems of Definition and Explanation." In: *Anthropological Approaches to the Study of Religion,* M. Banton, ed. London, Tavistock. Pp. 85-126.
1966b "Buddhism and Economic Action in Burma." *American Anthropologist,* 68: 1163-1173.
1967 *Burmese Supernaturalism.* Princeton, Prentice-Hall.
Srinivas, M. N.
1952 *Religion and Society among the Coorgs of South India.* London, Oxford University Press.
Stanley, A. and Freed, R. S.
1964 "Spirit Possession as Illness in a North India Village." In: *Magic, Witchcraft and Curing,* J. Middleton, ed. New York, Natural History Press, 1967. Pp. 295-320.
Stanner, W. E. H.
1958 "On the Interpretation of Cargo Cults." *Oceania, 29:* 1-25.
1959 "On Aboriginal Religion. I: The Lineaments of Sacrifice." *Oceania, 30:* 108-127.
1960a "On Aboriginal Religion. II: Sacramentalism, Rite and Myth." *Oceania, 30:* 245-278.
1960b "On Aboriginal Religion. III: Symbolism in the Higher Rites." *Oceania, 30:* 100-120.
1961a "On Aboriginal Religion. IV: The Design Plan of the Riteless Myth." *Oceania, 31:* 233-258.
1961b "on Aboriginal Religion. V: The Design Plan of the Mythless Rite." *Oceania, 32:* 79-108.
1963 "On Aboriginal Religion. VI: Cosmos and Society Made Correlative." *Oceania, 33:* 239-273.
Starr, Chester G.
1963 "Reflections upon the Problem of Generalization." In: *Generalization in the Writing of History,* L. Gottschalk, ed. Chicago, University of Chicago Press. Pp. 3-18.
Stefaniszyn, B.
1964 *Social and Ritual Life of the Ambo of Northern Rhodesia.* London, Oxford University Press.
Steward, Julian H.
1955 *The Methodology of Multilinear Evolution.* Urbana, University of Illinois Press.
Streng, Frederick J.
1969 *Understanding Religious Man.* Belmont, California, Dickenson Publishing Company.
Streng, F. J. et al.
1973 *Ways of Being Religious.* New Jersey, Prentice-Hall.

Sturtevant, William C.
1964 "Studies in Ethnoscience." *American Anthropologist,* 66: 99-131.
Sundkler, B.
1961 *Bantu Prophets in Africa.* London, Oxford University Press, 2nd. ed.
Swanson, Guy E.
1960 *The Birth of the Gods. The Origins of Primitive Beliefs.* Ann Arbor, University of Michigan Press.

Tax, Sol
1941 "Word View and Social Relations in Guatemala." *American Anthropologist,* 43: 27-42.
1964a "The Setting of the Science of Man." In: *Horizons of Anthropology,* Sol. Tax, ed. Chicago, Aldine. Pp. 15-24.
1964b "The Uses of Anthropology." In: *Horizons of Anthropology,* Sol. Tax, ed. Chicago, Aldine. Pp. 248-258.
Taylor, J. V.
1963 *The Primal Vision.* London, Fortress Press.
Taylor, Robert B.
1973 *Introduction to Cultural Anthropology.* Boston, Allyn and Bacon.
Temples, Placide
1959 *Bantu Philosophy.* Paris, Presence Africaine.
Textor, Robert B.
1967 *Cross-Cultural Summary.* New Haven, HRAF Press.
Thass-Thienemann, Theodore
1968 *Symbolic Behavior.* New York, Washington Square Press.
Thrupp, Sylvia
1962 "Millennial Dreams in Action: A Report on the Conference Discussion." In: *Millennial Dreams in Action,* S. Thrupp, ed. The Hague, Mouton, Pp. 11-27.
Tierney, Emiko Ohnuki
1973a "Sakhalin Ainu Time Reckoning." *Man,* 8: 285-299.
1973b "The Shamanism of the Ainu of the Northwest Coast of Southern Sakhalin." *Ethnology,* 12: 15-29.
Tillich, Paul
1963 *Christianity and the Encounter of the World Religions.* New York, Columbia University Press.
Titiev, Mischa
1960 "A Fresh Approach to the Problem of Magic and Religion." *Southwestern Journal of Anthropology,* 16: 292-298.
1963 *The Science of Man: An Introduction to Anthropology.* New York, Holt, Rinehart and Winston.
Tokarev, S. A.
1966 "Principles of the Morphological Classification of Religions, Part I." *Soviet Anthropology and Archaeology,* 5: 3-10.
Toynbee, Arnold J.
1965 *A Study of History, abridged version by D. C. Somervall,* vol. 1. New York, Dell.
Turner, D. H.
1972 "Nimda Rites of Access: A Comparative View." *Anthropological Forum,* 3: 121-135.
Turner, Terrance S.
1969 "Oedipus: Time and Structure in Narrative Form." In: *Forms of Sym-*

bolic Action, R. Spencer, ed. Seattle, Washington University Press. Pp. 26-68.

Turner, Victor W.

1957   "Symbols in Ndembu Ritual." In: *Closed Systems and Open Minds,* M. Gluckman, ed. Chicago, Aldine, 1964. Pp. 20-51.

1960   "Ritual Symbolism, Morality and Social Structure among the Ndembu." In: *African Symbols of Thought,* M. Fortes and G. Dieterlen, eds. London, Oxford University Press, 1965. Pp. 48-58.

1962a "Themes in the Symbolism of Ndembu Hunting Ritual." In: *Myth and Cosmos,* J. Middleton, ed. New York, Natural History Press, 1967. Pp. 249-269.

1962b. "Three Symbols of Passage in Ndembu Circumcision Ritual: An Interpretation." In: *Essays on the Ritual of Social Relations,* M. Gluckman, ed. Manchester, Manchester University Press. Pp. 124-173.

1962c *Chihamba: The White Spirit.* Manchester, Manchester University Press.

1963   "Colour Classification in Ndembu Ritual." In: *Anthropological Approaches to the Study of Religion,* M. Banton, ed. London, Tavistock. Pp. 47-84.

1964a "Betwixt and Between: The Liminal Period in Rites de Passage." In: *Symposium on New Approaches to the Study of Religion,* J. Helm ed. Seattle, University of Washington Press. Pp. 4-20.

1964b "Witchcraft and Sorcery: Taxonomy vs. Dynamics." *Africa,* 34: 314-325.

1964c "A Ndembu Doctor in Practice." In: *The Forest of Symbols,* by V. W. Turner, Ithaca, New York, Cornell University Press, 1967. Pp. 359-393.

1964d "Lunda Medicine and the Treatment of Disease." In: *The Forest of Symbols,* by V. W. Turner, Ithaca, Cornell University Press, 1967. Pp. 299-358.

1965   "Some Current Trends in the Study of Ritual in Africa." *Anthropological Quarterly,* 38: 155-166.

1966   Review of: *Theories of Primitive Religion* by E. E. Evans-Pritchard. *Man* (N.S.), 1: 256-258.

1967   "Aspects of Saora Ritual and Shamanism. An Approach to the Data of Ritual." In: *The Craft of Social Anthropology,* A. L. Epstein, ed. London, Tavistock. Pp. 181-204.

1968a "Religious Specialists." *International Encyclopaedia of the Social Sciences,* vol. 13: 437-443.

1968b "Myth and Symbol." *International Encyclopaedia of the Social Sciences,* vol. 10: 576-581.

1969a *The Ritual Process.* Chicago, Aldine.

1969b "Forms of Symbolic Action: Introduction." In: *Symposium: Forms of Symbolic Action,* R. Spencer, ed. Seattle, University of Washington Press. Pp. 3-25.

Tyler, Stephen A.

1968   "Introduction." In: *Cognitive Anthropology,* S. A. Tyler, ed. New York, Holt, Rinehart and Winston. Pp. 1-23.

Tylor, Edward B.

1871   *Primitive Culture.* 2 vols., New York, Harper and Row, 1958.

1889   "On the Method of Investigating the Development of Institutions: applied to the Laws of Marriage and Descent." *Journal of the Royal Anthropological Institute,* 18: 245-269.

Udy, Stanley H.

1973   "Cross-Cultural Analysis: Methods and Scope." *Annual Review of*

Anthropology, vol. 2, B. J. Siegel, ed., California, Annual Reviews Inc. Pp. 253-270.

Van Gennep, Arnold
1909 *Rites of Passage.* London, Routledge and Kegan Paul, 1960.

Waardenburg, Jacques
1972 "Religion between Reality and Idea. A Century of Phenomenology of Religion in the Netherlands." *Numen,* 19: 129-203.

Wach, Joachim
1947 "The Place of the History of Religions in the Study of Theology." *Journal of Religion,* 27: 157-177.
1958 *The Comparative Study of Religions.* New York, Columbia University Press.
1967 "Introduction: The Meaning and Task of the History of Religions." In: *The History of Religions,* J. M. Kitagawa, ed. Chicago, University of Chicago Press. Pp. 1-20.

Wallace, Anthony
1956 "Revitalization Movements." *American Anthropologist,* 58: 264-281.
1966 *Religion: An Anthropological View.* New York, Random House.
1968 "Cognitive Anthropology." *International Encyclopaedia of the Social Sciences,* vol. 2: 536-540.

Watts, Alan W.
1963 *The Hands of God. The Myths of Polarity.* New York, Collier.

Wax, Murray
1968 "Religion and Magic." In: *Introduction to Cultural Anthropology,* J. A. Clifton, ed. New York, Houghton Mifflin. Pp. 224-243.

Weber, Max
1905 *The Protestant Ethic and the Spirit of Capitalism.* New York, Scribner's Sons, 1958.

Welch, Claude
1971 *Graduate Education in Religion: A Critical Appraisal.* Montana, University of Montana Press.
1972 *Religion in Undergraduate Curriculum: An Analysis and Interpretation.* Washington, Association of American Colleges.

Werner, Oswald
1972 "Ethnoscience." In: *Annual Review of Anthropology,* vol. 1, B. J. Siegel, ed., California, Annual Reviews Inc. Pp. 271-308.

White, Charles
1967 "A Note of Field Method in Historico-Religious Studies: The Vallabhasampraday." In: *The History of Religions,* J. M. Kitagawa, ed. Chicago, University of Chicago Press. Pp. 161-175.

White, Leslie
1949 "The Symbol: The Origin and Basis of Human Behavior." In: *The Science of Culture,* by L. White. New York, Farrar, Strauss and Cudahy. Pp. 22-39.
1959 *The Evolution of Culture.* New York, McGraw-Hill.
1962 "Symboling: A Kind of Behavior." *Journal of Psychology,* 53: 311-317.

White, M.
1965 *Foundations of Historical Knowledge.* New York, Harper and Row.

Whitehead, A. N.
1958 *Symbolism: Its Meaning and Effect.* Cambridge, Cambridge University Press.

Whiting, B.
   1950   *Piaute Sorcery.* New York, Wenner-Gren Foundation.
Whiting, John W. and Child, Irvin L.
   1953   *Child Training and Personality: A Cross Cultural Study,* New Haven
          Yale University Press.
Wieschoff, H. A.
   1938   "Concepts of Right and Left in African Cultures." *Journal of the Ame-
          rican Oriental Society,* 58: 202-217.
Williams, Th.
   1966   *Field Methods in the Study of Culture.* New York, Holt, Rinehart and
          Winston.
Wilson, Monica
   1951   "Witch Beliefs and the Social Structure." *American Journal of Sociology,*
          56: 307-313.
   1954   "Nyakyusa Ritual and Symbolism." *American Anthropologist,* 56: 228-241.
   1957   *Rituals of Kinship among the Nyakyusa.* London, Oxford University
          Press.
   1959   *Communal Rituals of the Nyakyusa.* London, Oxford University Press.
Winter, E. H.
   1955   *Bwana. A Structural-Functional Analysis of a Patrilineal Society.* Cam-
          bridge, Heffer and Sons.
   1956   "Amba Religion." In: *Gods and Rituals,* J. Middleton, ed. New York,
          Natural History Press, 1967. Pp. 21-40.
Wolf, Eric R.
   1964   *Anthropology.* Englewood Cliffs, Prentice-Hall.
Worms, E.
   1963   "Religion." In: *Australian Aboriginal Studies,* H. Sheils, ed. Melbourne,
          Oxford University Press. Pp. 231-247.
Worsley, Peter
   1957   "Millenarian Movements in Melanesia." In: *Gods and Rituals,* J. Middle-
          ton, ed. New York, Natural History Press, 1967. Pp. 338-352.
   1968   *The Trumpet Shall Sound.* New York, Schocken, 2nd ed.

Yinger, Milton
   1970   *The Scientific Study of Religion.* New York, Macmillan.
Young, Frank
   1965   *Initiation Ceremonies: A Cross-Cultural Study of Status Dramatization.*
          New York, Bobbs-Merrill.
Yulman, Nur
   1964a "The Raw: The Cooked : : Nature : Culture—Observations on Le Cru
          et le Cruit." In: *The Structural Study of Myth and Totemism.* London,
          Tavistock, 1967. Pp. 71-89.
   1964b "The Structure of Sinhalese Healing Rituals." In: *Religion in South
          Asia,* E. B. Harper, ed. Seattle, University of Washington, Press. Pp.
          115-150.

Zaehner, R. C.
   1958   *At Sundry Times.* New York, Humanities Press.
   1962   *The Comparisons of Religions.* Boston, Beacon Press.
Zogorin, P.
   1959   "Historical Knowledge: A Review Article on the Philosophy of History."
          Journal of Modern History, 21: 243-255.